AMERICAN MASTERS
OF SOCIAL SCIENCE

AMERICAN MASTERS OF SOCIAL SCIENCE

An Approach to the Study of the Social
Sciences Through a Neglected
Field of Biography

BY

HOWARD W. ODUM
WILLIAM R. SHEPHERD
JAMES QUAYLE DEALEY
JOHN MARTIN VINCENT
CHARLES EDWARD MERRIAM
EDWARD CARY HAYES
JOHN L. GILLIN
PAUL T. HOMAN
CARL BECKER
HARRY ELMER BARNES

EDITED BY

HOWARD W. ODUM

KENNIKAT PRESS, INC./PORT WASHINGTON, N. Y.

PREFACE

THIS volume is devoted to the stories of an unusual group of " Masters of Social Science," the span of whose lives has witnessed such a development in the social life and culture of man as had not occurred in all previous history. The half century during which they have worked has witnessed, too, remarkable progress in each of the several social sciences and the beginnings of a more co-ordinated science of society. The part which they, and others like them, have played in this phenomenal development is far more important than has hitherto been recognized.

And yet while this neglected field of biography is of sufficient importance in itself to justify the presentation of the chapters in this volume, the primary purpose of the book is not biography but an approach to teaching and research in the social sciences. That the study of the social sciences will be made more vivid and concrete by these portraits will not be doubted. That scope, content and method will be interestingly interpreted is equally apparent. That these nine masters have been presented by nine other social scientists representing a wide range of institutions, can but add to the pedagogical value of the work.

On behalf of the increasing number of students of modern social science I wish to thank the authors of these chapters for their willingness to turn aside from pressing tasks and help construct the pillars and arches for a new

v

gateway to the social sciences. Their work appears as a labor of love for the " Masters " portrayed. What they have written is designed to aid the social science student seeking example, inspiration and guidance.

In addition to the authors whose chapters make up this volume, I wish to thank Professor Wesley C. Mitchell, of Columbia University; Professor Walton Hamilton, of the Brookings Graduate School; Professor A. M. Schlesinger, of Harvard University; Dean Guy Stanton Ford, of the University of Minnesota; and others for their suggestions concerning this study and those to follow in the life and work of American and European social scientists.

Some of these stories have been published in *Social Forces*. Beginning in Volume V, a second series will be devoted to other American " Masters " and certain of their peers in Europe. The initial set is offered only as a representative group suitable for the purpose and space limitations of this book, and has been selected in accordance with what appear to be prevailing preferences in each of the several disciplines. Four stories of other " Masters " in the fields of economics, jurisprudence, and anthropology, originally planned for inclusion, are not yet ready for publication. It is hoped, however, that the series in its present form and scope will be found indispensable to every mature student of the social sciences.

H. W. O.

CHAPEL HILL,
September, 1926

CONTENTS

CHAPTER I

PIONEERS AND MASTERS
OF SOCIAL SCIENCE

By

HOWARD W. ODUM

*Kenan Professor of Sociology in the University
of North Carolina*

CHAPTER I

PIONEERS AND MASTERS OF SOCIAL SCIENCE

The record of the social sciences in America during the half century from 1875 to 1925 is at once a story of achievement and of promise. Told in terms of progress from meager beginnings to the larger accomplishments of a new era, their annals appear as among the most important of the modern scene. And while the ultimate measure of achievement during the half century just passed must inevitably be gauged by the degree to which that distinctive era, well grounded in social foundations and scientific method, may become an effective forerunner of the half century just beginning, the story itself is full of promise. Recording notable advances in each of the separate fields of instruction, research, publication and promotion, which have marked the successive stages of the development of the social sciences, it may be told most effectively in the lives and deeds of pioneers and masters.

In his chapter on Dunning, Professor Merriam says: "It is difficult to realize that prior to 1880 there had been no systematic organization of research in the United States either in the field of history or of government." Writing of Burgess and his initial opportunity of 1876, Professor Shepherd reminds us that "at that time there existed in the United States no institution properly entitled to the name of 'university.' . . . Research as a scientific pursuit, distinct from investigation for the at-

tainment of some material end, was nowhere to be found."
And progress from this situation, so lacking in university
and research facilities and in coördinated social sciences, began with that other progress of which Professor
Barnes speaks: "In many ways the changes in culture,
knowledge, and outlook of man from 1885 to 1925 have
been more striking than those which have occurred in
the whole previous history of humanity upon the earth."
Has progress in the social sciences, then, been commensurate with that in the general material and cultural
achievement of mankind? What has been the nature of
progress in the social sciences since the beginning of the
professional careers of the "Masters" portrayed in this
volume? How is it to be measured? What methods and
influences may be set forth as guiding factors in that
progress?

A little more than a decade before any of the masters
whose careers are sketched began his professional work,
there was organized the American Social Science Association with an official organ, *The Journal of Social Science.*
This association, organized in 1869, as the successor to
the American Association for the Promotion of Social Science, which was organized in 1865, was thus the forerunner of a notable line of later efforts. Since then,
numerous social science organizations have been founded
and various journals established successfully in the several disciplines. The American Historical Association
came first in 1884, followed by the American Economic
Association in 1885, the American Political Science Association in 1904, the American Sociological Society in
1905, and later by the American Statistical Association,
the American Anthropological Association, and the Social

Science Research Council in 1923. Many institutes, foundations and societies for study, research, and the promotion of the social sciences have grown up, and the number and quality of scientific journals represent a high order of energy and scholarship.

From Burgess' starting-point, with no university, there have developed in the United States more than a score of larger institutions of the sort, as measured by the standards of the Association of American Universities. In these universities, with varying degrees of development and emphasis, teaching and research in the social sciences have been promoted with vigor and success. Professor Shepherd says, for instance, that " during the 36 years' activities of Burgess at Columbia up to his retirement in 1912 as emeritus professor of political science and constitutional law, the faculty that was his intellectual offspring grew from three professors to twenty-five, and from virtually a single department of political science into the four departments of history, public law, economics and sociology," with a baker's dozen outstanding teachers and scholars at the helm. To what has been turned out by these departments might be added the contributions of anthropology, social philosophy and social psychology, with such masters as Boas and Dewey. A similar story might well be told in the cases of many other universities, with their departments of history, economics, political science, sociology, anthropology, jurisprudence, social psychology and social ethics. In spite of all of the limitations of American universities as pointed out by their critics, there has been remarkable progress in the personnel and facilities for teaching and research in the social sciences.

General progress is reflected further, not only in the organization of the work and its agencies with their media for publication, but in the very large number and wide range of articles and books being published. A study of the book-review departments of a dozen social science periodicals reveals hundreds of contributions of great variety and of scientific value, while abstracting the articles in these same periodicals has come to be a task of magnitude and importance. In the more important quarterly, monthly and weekly general periodicals of America are many articles and discussions dealing with the problems of social relationships. Likewise in the field of fiction, literary criticism, biography, religion and general social interpretation, each year sees the publication of literature unprecedented in scope and quality.

A particularly important indication of progress is found in the number and range of the newer textbooks concerned with the several branches of social science. These manuals afford great promise, not only of effectiveness in college teaching and research, but of extending instruction to increasingly larger numbers of the adult population, and paving the way for still better technique in textbook writing. Noteworthy phases of the situation in this respect are reflected in the many new series of social science textbooks now being announced by the publishers. One result of their production is the development of specialization and intensive study of given aspects of the several social sciences. Another consequence, moving rather in the opposite direction, is the trend toward the breaking down of artificial partitions among those fields of thought. Coördination of the social sciences ought to produce in the aggregate a social science capable of directing progress and of working out effectively better results in human relationships. This latter tendency seems to be one of the most hopeful measures of progress, if it can be evolved along with the production of scientific material of real permanence and value.

There are, of course, grave dangers in the too rapid evolution of the social sciences after either fashion. Some of the " Masters," as for instance, Burgess, are apprehensive on this point. As Professor Shepherd writes of him, " The tendencies that appear to accompany in recent years the evolution of the fields of study, more or less related and yet more or less distinct, which have been grouped under the general designation of social science, Burgess regards with a measure of mistrust. They reveal at times, he believes, a disposition to convert an intrinsic interest in fundamental principles into a zest for manifestations of easy inexactness in thought and expression. Rather than producing actual sciences that require precise knowledge, sound reasoning and correct definition for their understanding and elucidation, their development would seem to indicate the presence of a bent for gathering multiplicities of detail and the absence of a zeal for coherent organization and logical formulation. Too much is being assembled in the shape of things of transience which float about on a readily perceptible surface, and too little of the things of permanence which lie deep-rooted beneath. Instead of displaying a vital concern for ascertaining the really basic relations of man to the state and to society, sciences of opinion would appear to be the outcome — not categories of consecutive thought derived from accuracy of information. Quantitatively, their output may be impressive; qualitatively, they are apt to ex-

hibit the earmarks of a pseudo-science animated by mental
and often sentimental emotionalism. The net result thus
would be the fostering of a cult of generalities in loose
and impulsive utterance, of an acreage of pages, of the unlimited expanse of speech."

Others of the " Masters " look with great expectation
to results which shall be more impressive qualitatively
than quantitatively. They recognize the magnitude of
problems of human relationships, and they seek to apply
the social sciences to the ends in view, regardless of the
details of separate disciplines. The projection of an encyclopedia of the social sciences is an evidence of this
tendency. Ward perhaps represented the extreme view,
when he declared that " each particular science is merely
a differentiation of science, so that all sciences are interrelated and may be synthesized into one philosophy. . . .
Or in other words, sociological fundamentals must be integrated with the teachings of psychology and these with
the teachings of biology and these again with the teachings derived from the study of the inorganic in the universe."

Professor Barnes writes of Robinson's objective of
making history " a genetic science concerned with tracing
the development of civilization as totality." He calls
attention also to Robinson's acquaintance with the works
of Veblen, "which impressed upon him the importance
of the interrelationship between the history of technology
and economics, on the one hand, and the history of ideas
and institutions on the other." Professor Hayes indicates how Small " became convinced of the inadequacy
of methods of attacking the problem. . . . That we can
understand social life only as a whole." Elsewhere it is

pointed out how Giddings, Turner, Veblen and the others have entered vigorously into the study of social relationships with all the better methods and newer ideals of the social sciences.

Many questions are being raised, nevertheless, as to whether the social sciences are meeting the opportunities and obligations that now await them. This present consciousness of their needs and limitations is itself one of the most dynamic forms of progress. It will scarcely be doubted that there is almost universal recognition of what may be accomplished. Democracy, institutions, learning, social progress, depend upon the capacity of the race to develop and utilize the social sciences as they have those in the physical realm. On this point engineers and physical scientists, no less than social scientists, are of one mind. Involved, too, are the larger development and utilization of the physical sciences in the service of human welfare. There is, therefore, a general self-examination process getting under way, accompanied by very definite means and methods of producing results. Turning back again to our " Masters of Social Science," we find some such critical state today as they found fifty years ago when they ushered in a new era. To examine, accordingly, some of the factors which entered into their effective work will be of great value and interest to those who must contribute to the further evolution of the social sciences.

One important question raised by the reading of these chapters is that of a substitute in the present generation of younger social scientists for the distinctively European influence which was so manifest in the lives of the pioneers. Burgess studied at the Universities of Berlin, Leipzig and Goettingen, under masters characterized by

Professor Shepherd as "intellectual giants" in the fields of history, politics, economics and philosophy. Adams, in addition to studying and travelling in France, Switzerland and Italy, worked under still other "giants" at Heidelberg, later toured northern Germany and attended courses at the University of Berlin. Small not only secured a substantial part of his education abroad, but "mediated thus the results of European scholars." After two years at the University of Leipzig, Dunning and Robinson continued their studies at other European universities. The "influence which these master minds of Germany wielded over the ambitious young Americans" left an enduring impression upon their thought and gave permanent direction to their methods. Working upon the minds of these young social scientists were such teachers as Curtius, Mommsen, von Ranke, Droysen, von Treitschke, Zeller, Roscher, Waitz, von Gneist, Ihne, Fischer, Grimm, Lepsius, Bluntschli, Knies, Erdmannsdorffer, Winkelmann, Starke, Ribbeck, Weil, von Holg, Guizot, Taine, Lamprecht, L'aurent, Stein, Schmoller, Wagner, Dietzel, Brentano, Boehm-Bawerk, Wundt.

Scarcely less powerful was the influence that other European scholars, contemporary and otherwise, through their writings, exerted upon Giddings, Small, Ward, Turner, Robinson and the others. Among them were, for instance, Spencer, Bagehot, Bosanquet, Comte, Darwin, De-Greef, Galton, Gumplowicz, Simmel, Durkheim, Mill, Montaigne, Condorcet. Granted that the writings of the old teachers are still influential and that the American university and the American scholar have advanced farther than their European progenitors, the fact remains that the earlier students had the advantage not only of their

American education but of first hand European contacts as well.

Another characteristic of the " Masters " was the versatility of their interest and training. Here was Burgess, well grounded in the fields of politics, public law and constitutional history. Ward, scarcely surpassed in the breadth and depth of his scientific information, startled his colleagues by announcing a course on " a survey of all knowledge." Adams excelled in political science, history, practical affairs and language. Small's range of training, like that of William Graham Sumner and G. Stanley Hall, began with theology, and extended through varied channels to later excellence. Giddings' scope of interest and grasp began with his newspaper work and brought him special recognition from the American Statistical Association, the American Economic Association, the American Political Science Association, and the Amercian Sociological Society. Dunning was president of both the American Historical Association and the American Political Science Association, and may readily be classed as either historian or political philosopher. Turner's economic background in history and regional geographic interpretation has made him master of a splendid field. The stories of Robinson and Veblen are those of additional master minds whose creative effort and variety of contacts spread far and wide.

This broad range of interest and training had its logical basis in long and careful preparation, in patience and persistence, and in cosmopolitan contacts over long periods of years. None of the masters has sought the easy road to scholarship and achievement; none has attained success without arduous intervening tasks. American college, American university, European university — years of

interneship as fellow, instructor, professor, educator, committee worker, administrator, publicist, citizen — these
were all so many stages through which the final products
have been brought forth. The fruition came in maturity
of life, and the history of their scholarship and work reads,
if not always like romance, often like a long tale of dubious
ending.

Burgess, from a planter's home in Tennessee to war, to
youthful questionings, to college, to law, to Europe, to research, to teaching, to administration, to organization, to
editing, and to a composite pioneering in all of these respects, presents a portrait altogether worthy of his still
dominant personality. Ward, from a New England
family, through New York, Illinois, back to Pennsylvania,
farming, teaching school, learning through the hard
knocks of experience, developing a fondness for language,
barely entering an academy, then, like Burgess, to war,
wounded, and discharged — vies with Burgess in an early
career reminiscent of the American frontiersman. Then
with forty years in governmental service, with prodigious
labors in the fields of geology and paleontology, Ward built
a remarkable foundation for his comprehensive knowledge
and his scientific methods. Adams, Dunning and Turner
represented that large group of American scholars whose
efforts and allegiance to university and scholarship extended successively from student, fellow, instructor, associate professor and professor, with long years of intermediate
apprenticeship. Small was typical of another large group
whose final products of education and research grew out of
varied studies in American and European institutions,
teaching in the small college as well as the university, and
carrying on administrative work.

Giddings stands for still another group whose achievements take on the proportions of the heroic, if measured by energy, thoroughness, comprehensiveness and scholarship. For, starting without the usual academic degree, he produced monumental contributions, directing his own studies and readings with remarkable effectiveness, taking a vigorous part in the formation of American ideals, all the while teaching, writing, editing and publishing. And Turner's thirty-five years, from Wisconsin to Harvard, may be literally described in terms of frontier effort: " a fresh and original mind that goes on its way, careless of the proprieties, inquiring into everybody's business, hobnobbing with cartographers, economists, sociologists, geographists, census compilers, editors of *Who's Who*." As for Robinson and Veblen, no more varied, persistent, difficult and triumphant careers have been recorded in the fields of American education and social statesmanship.

It was inevitable that men of such preparation, scholarship and personalities would have an important part in the shaping and development of the social sciences. Each has been peculiarly a pioneer in the larger and broader sense of the word. In the case of Burgess, Professor Shepherd gives ample evidences " of achievement which make him, not the pioneer alone, but the progenitor of much that is noteworthy during the past fifty years in the advancement of research by productivity within the field of thought to which his life has been devoted." Among these evidences, in addition to those mentioned elsewhere, are his efforts in creating a genuine university, founding the first graduate school of the social sciences, and introducing the systematic study of politics and public law. Ward pioneered in America, as did Auguste Comte in France and Herbert

Spencer in England, and was the first president of the American Sociological Society. Adams played a like rôle in the organization of his historical and political science association, in the founding of the American Historical Association, in the promotion of the Johns Hopkins studies in history and political science, and in the formulation of historical inquiry. Through his courses in sociology and his studies of European sociologists Small wielded a wide influence over the entire field of social study. Giddings has been instrumental in transforming the treatment of sociology from discussion on the old metaphysical basis to a scientific and objective examination of social phenomena, and has been twice president of the American Sociological Society, and once of the Institut Internationale de Sociologie. Turner and Robinson have created an era in the new history, while Veblen's record has set a pace to be reckoned with for many years to come.

Another field in which trails were blazed was that of editorial work. Burgess founded the *Political Science Quarterly*. Adams edited the papers of the American Historical Association, government publications, some ninety historical volumes and much other special material. Small founded and edited until his death the *American Journal of Sociology*. Giddings performed a decade's outstanding newspaper editorial work and was co-editor of the *Annals* of the American Academy of Poetical and Social Science, of the *Political Science Quarterly*, of the publications of the American Economic Association, and later of the *Independent*. Dunning was long editor of the *Political Science Quarterly*. Ward, Robinson, Turner, and Veblen have all made notable contributions in the editing of articles, texts, series and varied papers.

These masters were social scientists, not only in their scientific methods and achievements over a broad field of social interest, but in their participation in matters of social statecraft as well. Burgess had a vigorous share in many matters of social concern. He was much opposed, for example, to the institution of the state or national university. Adams was a critic of many national and local policies, and took an active part in their discussion. Small made many group contacts, while Giddings has always been forceful in the criticism and defence of public policies, serving on citizens' committees, city-planning groups and international organizations. Turner was no less versatile in other spheres of public concern. Robinson and Veblen, on their part, have excelled in their critical interpretations of a wide range of human experience.

To emphasize the vigor of personality manifest in the lives and work of this group of social scientists would seem almost a commonplace. They were not only born with capacity, but what is more important and too often neglected, they developed a personality to match. That of Burgess, " dignified, gracious, urbane, and kindly; calm yet never rigid; reserved yet never aloof; austere perhaps, yet never forbidding," may be set over against Turner's, possessed of a " lively and irrepressible intellectual curiosity; a refreshing freedom from personal preoccupations and didactic motives; a quite unusual ability to look out upon the wide world in a humane friendly way, in a fresh and strictly independent way, with a vision unobscured by academic inhibitions." Despite his vigor, Ward was modest and almost bashful, having a quiet dignity, deep emotion, and fine sympathy. Small has been described by Professor Hayes as the ideal of a gentleman in spirit and conduct, bearing himself with the quiet elegance of an ambassador yet without pretense, appreciative of the work of others, and unmindful of self. Giddings the man is synonymous with his teachings and writings. Curiosity, persistence, insight, forcefulness, charm, humor,— all are characteristic of him. Dunning was the genial, winsome soul, in whom wit and wisdom were happily joined. Robinson's personal charm and easy poise set off to advantage his broad interests and intellectual vim. Veblen's elusive self could not fail to provide an effective background for stinging phrases, effective satire and critical essay.

It is of course absurd to refer to the above characterizations as anything other than indicative of the vigorous personalities that so dominated the last half century of social science. Bertrand Russell, in his recent volume on "Education and the Good Life," has deemed four major traits essential. These are vitality, courage, intellect and sensitiveness. Each of the masters portrayed in this volume certainly exemplifies them. Broad minded, judicious, capable of leading and of following, inspiring both esteem and work, to know any one of these men, to observe closely their careers, is to become imbued with the spirit and atmosphere of social study, and to be stimulated to effective effort.

Such personalities were dominant in many ways. In order to understand even a small part of their influence upon scholarship one must read and ponder the stories of their work. What they have done in particular is to inspire and direct the new generation of students, teachers, authors, publicists — whether in classroom, in seminar, on the campus or in the community. Their influence upon thousands of their students is one to challenge study and emulation. Quoting again from the biographical sketches in this volume: " Burgess has ever been a man whom his students remember with affection, in which there is just a bit of awe. . . . He inspired them with trust in his learning, confidence in his guidance, and belief in their own capacity to accomplish the things worth while. . . . They remember with gratitude the conferences in seminar and office, where the master gave the pupils the best of his mind and spirit, instilling in them a desire to seek the truth and resolutely to make it known." Of Turner, Professor Becker says: " I do not ask of any historian more than this: that he should have exerted during his generation a notable influence upon the many scholars, in many branches of humanistic studies. This is enough; and this, I think, must be accorded to Turner . . . and his pupils understand it better than any others that the man is more than his work. And so I end as I began with ' that man Turner ' who laid and still lays upon us all the spell of his personality. Some indelible impression of him, some virtue communicated to us from the alert independence and the fine integrity of a high-minded gentleman, still shapes our lives and gives added substance to our work." " Adams' connections," writes Professor Vincent, " made in his seminary became life-long associations, for Adams' counsel and interest continued without stint. . . . Few American teachers more clearly recognized the value of close personal relations with his students. Doctor Adams, the man, overshadowed the professor." The recent memorial meeting held at the University of Chicago in honor of Small, together with the published proceedings, gives fresh evidence of the large body of scholars who owe allegiance to him. As for Giddings, a forthcoming volume of unusual proportions devoted to the newer emphasis upon the scientific study of human society, and written solely by his former students, will bear testimony to his far-flung influence. Of him Professor Gillin says: " His lectures amazed one at his power of exposition and illustration. The comprehensiveness of his scheme challenged thought. No one who heard him lecture could ever be narrow in his outlook." Of Dunning, Professor Merriam says: " The finest quality in Dunning was his power to arouse in students sustained enthusiasm for research, and for high standards of emphasis and expression. . . . His all-effectiveness was multiplied by the number of those who were interested by him and who became independent tillers of the soil." His was the task " to kindle in many minds the divine spark of enthusiasm for research without which the great intellectual adventure of mankind would close." Professor Barnes says of Robinson: " Though he was one of the most popular teachers of very large classes, his success was due to sheer intellectual ability and feats of psychic dexterity. . . . With a method utterly devoid of dramatic appeal Robinson interested and amused his students far more than any other teacher of history with whom the writer has ever had any association. . . . His command of subtle but penetrating irony and satire was almost unique and served to keep his students intellectually alert at all moments. . . . Robinson's success in the classroom will remain an outstanding example of what may be achieved in the way of pedagogical success through turning loose a profound but playful mind upon vital historical materials."

It will be understood that inseparably related to these masters and their work have been still other masters. One might easily select four score major teachers and scholars in the field of the social sciences, and point out how they, too, have blazed many a trail and achieved the frontiersman's task. Much of the training and experience, and not a few of the qualities of this larger group, coincide with those portrayed in this volume.

Much has been made in recent years of the lives and work of physical scientists, musicians, men of letters, statesmen, politicians and a varied group of individuals whose memoirs have rivaled fiction in the interest which they have aroused. And yet a comparison of the neglected field of biography of great teachers and scientists in the field of social study inevitably results in favor of the social scientists. A survey, for instance, of two score astronomers, physicists, botanists, geologists, bacteriologists, chemists and electricians shows the following positive qualities as most marked: Patience, perseverance, singleness of purpose, concentration, energy, love of work, desire for eminence, faith in the ultimate outcome, inquisitiveness, devotion to truth, courage, enthusiasm and the wise use of time. All of these qualities our social scientists possess, and more, in that their fields of knowledge, interests, experiment, and contact have been as wide as human society itself.

Further comparisons with the masters in other fields — of music, art, medicine, physical science, invention, education, statesmanship — may be made with profit and zest, by an examination of three score biographical sketches which have appeared within the last decade. Of the scientists, there are some fifteen volumes, some of which read like romance: books by Avery, Bachman, Darrow, De Kruif, Gibson, Hart, Holden, Murray, Osborne, Van

Wageman, and others. Of the musicians, ten volumes are worthy of special study, including those by Bridge, Brower, Crawford, Dole Lavel, Rosenveld and Sharp. Concerning the masters of art and of painting, there are a dozen, such as the stories by Caffin, Carrington, Chubb, Cortissiz, McSpadden, Pach and Pennell. Graves' story of great educators, Hagan's of great American lawyers, Kingston's study of famous judges, Newton's tribute to living masters of the pulpit, are types of biographies of other personalities. To these may be added such a distinguished array of general biography as has never appeared before, the reading of which will accentuate the value of the stories of the great social scientists and social statesmen.

Other biographies may be read with pleasure and profit and without detracting from the appreciation of the sketches which follow in this volume. Three recent stories of special interest are Starr's *William Graham Sumner*, Pruette's *G. Stanley Hall*, and Goldberg's *Havelock Ellis*. In addition to these, the student will profit immensely if he will turn aside to read such critical volumes as Spengler's *The Decline of the West*, Johnson's *The Historian and Historical Evidence*, and other similar volumes. He will find by comparison that many of the early contributions of the " Masters," not only in their scientific methods and results but in matters of public policy, appear peculiarly modern and timely. These and other observations will be apparent, but it must suffice now to turn our attention to the " Masters " themselves, keeping in mind the viewpoint suggested, but remaining none the less expectant of the pleasure and profit to come from a careful reading of the stories that follow.

CHAPTER II
JOHN WILLIAM BURGESS

By

WILLIAM R. SHEPHERD

Seth Low Professor of History in Columbia University

JOHN WILLIAM BURGESS

CHAPTER II

JOHN WILLIAM BURGESS

BECAUSE of his eminence as educator, publicist and historian, John William Burgess should be considered one of the first among scholars in this country who are accounted masters of social science. The services that he has rendered in all three capacities endow with right his post of honor. Helping actively to create a national university out of an urban college, introducing the systematic study of politics and public law, and expounding with singular forcefulness the constitutional history of the United States are evidences of achievement which make him, not the pioneer alone, but the progenitor, of much that is noteworthy during the past fifty years in the advancement of research and productivity within the fields of thought to which his life has been devoted.

The career of a scholar is more subject perhaps to influences wielded by training and experience in childhood and youth than is true of other walks of life. Impressions formed at that time and left upon a sensitive mind are wont to establish a tenacious hold that a subsequent change of environment loosens in but slight degree. Heredity, to be sure, has its share in the process of moulding thought and character; yet what is impressed heavily upon the consciousness at the period when it is most receptive leaves indelible traces upon the spirit and outlook of the youth become a man. The career of Burgess illustrates the effects of just such forces early operative in shaping it.

Born in Giles County, Tennessee, August 26, 1844, he comes, on the paternal side, of old Flemish stock that traces its ancestry to one John of Bruges, a weaver, who in the sixteenth century became lord mayor of London. A daughter of this magistrate married Robert Sackville, father of Thomas Sackville, the poet, and later Earl of Dorset, thus identifying the family with Dorsetshire. From that county Thomas Burgess migrated to America in 1638, where he settled at Sandwich, Massachusetts. Thence his descendants have spread into many parts of the United States. On the maternal side, the subject of the present essay derives his ancestry from the Virginia branch of the Edwards family.

The parents of the future scholar were slave-owners. In political beliefs they were " old-line Whigs," and staunch upholders of the Union. With neither the abolitionists of the North, who would destroy the nation if only thereby they could put an end to slavery, nor the secessionists of the South, who would tear it asunder if only thereby they could retain their " peculiar institution," had they any sympathy. John William, their eldest-born, inherited that devotion to an undivided nation, and that aversion from extremists of any sort who might design its overthrow. American nationhood, free of sectionalism at home and of control abroad, was an inspiration of the boy's childhood, an ideal of his later years. From this source sprang ultimately the firm conviction with which Burgess has ever been imbued: that his country was a great creative and regenerative force for the welfare of mankind; it must suffer therefore no attempts at disruption from within and the exercise of no untoward influences from without; independent and sovereign, it had both the right and the duty to develop its internal power unhindered, and to render that power effective for good elsewhere.

These impulses which arose from parentage and home surroundings were reinforced by what the child was told of Henry Clay. His earliest recollections centered on the days of 1850–1851. Upon his memory was graven the picture of that incomparable orator whose eloquence pleaded nobly, but in vain, for the preservation of the Union. Had any doubts emerged in the minds of parents and son as the pressure in favor of secession grew, the example of Henry Clay gave courage when the supreme test came.

Early instruction completed, young Burgess attended from 1859 to 1862 the species of high school in Lebanon, near Nashville, which pride of the commonwealth dignified with the title of Cumberland " University." Though most of his immediate comrades were Southern hotspurs, he himself revealed a strength of character unusual in one of his years in adhering to parental principles. While attending this institution he frequented the home of Jordan Stokes, one of Tennessee's most prominent and brilliant lawyers, and a devotee also of the cult of Clay. Here the men whom he met and the opinions to which he listened served to intensify still more his sense of attachment to the Union.

When, in February, 1862, the Federal armies entered Tennessee, driving the Confederates before them, the youth of seventeen who had now reached military age must show his colors. Unless he could escape to the Union lines, he would have to join a Southern regiment. Enrolling forthwith in the Army of the Ohio, commanded at the time by General Don Carlos Buell, he saw active service for a period of two and a half years, until the autumn of 1864.

Subjected to every sort of trial and hardship, having sacrificed his entire patrimony, forfeited the social prestige of his homeland, and witnessed all the horrors of war, the youth of twenty found himself one day in Nashville, Tennessee, having two thousand dollars of army pay in his pocket and yet not knowing what to do with it or with himself. By chance he met his old friend of earlier days, Jordan Stokes, who advised him to spend the money on an education. The college that he suggested for the purpose was Amherst, where his own sons were in attendance.

To the young Southerner who now betook himself northward the tight little New England environment, so unlike the open life in the big places of the plantation in Tennessee, proved to be another factor of great importance in determining his career. Here he was, an undergraduate of a

Puritan country college, where nothing was considered worth while except scholarship and character; where work began at 7 A. M. and ended at 10 P. M.; where academic rank was the one thing above all else which was coveted; where the Thursday evening prayer-meeting was the chief recreation; where teachers and students were intimately acquainted; where the students, coming from all parts of the country, lived together in the community of the dormitory; where dress was simple, meals were frugal, society was natural and sport unknown; where physical and mental vigor in the bracing air of the country made for work and clean character, and the premium was placed upon the man who won the valedictory and yet worked his way through, as the phrase went.[1]

[1] John W. Burgess, " Reminiscences of Columbia University in the last quarter of the last century," *Columbia University Quarterly,* XV, 321–322.

The spirit pervading such an institution, attuned so completely to the feelings and desires implanted by early associations, could not fail to stimulate the seriousness of purpose with which the collegian was now resolutely to cross the threshold of his life's work. At Amherst the soldier of yesterday became the scholar of to-morrow.

The professor from whom Burgess received his earliest systematic instruction in history and politics was Julius H. Seelye, whose primary fields of interest lay in philosophy, psychology and ethics. From that great teacher came also the first encouragement to specialize in those subjects. On one occasion he told Professor Seelye how, during the campaign of 1863, the query had arisen in his mind, whether it were not possible for men made in the image of God and endowed with reason and conscience to settle questions arising out of their relationships without recourse to the destruction of war, and how then and there he had made the silent resolve to dedicate his whole life to the work of discovering the ways for such settlement and of teaching them to others. Where, he asked, could he find the instruction needful to equip him for the task. The answer was — Germany.

Graduating from Amherst in 1867 with this thought deeply rooted in his mind, Burgess studied law at Springfield and two years later was admitted to the Massachusetts bar. Hardly had he begun to practice, when he was offered an appointment as professor of history and political economy at Knox College, Galesburg, Illinois. This he accepted, only to become convinced that his future lay in the study and teaching of public law. Then he remembered the advice about Germany, and decided forthwith to heed it.

Probably at no period in the life of man before or since
was there ever assembled in any one country such an array of intellectual giants in the fields of history, politics,
economics and philosophy as those under whom, from
1871 to 1873, Burgess was privileged to study at the universities of Berlin, Leipzig and Goettingen: Curtius and
Mommsen, von Ranke and Droysen, von Treitschke and
Zeller, Lotze and Helmholtz, Roscher, Waitz and von
Gneist. Nor is it strange that the influence which these
master-minds of Germany wielded over the ambitious
young American should have left an abiding impress upon
his thought.

Profoundly interested in tasks of research, Burgess reluctantly had to abandon them when, in 1873, Amherst
called him to assume charge as professor of the newly established departments of history, political science and political economy. Upon these duties he entered zealously,
with the idea of bringing to bear some of the fruits of his
work of investigation in Germany. For the realization of
this object he sought to gather about him a few unusually
gifted pupils whom he might train in the use of original
sources. He forgot, however, that he was in New England.
A project so bold and so radical proved to be the " stern
and rock-bound coast " on which his young bark foun-
dered. Rumor had it that in the privacy of his home he
was teaching his selected pupils a rationalistic philosophy.
To the college folk of the time and to their immediate
neighbors truth could come only by revelation from above
— professorial and otherwise; and such a thing as independent research conducted in a scientific spirit was taboo.
Henceforth the German-trained professor must spend so
much time teaching the general run of undergraduates that

he would be unable to direct superior minds of the student-body into the dubious paths of investigation for its own sake.

In 1876 came at last the opportunity for Burgess to render his ideas effective. It appeared in the form of an invitation to lecture on constitutional law and government at the Law School associated with Columbia College, New York. At that time there existed in the United States no institution properly entitled to the name, " university." Colleges and professional schools made up a loose educational aggregate, dignified in some instances with that appellation. They lacked correlation, however, and none of them possessed such a thing as a faculty of philosophy. Research as a scientific pursuit, distinct from investigation for the attainment of some material end, was nowhere to be found.

Having the German faculty of philosophy in mind, Burgess now proposed that a nucleus of an organization for research be created within the Columbia group of teaching-bodies. It should take the form of a faculty and school of political science. In order further to signalize this union of instruction with investigation, which was to make possible the establishment of a genuine institution of higher learning on the European model, he urged that, as an expression of hope at least, the name "college" be changed to that of " university." This, however, was too sweeping an innovation for even the best disposed of Trustees to accept. Instead, they offered the innovator appointment to a professorship of political science and constitutional law, during the tenure of which he might carry the project onward.

With the approval of the Trustees, and supported by

three successive presidents — cautiously by Frederick A. P. Barnard, deliberately by Seth Low and whole-heartedly by Nicholas Murray Butler — Burgess pursued an active campaign of education among his colleagues on behalf of converting Columbia into a genuine university until, after years of tireless perseverance, he beheld his hopes realized. In 1880 he organized the first faculty and school of political science to be founded in the United States. A decade later, when the office was established, he became dean. As other non-professional graduate faculties were set up, broad educational policies affecting the entire institution were coördinated under a university council and, to signalize the transformation that had taken place, " Columbia College " assumed the name of " Columbia University." Then, after the work of the several faculties had become closely interrelated, he was made their joint dean.

The more immediate impulses, however, to the creation at Columbia of the Faculty and School of Political Science came from further experiences abroad. In 1878 Burgess had visited the " École Libre des Sciences Politiques " at Paris and had attended the sessions of the Congress of Berlin. As the latter afforded him something of a practical insight into European international politics, so the former gave him a chance to observe the actual workings of the only independent institution of the sort in the world. From it he appears to have derived the idea of seeking to make what was to be more or less its counterpart in the United States fulfill a threefold function: the advancement of research, the preparation of teachers and training for public service.

During the thirty-six years of the activity of Burgess at

Columbia, up to his retirement in 1912 as emeritus professor of political science and constitutional law, the Faculty that was his intellectual offspring grew from three professors to twenty-five, and from virtually a single department of political science into the four departments of history, public law, economics and social science. The historians included Herbert L. Osgood, William A. Dunning, William Milligan Sloane and James Harvey Robinson; the publicists, John Bassett Moore, Frank J. Goodnow and Munroe Smith; the economists, Richmond Mayo-Smith, Edwin R. A. Seligman and John Bates Clark; and the sociologists, Franklin H. Giddings. Among the men, furthermore, whom Burgess trained at Columbia and Amherst many gained nation-wide distinction as lawyers, judges and statesmen. In official life the most famous of his pupils were Theodore Roosevelt and Frederick H. Gillett.

Stimulated by his example, colleagues and students alike have produced a rich literature in history, political philosophy, constitutional, administrative and international law, economics and sociology. From the school that he created have come forth many of the most successful teachers of those subjects in the institutions of higher learning throughout the United States. It was Burgess also who founded the *Political Science Quarterly,* the first periodical of its kind in this country, and numbering among its contributors such men as Theodore Roosevelt, Woodrow Wilson, F. W. Maitland, W. J. Ashley, J. A. Hobson, Charles Gide, Charles V. Langlois, Charles Borgeaud, Georg Jellinek and Vilfredo Pareto.

The share of Burgess, accordingly, in the development of the facilities for higher education in the United States was not confined to what he accomplished at Columbia alone. So far as the organization of the American university as an institution comparable with those of Europe in the promotion of critical investigation and the spirit of liberty indispensable to scholarship may be attributable to the work of one man, he deserves the major credit. The exercise of wise academic statesmanship, derived from the possession of exceptional foresight, constructive genius and marked powers of leadership, made it possible for him to imbue an old college and its associated schools with university ideals and to devise for them an appropriate organic form. In fomenting that spirit and those ideals he aimed to maintain and foster the essential traditions of a true university: "liberty of thought and of speech; equality of all conscientious and capable inquirers, and fraternity of all members of the republic of letters and sciences." [2] From the fruition of the reforms that he introduced at Columbia, from the wide extent to which they have been adopted or adapted at other centers of learning and from his writings, the influence of the ideas that he was the first to advocate has radiated over the entire country.

Six years before the retirement of Burgess from academic service occurred an event of considerable importance to the cause of international education. This was the establishment of a system of exchange professorships in the history and institutions respectively of Germany and the United States between the University of Berlin and Columbia University. The American scholar selected to represent his country for the purpose was to be known as the "Roosevelt Professor," in honor of the President of that name, and his German compeer, to bear the title of

[2] Editorial in *Columbia University Quarterly*, xv, 64.

" Kaiser Wilhelm Professor," in honor of the German Em-
peror from whom the proposal for closer intellectual ties
of the sort had originally come. Of this Roosevelt professorship Burgess was the first incumbent.

In his inaugural lecture at Berlin, in 1906, Burgess declared that, in the opinion of President Roosevelt and of
the American people, an international exchange of professors was the " most pregnant idea " that had come
forth in our time, because it made possible a subjection of
" questions of the highest importance which can scarcely
be touched upon in a diplomatic way to the most fundamental examination and the most friendly consideration."

" There are, for example," he continued,

two doctrines in the policy of the United States which are regarded almost as holy doctrines, the discussion of which may
not even be proposed by a foreign power without risk of awakening hostility in the United States. These are the high protective
tariff theory and the Monroe Doctrine. Our politicians do not
seem to have the slightest notion that both of these doctrines are
virtually out of date; that the reconstruction of the European
states and their constitutions, and the assumption by the United
States itself of the position of a world power have made them
appear well-nigh meaningless.[3]

This was the calm and deliberate utterance of a student of
politics, and intended for students like himself. Certain
representatives of the press in the United States, however,

[3] *Antrittsrede des ersten Inhabers der Roosevelt-Professur an der
Königlichen Friedrich-Wilhelms-Universität zu Berlin, Prof. John W.
Burgess, von der Columbia Universität zu New-York, und Erwider-
ung des Rektors der Universität, Oberkonsistorialrats, Prof. Dr.
Kaftan, in Gegenwart Seiner Majestät des Kaisers und Königs, Ihrer
Majestät der Kaiserin und Königin und Seiner Königlichen Hoheit
des Prinzen August Wilhelm, in der Aula der Königlichen Friedrich-
Wilhelms-Universität zu Berlin, am 27ten. Oktober, 1906. Berlin,
1906. 7–8.*

saw fit to characterize it as "undiplomatic," indicating that the President and the people of the country were committed in some way by it. His opinion even was denounced hotly as "premature" and "dangerous," and he himself berated as a "missionary of mischief" who ought to be recalled forthwith! But, as one journal, though disagreeing with the statement of Burgess about the Monroe Doctrine, very properly remarked, an object of the founding of the Roosevelt professorship was to secure an "academic and undiplomatic freedom of discussion" of American topics in a foreign forum. All, it added, that the professor really had done was, to tell German students what *he* thought, and not "what he thought other people thought he ought to think!" [4]

Apart from his lectures at the universities of Berlin, Leipzig and Bonn on American history and institutions, perhaps the chief service rendered abroad by Burgess to the study of social science was the series of addresses that he gave at Vienna before the Juristic Society of Austria-Hungary. Here, in the presence of the heir apparent, Franz Ferdinand, and of the leading officials and lawyers of the Dual Monarchy, he was called upon to explain the federal system of government prevailing in the United States, as a possible pattern upon which in greater or less degree the future organization of Austria-Hungary itself might be modelled.

From his view as to the potential value of an exchange of professorships between countries Burgess has never departed. In spite of all that war has done to shatter previous relations of friendship, he believes that an educational device of the sort constitutes a "beginning at the right end

[4] *The Outlook*, lxxxiv, 591–592.

for the attainment of a consensus of international opinion."
That object might well be reached " through the approach
of the intellectual aristocracy of the different countries to
each other, by means of the presentation of the civilization
of each country to the educated classes in the others by
representatives of each." [5]

All these characteristics of Burgess revealed in his career are no less manifest in his writings. As early as 1884
he had formulated definite conclusions about the American
type of university and its relation to government.[6] In his
opinion,

> The rapidly shifting policies in legislation and the rapidly
> rotating personnel of administration render the government,
> either of the Nation or Commonwealth, utterly unfit to direct
> the development of the higher education. Moreover, there is
> nothing which would offer to the universal demagogism of Amer-
> ican politics so capital a point of attack as the appropriations
> necessary to the support of the University. No party would
> be able, in all probability, to hold the reins of power here for a
> second term which should dare to expend the public moneys, in
> any sufficient amount, upon what, in the eyes of the great ma-
> jority of voters, is a useless luxury.

> The American University must therefore be a private insti-
> tution, supported by private donations, and directed by an asso-
> ciation of private persons. . . . The higher education can
> not, in my opinion, be too far emancipated from governmental
> interference in a political system where nothing is done except
> with a partisan purpose.

For the administration of the university he deemed a self-
perpetuating corporation the most practicable instrument.
Of the several faculties that ought to be provided, that

[5] Letter to the present writer, January 27, 1926.
[6] *The American university: when shall it be? where shall it be?
what shall it be?* Boston, 1884.

given over to research in the fields represented by the German type of Faculty of Philosophy he thought the one of paramount importance — the " life and glory." " It is the foundation for everything further. Without it Theology becomes a dreary dogmatism, Law a withering letter, and Medicine a dangerous empiricism." As in the German system, moreover, the methods of instruction should comprise three fundamental principles: " the combination of studies at the election of the student, the giving of the instruction by original lecture and the exercise of the student in the Seminarium. There is, however, nothing exclusively German in these principles. The reasons for them are as general as humanity, and have the same force here as there."

That Burgess clung steadfastly to his views on the general subject is shown by an article published shortly after he relinquished his work at Columbia. In it he averred that the " finest thing which civilization has yet produced is a great American university upon a private foundation. . . . No other nation on earth has brought the like of it forth. It is the peculiar offspring of American conscience and American liberty." [7] Again, in 1914, when a project of erecting at Washington a " national university," was mooted, he assailed it vigorously. An institution of the sort he regarded as superfluous, prejudicial to American traditions of liberty, a symptom of political retrogression, inimical to freedom of inquiry and financially wasteful. To quote his trenchant language:

When our forefathers founded this republic they were chiefly concerned with the preservation of liberty, and they valued government chiefly as a means to that end. They carefully

[7] " Reminiscences " etc., *Columbia University Quarterly*, xv, 321.

kept its clumsy hand off the finer instruments and institutions of civilization, such as the church and the colleges and universities. This is the one thing more than any and every other which has distinguished American from European civilization and which has preserved American liberty against the despotism of government.[8]

Let the public authorities once get the control of higher education within their grasp, they will seek to monopolize it. The inevitable tendency of government is to " encroach more and more upon the domain of liberty, and if liberty would live, it must resist this tendency at the outset." Too much, in his judgment, does the present generation exaggerate the part that government should play in the civilization of the republic. " No clearer evidence of retrogression in the ability and character of a people is possible than the demand that the government shall undertake what has, heretofore, been accomplished through the free impulse and action of individuals and associations of individuals." In a university, not the spirit of government, but the spirit of liberty, ought always to prevail.

We have already too many universities and too many students attending them. We are not suffering from lack of quantity, but far more from lack of quality, in university professors or university students. . . . We ought not to create any more opportunities for attracting the natural hewers of wood and drawers of water into lines for which they are utterly without genius or aptitude.[9]

His views on education bear a close resemblance to certain of the theories and principles laid down by Burgess in his treatises dealing with the state and with comparative

[8] "A government university at Washington," *Educational Review,* xlvii, 183–187.   [9] *Ibid.*

constitutional law, upon which so much of his fame as a political scientist rests. Initiated as early as 1886 and developed in many articles,[10] they were embodied also in a number of systematic works. Of the latter the first to appear was his *Political science and comparative constitutional law*, published in two volumes, 1890–1891. Of it an English reviewer wrote:

> Professor Burgess's work is an outcome and an evidence of the vigorous study of political science now being carried on in America. . . . The volumes before us claim the attention of European as well as of American readers. They constitute a contribution to the comparative study of existing political institutions, of which there are too few examples in French and English literature.[11]

The distinctive theory that pervades it, he ascribes to the patent influence of American institutions. Moreover, just as Calhoun's *Disquisition on government*, brought out posthumously in 1851, was the first political treatise composed by an American, which portrayed the state as an institution having a legally omnipotent will and expressing it through law, so the volumes of Burgess provide the first attempt by an American to offer a complete theory of the state, through an analytical examination of the nature and functions of government and an elaborate comparison also of foreign constitutional law with that of the United States.

The initial volume of the work treats of sovereignty and

[10] *Political Science Quarterly*, i, 9–35, 259–94, 612–35; ii, 313–68; iii, 123–35, 334–84, 633–53; vi, 338–400; x, 404–25; xi, 44–67; xiii, 201–12; xiv, 1–18; xv, 381–98; xvi, 486–552; xvii, 650–63; xix, 1–19, 545–78; xxiii, 385–407. Cf. also *Annual report of the American Historical Association for the year 1896*, i, 201–11.

[11] *The Westminster Review*, cxxxv, 541.

liberty. It defines political science as the science of the national country-state of modern times, in contradistinction to the country-state and city-state of antiquity. Territorial expansion, representative government and national unity have made that science to consist of three doctrines — of sovereignty, of liberty and of government. Of the three doctrines sovereignty, as the basis of both liberty and government, is the most fundamental.

By the term " state " is meant " organized society as sovereign over all its individual members and over all other organizations within it." Sovereignty is the original and absolute power to command and enforce obedience. It operates through the agency that amends the constitution, and the location of it determines the form of the state. Liberty, the body of civil rights and immunities pertaining to the individual, is a direct creation of the state. Government, on the other hand, refers to the organization of the three branches of political authority, the executive, legislative and judicial, within the constitution. The defense of liberty against government forms an essential part of modern constitutional law. This in turn consists of a series of provisions that designate where sovereignty is found, prescribe its mode of action, define and guarantee the realm of individual liberty, and construct the organs of government, vesting in them the powers which they lawfully may exercise. So regarded, constitutional law would be the more or less perfect objective realization of all three doctrines of political science itself.

In his second volume Burgess applies the principles enunciated in the first. He presents here a detailed survey of the constitutions of the United States, Great Britain, Germany and the French Republic. These he examines and compares accordingly in respect of their formation, the ultimate seat of sovereignty, the guarantees of liberty, and the organization and operation of the several branches of government.

Apart altogether from its value as a contribution to the literature of the subjects with which it primarily deals, the work possesses an especial interest because of the manner in which it foreshadows the policy that the United States was to adopt a few years later. It asserts and demonstrates the right and the duty of civilized nations, not only to acquire and rule territories occupied by savage or barbaric peoples, but also to " interfere in the affairs of populations which are no longer barbaric, yet which manifest incapacity to solve the problem of political civilization with any degree of completeness." Among such nations, moreover, the author singles out those of basically Teutonic origin and culture as the ones best fitted to perform the task, and preëminently the United States, Germany and Great Britain.

A quarter of a century later, in 1915, Burgess published his second systematic treatise on political science: *The reconciliation of government with liberty,* which reflects the judgments that he had reached on men and events during the intervening period. Of its significance a competent reviewer has this to say:

Many histories of human government have been written, and several histories of human liberty. It has remained for an American scholar to attempt a history of the age-long efforts of men to reconcile government with liberty. It may be doubted whether any American is more adequately equipped for the performance of such a task than Professor Burgess. To a full knowledge of comparative government, accumulated through a long life of study and teaching, he adds a notably independent

spirit and an exceptionally keen judgment. Whether or not
the interpretation of men and events which he gives appeals to
one as valid or final, one may rest assured that it is based upon
carefully ascertained facts and conscientiously framed conclusions.[12]

" It has been the search of the ages," declares the author, " to find a political system, the travail of the ages to
construct one, in which government and liberty shall be
reconciled." The results of the search he then proceeds
to record and analyze, tracing them through the development of civilization in Asia, Africa, Europe and the Amer-
icas. Of the four areas he selects the last two for the purpose of an elaborate discussion and comparison of modern
constitutional government and its operation in the political
systems of the various nations concerned. These phenomena he measures and evaluates in accordance with certain abstract standards of excellence. In European constitutions he notes as defects the lack of an " organized
sovereign back of both government and liberty," the absence of a " well-defined sphere of individual liberty " over
against governmental power — such as would be provided
by an inviolable bill of rights, and the subordination of one
legislative body to another; whereas " political science insists upon a parity of powers " between the parts of a dual
legislature. Countries that maintain this parity are the
ones in which " men of intelligence, character, thrift and
wealth still occupy stations in political society," and the
" higher classes have retained their vigor and courage."
Since in most of the nations, however, liberty has been sacrificed to government, the sole forces counteractive of dis-
aster are those supplied by the returning influence of a ra-

[12] Frederick Austin Ogg, in *The Dial*, lx, 69.

tional philosophy of the state in the Teutonic lands and the strength of the Roman Church in the Latin.

The experience of other countries forms the background upon which Burgess depicts with bold and colorful strokes what has befallen the constitution of the United States in recent years. His original design now becomes apparent: to demonstrate that before 1898, when this land of ours entered upon courses of action which have tended to grow increasingly subversive of so much that is beneficent in American political life and thought, it had the " most perfect system of civil liberty, the best protected and guaranteed against governmental power, ever attained in the civilized world." The constitution of the United States, embodying the finest results of the accumulated experience of mankind, offered then the most satisfactory solution yet devised of the greatest of all political problems — that of the reconciliation of government with liberty.

For the process of deterioration which set in after 1898 and has enabled government more and more to encroach upon the legitimate domain of individual rights and immunities, Burgess holds in a measure responsible the decisions of the Supreme Court in the Insular Cases. The precedent thus established for omnipotence of government control, he avers, has been followed by a demagogic onslaught upon private wealth and other evidences of the enjoyment of individual liberty. Visible alike in legislation and constitutional amendment, a paternalism exercised in the name of a despotic popular majority has rendered the individual helpless before the " whims or the cupidity of a mob." In Europe an indiscriminate extension of the suffrage has enhanced the tyrannical power of the legislature, creating a tendency toward the erection of the socialistic state that disregards ruthlessly any and every sphere of individual immunity which may be defined and guaranteed by the constitution against the arbitrariness of government. Similarly, under the ultra-democratic system prevailing in the United States the will of the people, made manifest by the force of numbers alone, tends to ignore the distinction between government and the sovereign power " organized back of both government and liberty, independent of both, supreme over both, the originator of both and the determiner of their relations to each other," vesting that government instead with an unlimited mandate over the lives and property of all its subjects. An elected legislature, indeed, can be depended upon to protect the individual

only where the suffrage is limited to men of intelligence, character and means, and eligibility to a seat in the legislative body is conditioned upon the same qualities. Where universal suffrage is the source of legislative mandate, the legislative authority is a far more consummate despot than any king or prince has shown himself to be.

" It is high time for us," concludes the author, " to call a halt in our present course of increasing the sphere of government and decreasing that of liberty."

Following along similar lines of thought, *Recent changes in American constitutional theory*,[18] the latest work from the pen of Burgess, is a treatise addressed to the ten thousand and more of his former students as a " maybe final word from their old teacher." Like its predecessors, it expounds certain principles of political science arising out of basic concepts that in turn are posited by *a priori* reasoning and, in his judgment, demonstrated

[18] New York, 1923.

by experience. The dominant theme is the separation which should be upheld of government from sovereignty, in order that the latter shall protect the constitutional rights and immunities of the individual through the decisions of an independent judiciary, and that the use of power by the former shall be restrained within the bounds of interests genuinely national. Lacking the safeguards of a strict observance of the distinction between government and sovereignty, the freedom of institutions which our political system was designed to conserve, becomes subject to a double menace: that of despotism from above and that of intolerance from below. Differences of opinion, by which alone that freedom may continue to flourish, are liable to destruction by a government that exceeds its legitimate powers and by a radical democracy scornful of individual rights. Divergence of view, therefore, must be endured and respected, nay " sought, invited and encouraged; for only through the clash of opinion and the attrition of thought can man press onward toward the goal of truth and the perfection of civilization."

These principles Burgess brings into play in discussing what he deems to be the proper limitations resting upon the government of the United States in its relation both to individuals and to foreign nations. The addition of the four recent amendments to the Federal Constitution he regards as an error, because of their actual or potential encroachment upon the sphere of separateness which should obtain between the government and the supreme power behind it, and also upon the powers reserved to the States of the Union. They have served thus unduly to exalt the degree of control wielded by the authorities at Washington. Legislative enactment similarly has violated certain constitutional principles laid down by the Fathers of the Republic. It has forced conscripts to fight in a foreign war, and in this connection has sanctioned the loaning of money to foreign governments. Through the device, furthermore, employed in the " espionage act," of a new name for treason, legislation has made possible the prohibition of seditious utterance and imprisonment for difference of opinion, thereby evading the constitutional restrictions upon the definition and punishment of treason. In the same objectionable realm of enlarging immoderately the powers of the government at Washington belong all efforts aimed at entry of the United States into the League of Nations.

What Burgess thinks of the relation of political science to history is set forth in an address that he delivered in 1896 before the American Historical Association.[14] The categories of time and cause and effect, he believes, are insufficient to work out the true conception of history; for they do not distinguish it clearly from any other body of knowledge. That which supplies the crucial test is " self-progression." Whereas in nature the " chain of events returns into itself," on the principle that what has happened will happen again, in history the significant thing is the increment in succeeding events. What has befallen a given people ought never to occur again precisely as it did before. Should it do so, the fact indicates that where and when the recurrence takes place, as regards the underlying cause at least, history either is not being made or is being unmade. In evaluating the past, therefore, wisdom does not consist simply in knowing what has happened, but in apprehending correctly the variations in conditions as they change

[14] *Annual report of the American Historical Association for the year 1896,* i, 203–11.

and the accretions produced thereby in the events that follow.

Observation of phenomena from the standpoint of the category of self-progression leads to certain conclusions. Of these, the first would hold that the substance of history is spirit, since spirit alone " possesses the creative power of making the consequent contain more than the antecedent, of making the effect an advance upon the cause." The second would regard that substance as human spirit, because " progress can be predicated only to the finite and the imperfect." Thirdly, the events that constitute historical facts are specifically " those creations of the human spirit which are the symbols of its advance toward its own perfection."

History in the making, therefore, is the progressive realization of the ideals of the human spirit in all of the objective forms of their manifestation. In the writing, it is the " true and faithful record of these progressive revelations of the human reason marking the stages of advance toward ultimate perfection. Should there be retrogression in the experience of a given part of mankind, that portion then ceases to make history, or rather, unmakes it." The happenings of the time furnish material for tragedy and romance, but not the stuff out of which history is made.

Defining now the specific relation of history to political science, Burgess quotes with qualified approval an utterance of J. R. Seeley to his students at Cambridge University in 1885. " History," declared the English scholar,

is the name of a residuum which has been left when one group of facts after another has been taken possession of by some science; . . . the residuum which now exists must go the way of the rest, and . . . the time is not very distant when a science will take possession of the facts which are still the undisputed property of the historian — [15]

namely, political science. Burgess, on his part, declares that the process of casting the principles of the doctrines that this science posits " into the objective forms and institutions of positive law " is an "historical process and movement," just as the doctrines themselves are largely an historical product. Even if political science has attained a stage of completeness sufficient to regard it as the basis of constitutional law, its " propositions are being continually modified and readjusted by new practical experiences." Leading them at one moment, it is led by them at another. Hence its genesis and development meet all the requirements of a true historical process.

Of all the movements of history, the evolution of the principle of national popular sovereignty, as defined by political science and its concrete effectuation in constitutional law, is the most intricate and far-reaching. " It involves facts about race, language, tradition, custom, literature, ethics, philosophy and religion, in addition to those more commonly considered as belonging to the exhibitions of force and power." Doing so, it is in actuality the historical growth of a " consensus of opinion among the people of a country concerning the fundamental principles of government and liberty and the objective realization of that opinion as supreme law." '

With all due regard to the contention of Seeley, Burgess holds that " there is a vast number of the facts of human experience which can not be exclusively claimed by any science as yet developed." For such a body of knowledge an appropriate designation would be " history." When-

[15] *Introduction to political science*, 9, 12.

ever mankind " shall have reached that fullness of experience which shall enable it to become completely conscious of itself, it may then be able to turn all of its knowledge into science." Should such a degree of perfection in intellectual achievement be attained, history may be said to have done its work. But, " when that far-distant day shall have been reached and the historian shall be no longer needed, the retirement of the political scientist also will not be greatly delayed." Until the coming of that time, arrangement of the facts of history " in the forms and conclusions of science will only lift history to a higher plane, as the experiences of mankind approach more nearly to the ideals and the goal of civilization."

An element of political science which can not be classed as history is philosophical speculation. If "true and correct," it is the forerunner of history. For when

political facts and conclusions come in contact with political reason, they awaken in that reason a consciousness of political ideals not yet realized. Thrown into the form of propositions, these ideals become principles of political science, then articles of political creeds, and at last laws and institutions. . . . While this speculative element in political science must be kept in constant, truthful and vital connection with the historical component, and must be . . . regulated by the historical component, it is nevertheless the most important element in political science, because it lights the way of progress and directs human experience toward its ultimate purpose.[16]

In sum, " there are parts of history which are not political science and there is an element in political science which is not strictly history; " yet the two spheres so overlap and interpenetrate each other that they can not be dis-

[16] *Annual report of the American Historical Association for the year 1896*, i, 203–11.

tinctly separated. "Political science," concludes Burgess, "must be studied historically, and history must be studied politically, in order to secure a correct comprehension of either. Separate them, and the one becomes a cripple, if not a corpse; the other, a will-o'-the-wisp."

That history must be studied politically is a maxim that Burgess exemplifies in his writing of it. His theme is politics, the science of politics and the realization of that science in constitutional law, as interpreted in accordance with principles derived from philosophical speculation on the basis of experience. Clarity, compactness, vigor and readability mark his style; fearlessness, breadth of vision, freedom from sectionalism and demonstration of an intense national feeling distinguish his attitude. Whenever the occasion seems to demand it also, he can become a decided partisan of what he deems right in obedience to the dictates of reason and conscience. Familiar in the days of his youth with conditions in the South, knowing well the sentiments of its people — for he was one of them, inheriting and cherishing at the same time an ardent sense of devotion to the Union, which was enhanced by his service in the army that fought for its preservation, he sought and found in a Northern and a European education the instrumentalities of expression requisite to enable him to transmute a surging thought into the cogent word. Having himself lived through many of the phenomena that he describes, he had only to amplify his own recollections by what he could learn from the testimony of reliable witnesses, earlier or contemporary, and from other sources of independent worth, in order to paint a glowing picture of sixty years and more in the constitutional development of the United States. No other writer on the field who, like

him, had passed through the crucible of the years of conflict from 1860 to 1877, attained the poise and the sea-
soned judgment which are the singular possession of this
Southerner by birth, Northerner by adoption, and American by devotion to a common country.

In his initial work of an historical character — *The
Middle Period, 1817–1858*,[17] — the topic is the struggle
centering in Congress between the North that strove to
adapt an instrument of government and liberty to the successive needs of a nation in development, and the South
that held fast to the ideas of the men who framed the Constitution. Each labored according to its lights and on behalf of its own interests. The North, however, looked to
the present that had a future; the South, to the present
that had a past. These respective viewpoints, embodied
in legislative procedure and enactment, are described and
discussed with reference to the principles of political science and constitutional law involved in them. From that
mode of interpretation it becomes demonstrable that,
genetically speaking, the North was right and the South,
wrong. Historically alone the South may have had something of a case, but solely in the sense of let things be as
they were, or let them not be.

The second work, called *The Civil War and the Constitution, 1859–1865*,[18] though in substance a record of military occurrences, gives heed to a number of political questions that the sectional struggle had engendered. Like its
predecessor, it furnishes an extensive, yet well condensed
and skillfully ordered, mass of information interspersed
with frequent and pertinent comment. The judicial temperament again is manifest, as are also clearness and in-

[17] New York, 1901.   [18] 2 vols., New York, 1901.

dependence in expression; but the tone is more distinctly human. In his strictures upon individuals, certainly, Burgess displays no particular hesitancy in the selection of terms. His keen dislike for the extremists of the South finds a parallel in his utter disapproval of their ilk in the North.

The cause of secession he believes constitutionally and morally indefensible. The only real grievance of the South was, that the Republican party might legislate contrary to the wishes of the secessionists on matters admittedly within the legal competence of Congress. The South, moreover, had been offered compromises beyond anything that with any show of reason it might expect. As to the exercise of the war-power, the government of the United States undoubtedly

overstepped its ordinary limitations; but it had, and has, the constitutional right to do that in periods of extraordinary danger. The root of the error in denying this right lies in the claim that the Constitution made the Union. The truth is, that the Union made the Constitution, and that the physical and ethical conditions of our territory and population made the Union.

The third of the treatises on sixty-odd years of American national history bears the title: *Reconstruction and the Constitution, 1866–1876.*[19] It provides in the main a survey of the processes employed for rehabilitating the States that had lost the war. The purpose that pervades it is, to foster the spirit of reconciliation between North and South, through an impartial adducement of the facts and a candid admission of the errors — and worse — perpetrated in the course of Reconstruction.

The treatment of questions relating to or affected by the

[19] New York, 1902.

Constitution as such is keen, discriminating and eminently judicious. Here calmness of utterance imparts to the author's conclusions much of the weight and emphasis of a decision from the bench. But, although Burgess sustains the Congressional interpretation of the relation existing between the erstwhile States and the Union, in that through secession they became territories and continued such until reinstated, he condemns roundly the methods chosen by the Republican majority in Congress for making that interpretation effective. Not content with a presentation of facts and theories alone, he declares what in his opinion ought to have been done. Sharp criticism is the necessary accompaniment of his earnest desire to ascertain and set forth the true constitutional ground that should have been occupied at every stage in the momentous proceedings. Hence he censures and applauds alternately the executive and legislative branches of the government and individual statesmen of the time, according as they depart from or adhere to what he thinks the proper norm of action. The values of the various measures adopted he subjects to the test supplied by what he calls the principles of " sound political science and correct constitutional law." The conduct of men, on the other hand, he judges from a politico-ethical standpoint.

To this trilogy Burgess added thirteen years later an epilogue: *The administration of President Hayes.*[20] It appears in the form of lectures delivered at Kenyon College, Ohio, the *alma mater* of that President. Iterating a belief expressed in his previous work, that the personality and achievements of Hayes had not been duly estimated and appreciated, Burgess makes plain his conviction that

[20] New York, 1915.

the reëstablishment of constitutional normality in the United States was due to the presidential policy of the time more than to any other factor. In this light he pictures the party struggles, the disposition of the House of Representatives to override the Senate, their joint efforts to control the executive, and the peculiar difficulties that beset the task of political and financial recovery from the evils that had attended the era of Reconstruction. It was the wisdom, the courage and the steadfastness of Hayes which righted the keel of the ship of state, enabling it to sail forth once more out upon the open sea of a nation's welfare.

The portrayal of a President not reckoned usually among the most eminent of our chief magistrates reveals Burgess striving to do justice to the man as well as to the policies followed. This desire for rectitude in the estimate of an individual and his measures, coupled with enthusiasm for a cause that stands the tests of knowledge and reason, is a trait of the scholar whose gifts of mind and personality have made him so conspicuously a master of social science. The definiteness, moreover, with which he forms conclusions is equalled only by the tenacity with which he holds them. In the profound study and mature reflection upon which they are based he finds justification for their statement and maintenance. Doubt befits the man who does not know; certainty, the man who does.

Whether one agrees with Burgess or not, no one can in fairness question the sincerity of his convictions or accuse him of evading an issue. Of tergiversation he displays not a trace. Dogmatic he may be, but never domineering in his dogmatism. With all the fixity of his own sentiments, he has always shown the broadest tolerance of differences in opinion. That is what renders him so ardent an apostle of individual liberty, so implacable an enemy of whatever restricts its rightful enjoyment. Fearing not to say what he thinks, he demands the same spirit in others.

In his attitude toward education, political science and constitutional law, no less than in his treatment of the men and events of history, Burgess envisages them, it would seem, from the viewpoint of the aristocrat — not that of the devotee of an autocracy inherent in the few, the wise and the good, but that of a staunch believer in the privileges that are the guerdon of intelligence, ability and thrift. These indeed are not the right of the few to possess, but of the many to obtain. Honest in his partisanship for the power of mind over mass, of character and knowledge over instinct and emotion, he exalts the safeguards that are needed to uphold orderliness in thought and conduct against all agencies of action operating from above or from below, which would substitute the rule of sheer numbers for the governance of law and reason. If in the realm of politics and all that a scientific study of it connotes he has never produced an elaborate body of doctrine, if he has never cultivated allurements of style, if he has never sought the popularity that responds to the touch of personal magnetism, he has laid down nevertheless in terse phraseology and compact statement the absolute fundamentals upon which that body of doctrine would rest and which those who would know them may see.

The tendencies that appear to accompany in recent years the evolution of the fields of study, more or less related and yet more or less distinct, which have been grouped under the general designation of " social science," Burgess regards with a measure of mistrust. They reveal at times, he believes, a disposition to convert an intrinsic

interest in fundamental principles into a zest for manifestations of easy inexactness in thought and expression.
Rather than producing actual sciences that require precise
knowledge, sound reasoning and correct definition for their
understanding and elucidation, their development would
seem to indicate the presence of a bent for gathering multiplicities of detail and the absence of a zeal for coherent organization and logical formulation. Too much is being
assembled in the shape of things of transience which float
about on a readily perceptible surface, and too little of the
things of permanence which lie deep-rooted beneath. Instead of displaying a vital concern for ascertaining the
really basic relations of man to the state and to society,
" sciences of opinion " would appear to be the outcome —
not categories of consecutive thought derived from accuracy of information. Quantitatively, their output may be
impressive; qualitatively, they are apt to exhibit the earmarks of a pseudo-science animated by mental and often
sentimental emotionalism. The net result thus would be
the fostering of a cult of generalities in loose and impulsive
utterance, of an acreage of pages, of the unlimited expanse
of speech. An intensive tillage of the narrow strips lying
within that genuine field of the intellect where alone real
knowledge, close reasoning and exact definition can be
made to rise from the soil is, and must be, the true and the
sole function of science, whatever the import of the adjec-
tive that precedes the name.

On the personal side, Burgess has ever been a man
whom his students remember with affection, in which there
is just a bit of awe. An old-time Southern gentleman, dignified, gracious, urbane and kindly; calm, yet never rigid;
reserved, yet never aloof; austere perhaps, yet never for-

bidding, he inspired them with trust in his learning, confidence in his guidance, and belief in their own capacity to accomplish the things worth while. They can picture him now — the tall, spare figure entering the classroom and motioning to the nearest student to close the windows, so that his voice, none too strong, might be heard amid the clatter of a great city. They listen with attention to him expounding comparative constitutional law, and marvel at the power of intellect which enables him to lecture on an abstruse subject with not a scrap of paper on the desk before him. They wonder no less why, in his discussion of quite a different theme — the constitutional history of the United States, which has about it a connectedness that would necessitate seemingly little aid from notes — he always places before him a roll of manuscript, but never looks at it. They recall their eager interest when Burgess characterizes with graphic phrase and apt quotation the career and conduct of men who shaped the nation's weal or woe. They remember with gratitude the conferences in seminar and office, where the master gave the pupils the best of his mind and spirit, instilling into them a desire to seek the truth and resolutely to make it known.

Fifty years have elapsed since Burgess began at Columbia his long life of service to the cause of university education, political science, constitutional law and American history. During it he has been honored often in this country and abroad with the academic laurels that are among the rewards of learning. Here and in Europe he has interchanged ideas with men of national and international eminence. Mentally and physically alert, he sees ahead no years of decline, but only those of restful study and contemplation amid surroundings at his summer home in

Newport, Rhode Island, and his winter residence in Brook-
line, Massachusetts, which insure the comfort and serenity
that are his later heritage.   Many a chat has he had there
with that other grand old man of American scholarship —
Charles William Eliot; and many a member of younger
generations would have counted himself fortunate, had he
been privileged to listen!

CHAPTER III
LESTER FRANK WARD

By
JAMES QUAYLE DEALEY
Professor of Social and Political Science in Brown University

LESTER FRANK WARD

CHAPTER III
LESTER FRANK WARD [1]

LESTER F. WARD in the field of social science is to the United States what Auguste Comte is to France or Herbert Spencer to England. Great pioneer in the development of sociology on this side of the Atlantic, he was often referred to in his later years as the Nestor of American sociologists. At the same time his comprehensive knowledge and his scientific method make him, even yet, an admirable approach to the study of the social sciences.

Few, if any, Americans can compare with Ward in the breadth and depth of his scientific and philosophic information. In his teaching at Brown University he made his colleagues gasp by announcing a course entitled, " A Survey of All Knowledge." Aided by a chart [2] he, in the course of a year, worked up from astronomy and the physical sciences, into the organic and the psychic, and closed with an exposition of the laws and principles basal to sociology and a discussion of its numerous sub-divisions. Throughout he emphasized a monistic and synthetic explanation of the field of knowledge, with hints here and there as to the trend of future investigations.

This remarkable fund of knowledge on his part was the result of the study and meditation of a full half century,

[1] Born in Joliet, Illinois, June 18, 1841; died in Washington, D. C., April 18, 1913.
[2] A facsimile of this may be seen in Emily Palmer Cape's *Lester F. Ward,* pages 148–149.

during which he devoted, in his leisure time, all the energy of his mind to scientific study and investigation and to the expression of his thought in numerous writings. One wonders what he might have accomplished in the sociological field, had his last twenty-five years been freed from the necessity of economic task work for daily support, for Ward was born in poverty, his income throughout his life was rather meager, and his estate at death was of small value.

Ward was fortunate in his parentage. On the paternal side was an old New England family of English descent, honored by a recent genealogy.[3] On the maternal side was the Loomis family, famous for many distinguished members; the mother herself was the daughter of a clergyman and a woman of refinement and literary taste. The father was a mechanic of an inventive turn of mind, a veteran of the War of 1812, and a rolling stone of the pioneer type. He first moved his family from New York State to Illinois and then after some years the parents, with their two youngest children, Erastus and Lester, moved by wagon to Iowa, where the father died in 1857. After the father's death the mother with her two sons returned to Illinois.

The youngest son, Lester, the youngest of ten children, was at this time nearly sixteen years of age, and he at once sought work for self support; in the following year he moved to Pennsylvania, working, farming, and at times teaching school. The boy's education during his early years was chiefly in the school of hard knocks and experience, there being little opportunity for formal education. Yet he found mental stimulus in the family environment

[3] *The Genealogy of the Descendants of Andrew Ward of Fairfield, Connecticut.* Edition, 1910.

and through contact with the natural phenomena and teeming life of the prairies whence he got his great love for nature. In his early adolescent years young Lester mastered the contents of what books he could find, developed great fondness for languages, more especially French, German, Greek and Latin, and finally, by the time he was twenty-one years of age, he was able to spend a little over a year completing a course at an academy at Towanda, Pennsylvania, in preparation for college. But in 1862 the Civil War was raging and he could not resist Lincoln's call for additional troops, so that in the summer he enlisted in the army, marrying just before his departure Elizabeth Vought,[4] a love match followed by his lonely honeymoon in camp. He was severely wounded at the battle of Chancellorsville, three gunshot wounds, and was discharged from service November 18, 1864, because of physical disability.

Beginning in 1865 and for the next forty years he was in governmental service, at first as a clerk in the Treasury Department, then he became Chief of the Division of Navigation and Immigration and afterwards Librarian of the United States Bureau of Statistics. In 1881 he entered the United States Geological Survey, and in 1892 became chief paleontologist. His linguistic ability was recognized by appointments among the collaborators of the *Century Dictionary* and of the last supplement to Webster's *International Dictionary*. As special agent for the United States Bureau of Education also he prepared a report on " Sociology at the Paris Exposition of 1900," at which he spent several months. During the last twenty-four years

---

[4] She died in 1872, having had one child who died in infancy. Ward was later married to Miss Simons, who survived him by a few months, leaving no children.

of governmental service he specialized in botanical and geological work and in paleobotany. In the summer of 1906 he was able to gratify a life-long ambition — that of instructing in a university — by accepting a position as Professor of Sociology at Brown University, thus giving him leisure for authorship. This position he held until death came in the spring in 1913; he was buried at Washington and later reinterred in the Brookside Cemetery of Watertown, New York.

Ward's attainment in 1865 of a place in the Civil Service at Washington gave him at last a real opportunity for formal education. Columbian (now George Washington) University offered then as now evening classes in collegiate instruction and of these he took advantage. In rapid succession he secured the A. B. degree (1869), LL.B. (1871), A. M. (1872), and in 1897 was given the honorary degree of LL.D. He had a diploma in medicine also but once jokingly remarked that his conscience would not permit him to *practice* either in law or medicine. He was a member in many learned societies, holding high office in some, but those of which he felt especially proud were his election to the presidency of the Institut International de Sociologie, 1900–1903, and his election as the first president of the American Sociological Society, 1906–1907.

Ward's real education came not so much from the class room but rather through his own eager desire to add to his fund of knowledge by studying along the line of his interests. A glance at the list of his published articles in *Glimpses of the Cosmos,* aside from his formal works in the natural sciences and in sociology, shows his keen interest in astronomy, biology, anthropology, psychology, economics and political science. Education also was one of his favorite fields, the social aspects of which especially interested him. He studied deeply into philosophic systems, paying especial attention to Kant, and wrote much on religion, at first as a controversialist against the errors of the churches and the dogmatism of theology and in later years in attempts to work out a philosophic basis for a world religion freed from superstition. In all of these studies he was greatly aided by his facility in the knowledge of languages. In addition to the four already mentioned he read Italian, Spanish and Russian, besides having a bowing acquaintance with several others.

Obviously such attainments were not made by one in poor health or of weak physique. Ward hardly knew a sick day in his life until he had passed seventy years of age. He was in height fully six feet, broad shouldered, deep chested, and muscular from the experiences of early years, showing no tendency towards stoutness. Even in his sixties he was able to walk without apparent fatigue fifteen to twenty miles on a stretch, absorbed in the botanical or geological phenomena about him. In complexion he was blond, but tanned by much exposure to the sun, and had brown hair and the bluish-gray eyes of his race. In older years he acquired a "scholarly stoop" that detracted somewhat from his real height. He smoked with great moderation and rarely drank except on social occasions. His abounding health enabled him to work hard and long, day after day, with very brief intervals for rest or social intercourse, since he found his happiness, not in play or amusement, but in the contact of mind with mind or in reflection in his study or on the long jaunts away from the city into the country.

In personality Ward was rather modest and at times

almost bashful, especially in addressing gatherings of
women. Having traveled widely all over the United States
and in Europe, where he was well known and highly es-
teemed, he was an excellent conversationalist on worthwhile subjects but disliked small talk. He was fond of
home life and of children, though awkward with them
through lack of experience in their ways. He was twice
happily married, to women highly congenial and interested
in his studies and literary labors. Each was a constant
stimulus to him in his ambitions and daily tasks, and to
their influence doubtless may be ascribed much of his belief in woman's capacity and his stress on a marriage based
on love and mutual appreciation.

His natural dignity was best manifested in scientific
gatherings where he felt himself to be at home. In the expression of opinion he was clear, logical and brief, having
a fine command of English and was never at a loss for an
appropriate illustration. Like many who seem somewhat
distant and reserved he was at heart rather deeply emotional and affectionate and was highly appreciative of sympathetic attention, but his emotional nature was held in
check by circumstances and subordinated to the necessity
of intellectual tasks needing attention. In his work he was
systematic, painstaking and withal extremely conscientious, insisting always on the completion of his official tasks
before taking up the work of his leisure hours. He regularly verified his quotations or references, often spending
hours in finding the original source needed and his ambition was to make no statement not susceptible of proof.
He had a puritanic sense of duty, punctiliously fulfilling
his promises and engagements. In his last days he kept
at his class work long after other men would have taken to

their beds and even then he would not stop until assured that his classes would be continued during his illness. Since his income always had been rather small he had learned close economy and hence, of necessity, refrained from expenditures for amusement in itself. As long as he lived he worked hard, lived closely and steeled himself so as to " hew to the line " and to give little heed to the many distractions and enticements of social life. He lived, therefore, a rather lonely life, having, to be sure, many friends, but persons who for the most part were, like himself, devoted to their work, so that these were met chiefly at intellectual and scientific gatherings.

In the larger sense of the word Ward was deeply religious, not theologically nor ecclesiastically, but in the idealism of his morals and his aspiration to make achievements helpful to humanity. He had a strong belief that his sociological teachings would make possible a more rapid rate to human progress and that as these became accepted and put into effect the average man would become proportionately happier in his daily life. Raised as he was under frontier conditions and in poverty, used to work with hands as well as head, he was democratic through and through and hence preached the gospel of equal opportunity that each might attain the best of which he was capable.

As an intellectual worker Ward was the very embodiment of order and system. From 1860 to the time of his death he kept a diary, writing down scrupulously at the end of every day its chief events, especially those that bore upon his literary life.[5] He kept a careful record also of the

[5] After his death his relatives in a moment of thoughtlessness destroyed these priceless diaries, some forty in number.

facts respecting his numerous writings and in addition a complete scrap-book system of twenty-three volumes, classified under the headings, *Reviews and Press Notices, Autograph Letters* and *Biography*. In his reading he read systematically, noting important passages or thoughts and indexing them with cross references in his filing system, for, in order to be able to locate any item easily, he made a thorough card index of every name, subject, or important key word contained in his diaries or scrapbooks, or noted in his reading. A series of supplementary letter files systematically arranged completed his filing system. Whenever possible he worked standing at a high desk and in doing his literary work he used the pencil or the pen, not a typist or a typewriter, these being made use of only in official business. In *Glimpses of the Cosmos* he explains the methods he used in writing each of his several sociological works, but these are too lengthy for quotation.

When he entered Brown University as professor of sociology he was sixty-five years of age and practically without experience in class-room work beyond occasional lecture courses at summer sessions of universities. In the class room he was not inspirational in type but his age, dignity, and thorough knowledge became a sort of inspiration to his students who revered him and personally liked him, so that it became " the thing " to have at least one course under him as a valuable college experience. In preparation for a course he blocked out the entire subject for a year, wrote on cards the essential points of each part, and lectured from these. His arrangement of subjects was so orderly and his blackboard drawings so graphic, that the class had no difficulty in following him. He invited questions but preferred straight lecturing and relied much on papers prepared on assigned subjects. During his last five years, his wife being ill, he lived in a dormitory among the students, who often availed themselves of his invitation to call. There was much sadness on the campus when the half-masted flag gave information of the passing of the great teacher.

Mrs. Emily Palmer Cape, who collaborated with him in the preparation of *Glimpses of the Cosmos,* in her little volume, *Lester F. Ward,* stresses in her description of him his emotional nature, his kindly humor, and his deep sympathy with nature. She quotes as applicable to him Comte's characterization of a true leader of humanity — one who has " the mind of a sage, the heart of a woman, and the soul of a poet."

In mentality Ward was unquestionably a genius but not of the erratic abnormal sort emphasized by Lombroso. By heredity he had a strong physique and a capable mind; the outdoor life of his boyhood strengthened his physique but the absence of systematic schooling and broad intellectual contacts, coupled with the absence of libraries during these boyhood years, proved to be a real handicap to his mental development. His war experiences and their aftermath possibly account for the intense radicalism of his early anti-ecclesiastical attitude, but the times themselves were controversial since Darwinism and evolutionary teachings were under discussion and theology was on the defensive.

After that " period of storm and stress " he settled down definitely to his life work and during the next ten years in his leisure hours he completed the manuscript for *Dynamic Sociology.* He was then about forty years of age and embodied in this work practically all the main ideas of what may be called his system of sociology. In the next thirty

or more years of life still remaining he considerably broadened out his general knowledge by constant reading, discussion, and reflection, so that in his later works modifications of his earlier views and a changing emphasis may be
noticed. Hence, though in general it is true that his later
works contain nothing not stated or hinted in *Dynamic
Sociology,* yet it would be unfortunate had the later volumes not been written. These represent his matured conclusions as to the essentials of his teachings, omission indicating those that might best be ignored, and enlargement,
those that should receive more prominence than was given
them in his earlier work. His *Psychic Factors* and *Applied
Sociology,* for example, place vigorous emphasis on the
achievement of genius and the place of the psychic in a
sociocracy characterized by telesis.

Ward's chief sociological works are (1) *Dynamic Sociology,* two volumes, 1883; (2) *The Psychic Factors of
Civilization,* 1893; (3) *Outlines of Sociology,* 1898; (4)
Pure Sociology,[6] 1903; (5) *Applied Sociology,* 1906. All
of these have been translated into other languages, although not all into each language. Translations into German, French, Spanish, Italian, Russian, Polish and Japa-
nese are mentioned by Ward in his *Glimpses of the Cosmos.*
His other work, aside from the several volumes of botanical and geological material,[7] is his *Glimpses of the Cosmos,*
originally planned by him to be issued in twelve volumes,
but reduced to six after his death owing to lack of funds

---

[6] The *Textbook of Sociology,* 1905, by Dealey and Ward, is
mainly a condensation of this volume.

[7] His chief botanical work is entitled *Guide to the Flora of
Washington and Vicinity.* For an account of his botanical studies
see *Glimpses of the Cosmos,* Volume II, pages 448–464. His geological and paleobotanical works are contained in nine large illustrated
memoirs published by the United States Geological Survey.

for publication. This series is rather unique in that it presents a chronological arrangement of everything Ward ever published, " great and small, good, bad and indifferent," exclusive of books and large illustrated memoirs and monographs. Ward's thought was that by such an arrangement the development of his intellectual life might best be traced, from the callow productions of early youth to the matured reflections of later manhood. Volume I, for example, is made up almost wholly of articles written before he was thirty years of age, many of which were printed in the *Iconoclast,* of which he was editor, hitting at the errors and supposedly false teachings of religion. Volume II, the next ten years, is chiefly botanical, showing his absorption in that field. Volume III continues the botanical but also devotes itself largely to sociology, since *Dynamic Sociology* was now in print. The remaining three volumes cover almost the entire field of knowledge, though with the greatest stress on the teaching of the social sciences and of psychology. The whole set of six volumes covers a literary period of fifty-five years.

In order properly to appreciate Ward's system of sociology one should keep clearly in mind the social environment of his first forty years. His first sixteen years were spent on what was then the frontier, in the pioneer life of the middle west, in touch with nature and the soil, but with little opportunity for education. In the following five years he managed to secure, while supporting himself, education enough for college entrance, an education made up chiefly of languages, both ancient and modern, along with some mathematics, of which he was not fond. His next ten years included his first marriage, his war experience ended by three gunshot wounds, and then a governmental clerkship and his collegiate years at Columbian. The support of a family on a small salary, the pursuit of an education, and his clerical duties all combined drove him hard, yet he found time also to edit the *Iconoclast,* writing most of its contents during the brief duration of its existence.[8] This was the period of a post war psychology and a radicalism that revolted against the established order. Throughout this period of formal education he had no scientific studies of any value and his interests were largely in the field of philosophy and education. He started the next decade (1871–1881) with a clear conviction that education was the great panacea for human progress and began systematic reading in philosophy, religion and the sciences, being especially attracted by the works of Francis Bacon, Kant, and Draper, and of Agassiz, Lyell, Haeckel, Comte and Spencer. Meanwhile, he devoted himself to the study of botany, and later of anthropology and geology, and during the whole decade devoted himself to the preparation of the manuscript that ultimately became *Dynamic Sociology.* In Washington itself he was in contact with a large intellectual and scientific circle of kindred minds and in this cultural atmosphere, through discussion and the presentation of papers at literary and scientific gatherings, he broadened out in his attainment and in his world view of life. In this he was greatly aided by his second wife who was deeply interested in aesthetic studies and worked harmoniously with him until 1908 when she became permanently invalidic. This large social environment, therefore, formed the background for his *Dynamic Sociology,* which was completed in 1880 and published in 1883. Volume I of this work shows the influence of his scientific and other

[8] From March, 1870, to August, 1871.

reading during the seventies, and Volume II represents his earlier stress on progress and education. From this period also there survives a large unpublished manuscript on education, substantially in harmony with the famous Chapter XIV in Volume II.

After 1883 his reading widened in scope and became more systematic, making notes and indexing whatever he read. He rarely read for recreation merely but rather when in search of material for reflection and supplementary to his own scientific pursuits. In his special scientific studies — botany, paleobotany and geology — he was a close and exact observer and made many worthwhile contributions to the knowledge of these subjects, since he traveled extensively at home and in Europe and brought to his studies an eager interest and a keen and synthesizing mind. His theory of sympodial development [9] illustrates the originality of his thought in this field and his monistic application of this to social development.

In other scientific studies, both inorganic and organic, he followed carefully the newer teachings of the sciences that multipled so rapidly after 1860, more especially the kaleidoscopic development of biology, anthropology and psychology, realizing as he did that these were basal for sociology in which field he manifested a growing interest. His thorough training in science and scientific methods enabled him to criticize and to appreciate new points of view as they appeared, so that his numerous smaller writings from 1883 up to the time of his death testify to his wide knowledge of and his deep sympathy with the broadening field of knowledge.

As a sociologist his comprehension of the many fields of

[9] *Pure Sociology*, pages 71–79.

science enabled him to grasp the unity of knowledge, to stress the relationship or filiation of all the sciences, and to illustrate sociological teachings by analogous teachings in other sciences. This, however, to many made the reading of his works difficult since they were, in general, unfamiliar with the sciences; others also were repelled by the numerous words of Greek derivation that he coined so as to express his thought more concisely, so that his works never met with large sales. They were read by the few, not by the many. As a matter of fact his style is remarkably clear and logical, stressing a simple English vocabulary wherever possible. At times his sentences are eloquent and almost rythmic since much of his work he wrote when his head and his heart were so full that they demanded expression in literary form.

In the last third of his life he had become so absorbed in his teachings that the personal pronouns became prominent, giving the appearance of egotism. He did, to be sure, realize that he had a well trained and capable mind and that he had done some excellent work, yet at heart, as already explained, he was very modest and in gatherings never sought to dominate the discussion or to assert his own point of view, preferring to hear others speak when they had thoughts worthy of expression. The writer once sat by his side while he meekly listened to a young instructor in philosophy who was explaining to him a point in Kant's teachings, a subject Ward had studied for seven years. Yet not by a word did he intimate to the young man that the matter was very familiar to him. When prominence did come to Ward because of his recognized merit, he assumed it naturally and in action showed himself easily to be *primus inter pares*.

In the last five years of his life at Providence, the absence of his wife who was then a permanent invalid at Washington under her sister's care and the consequent loss of companionship, coupled with the constant drains on his purse, distinctly depressed him and probably shortened his life through a too close economy and unremitting labor without much relaxation. On the other hand, he often asserted that his years at Brown University were the happiest of his life, since he was free from the routine of governmental service and could devote all of his time to his studies in the midst of an intellectual atmosphere. Though past seventy years at death, he really died prematurely, when both body and mind were still powerful, and when many thoughts written in note form only were awaiting literary expression.

In the sociological world there is no definite agreement as to what constitutes the field of sociology. The field is becoming highly specialized and each specialist tends to assume that his is the real field, so that, as a graduate student once remarked, " I have studied fifty-seven different varieties and don't yet know what sociology itself is." To Ward all this sort of thing was anathema. All knowledge is one, he taught, each particular science is merely a differentiation of science, so that all sciences are interrelated and may be synthesized into one philosophy. The great fields of scientific knowledge may be arranged in logical order into a series, from the cosmic and the inorganic, through the organic and the psychic to the social, which supplies the crowning science from the anthropocentric point of view.

This theory of the classification of sciences, first worked out by Comte, Ward asserted to be, " the most sublime, interesting, and important idea of the nineteenth century."

It is clear, therefore, that Ward continued the Comtean, Spencerian tradition of a synthetic philosophy, but, with the advantage of another generation of intense research and scientific development, he was able to transcend their teachings and through his stress on the psychic factor in civilization to blaze out a new path in the study of sociology. If one may use Ward's botanical illustration, each of these three writers represents a sympode in the development of sociology.

In *Dynamic Sociology* [10] and in *Glimpses of the Cosmos* [11] Ward summarizes what, in his opinion, has been his contribution to the world's thought. In the first reference five contributions are named and in the second, eighteen. Hints or " adumbrations " of these he admits may be found before his views were in print, but he asserts that he was the first clearly to enunciate them and to give them place in a scheme of scientific philosophy. Many of these are not really sociological teachings but belong to the field of a monistic and synthetic philosophy. They illustrate well the type of thought that characterized Ward's genius. Surveying in his mind's eye the entire field of knowledge as he saw it, he sought by meditation and comparison to ascertain the few simple generalizations that should underlie all knowledge, if it is unitary. These broad universal generations, if known, would obviously illuminate the mass of endless detail of human knowledge, seemingly without order or significance, and would suggest the fundamental principles basal to each particular science, including, therefore, sociology. To Ward the complex mass of sociological data can not properly be comprehended unless it

---

[10] Preface to the first edition.
[11] Volume I, pages lxxviii to lxxxix.

be integrated with the other sciences in the series and its teachings coördinated with the broad generalizations synthesized from the deductions of these sciences. In other words, sociological fundamentals must be integrated with the teachings of psychology, and these with the teachings of biology, and these again with the teachings derived from the study of the inorganic in the universe. Ward, therefore, in his researches was continually seeking for laws and principles basal in a monistic, synthesized, coördinated field of sciences explanatory of cosmic phenomena. For that reason he had no special interest in particular fields of social science, except to show the relation of these to the fundamental teachings of a synthetic social philosophy. As one might put it, trees should be seen in their relation to the forest of which they form a part. Obviously few in any one generation possess the wide knowledge and generalizing type of mind needed to grasp clearly the synthetic aspect of the whole field of knowledge, so that, lacking such philosophic leaders, sociology is differentiating into innumerable specialized studies, each apparently complete in itself, yet lacking that integrating perspective that puts it into relations with kindred knowledge. Differentiation, however, without integration, leads on to chaos, so that from time to time sociologists must return to synthetic coordinating processes and in so doing must inevitably retrace somewhat fully the steps marked out in Ward's synthetic social philosophy. Space will not permit of a lengthy exposition of the cosmic teachings he would emphasize, but in brief they may be summarized as follows, prefacing with the remark that these, in his opinion, are not merely speculative, but are founded on scientific facts or on scientific hypotheses in process of proof or disproof.

The universe, he taught, is energy, pulsating, creative, since there is a constant compounding and recompounding of conflicting manifestations of energy (the principle of synergy), resulting in a series of cosmic creations, such as the so-called elements and their compounds in chemistry or the particular energies and mass bodies of physics including stellar systems, or the protoplasmic cell and its myriad compounds in biology, or the organic nervous system with its instincts, its feelings and its capacity to think, and finally the social group and the social phenomena and activity arising from the contact of mind with mind, or mind in contact with its manifold environment. These innumerable " synthetic creations of nature " are dynamos of stored energy, finding their highest expression to us in human kind, combining in itself the great sympodes — life, feeling, thought, and social creative achievement.

These synthetic creations of nature are evolutionary, each later one in the series evolving from what preceded and hence all are filiated. The scientific philosopher, therefore, should seek to show by study and research this filiated evolution, as, for example, the differential of protoplasm from chemical compounds, the slow evolution of feeling and then of intellect in protoplasmic compounds, and the rise of social groups from the undifferentiated horde of zoölogic man.

Obviously this teaching is throughout monistic and synthetic. Basal to the cosmos is energy, the nisus of nature, the God of religion, working, continuous, comprehensible to the human mind, itself part of the whole, manifesting itself in creations stored in structures functioning each after its own nature but all in harmony with one common principle, monistic, materialistic, yet at the same time deeply spiritual in its highest manifestations. The stars and the mind of man are but differentiations of world energy, having a common origin but differing structures and functions. Human beings are akin to animal and plant and these to the inorganic world and basally to the energy of the universe. Energy is creative, constructive, so that even apparent destruction is reconstruction. An appreciation of this teaching and of man's kinship in the universe was, in Ward's opinion, the essence of ethics and religion, since man is a part of the beginning and the end and is himself the highest manifestation of creative energy known to the mind. He is a part of all that is, the microcosm of the macrocosm, and is himself part of eternity.

Passing now more definitely to Ward's sociological teaching, he, after seeking to trace from biological bases the rise, differentiation and development of intellect, sought to show that the feeling aspect of the human mind is the dynamo, the " dynamic agent," back of human and hence of social activity. The essential teaching is that feelings, wants, desires, ambitions, aspirations drive men on to action and hence in sociology the psychology of feeling is fundamental. The Freudian, psychoanalytic school in psychology illustrates one aspect of such a study and the stress on " interests " in many aspects of social studies furnishes another.

Feeling, unregulated, he argues, leads to destruction and hence arises his contrast between feeling and function. Organisms function through structure and feeling is an aid to function because of the pleasant sensation involved in functioning and the pain arising from non-functioning. With the rise of awareness or " consciousness " the joy of pleasure and dislike of pain may result in making feeling

an end in itself, resulting in excess, as in gluttony, and ultimate death.   Hence arises the rational intellect as an aid
to feeling, which, when well informed through experience
and contact, perceives consequences both good and bad,
thus serving as a guide or " directive agent " to the feelings, so that it suggests inhibition when necessary for ends
perceived in the mind, or suggests expression when striving for ends approved.

In social life these restraints and approvals voice themselves in social institutions, in moral codes and laws, which
restrict, regulate, or allow expression to human feelings in
their various manifestations according as society in its wisdom or unwisdom determines.   From the standpoint of social psychology, therefore, it is essential that human feeling or feelings be clearly understood and then intelligently
controlled (social control), so as to attain socially desirable ends.   In order, however, that guidance or control
be intelligent, it is necessary that the intellect be well informed, so that when decisions are made they may be
approximately correct.   Feeling, therefore, in Ward's psychology is dynamic, it is energy, and energizes its organism
into activity; intellect, by contrast, is not energizing but
illuminative, it directs or guides and can best perform its
function when rightly informed or educated.

Feelings unregulated, or a social control that merely
suppresses or sternly regulates, is wasteful.   Feeling is
energy and should be utilized, not wasted.   The office of
the intellect is to eliminate waste.   Organic nature undi-
rected by intellect is extremely wasteful but when regulated and controlled by well-informed intellect, waste is
largely or wholly eliminated; this makes the contrast between the wasteful " economy of nature " and the efficient

" economy of mind." A well-informed intellect, familiar with its own nature and with human feelings and aims may serve as a guide to human activity, turning it aside from wasteful and destructive action towards those that make for constructive activities and human progress.

These psychological teachings of Ward became basal for his main teachings in sociology and these will now briefly be mentioned. The feelings, being the dynamic aspect of the mind, are the " forces " that urge to action. In group life similarly group needs or desires become the social forces. Of course all social forces are in individuals, felt in their minds, but general needs for the preservation and development of the group become group or social forces. Ward gives a classification of these, naming two chief aspects; those that stress group safety and continuity, and those that elevate or spiritualize, such as the ethical, the aesthetic and the intellectual.

Group feelings, like other feelings, are in need of guidance, or direction, if they are to function safely, so that there is need of social guidance or social control. Social control in its highest manifestation becomes social or collective telesis. Telesis implies that the social ends to be attained are well known and that the ways and means whereby the ends may be attained have been scientifically ascertained. Given this information, the next step is that the social forces move towards the ends desired, guided by the " directive agent," the intellect, following the ways and means determined in advance. *Telesis*, therefore, is not merely purpose, it is purpose combined with scientific knowledge of how to accomplish one's purpose. It is like a combination of an architect's plan and the contractor's estimates, so that when the desire wills compliance with the whole plan, the command is given, action begins and in due time the desired end is attained.

Telesis, it will be noted, is the "economy of mind," eliminating wastefulness in action. The ends sought are attained with the least possible expenditure of energy commensurate with the task. This telic notion applied to social progress is one of the great contributions made by Ward. Nature makes progress in evolutionary fashion, but the natural process is extremely wasteful, meandering in all directions like a slow current on a level plain, instead of going straight forward to the goal as a canal would, for example, if planned by competent engineers. Society, therefore, should not drift aimlessly to and fro, backwards and forwards, without guidance. Rather, the group should carefully study its situations, comprehend the aims it desires to accomplish, study scientifically the best methods for the attainment of these, and then concentrate social energy to the task set before it. The method of the Social Survey illustrates the telic method applied to social improvement.

If society should become fairly conscious of its desired ends, and should become intelligent enough to employ telesis, it would then become *sociocratic*, since stress would be placed on a form of control working constructively for the upbuilding of the whole of society, not merely of a segment of it, as in class control, and hence will furnish to all opportunity for the development of whatever capacity each may have. Intelligent social control eliminating the waste of energy through telesis, would result in *attractive legislation*. For social control, which includes the political, should so frame law and regulation that these would appeal to the individual as fair and worthwhile, thus tending towards a cheerful compliance with law, thereby eliminating much social friction. All repressive laws and those sternly regulative in sort are prima facie defective. As the human mind becomes scientifically known, and the feelings appreciated as the dynamic aspect of the mind, and the intellect acquires greater intelligence through wiser education so as to furnish wise guidance, society will develop systems of organization and control so completely that prohibitions and repressions will cease and law, meeting with the approbation of an intelligent public opinion, will become self-enforcing. Telesis applied to legislation will make it " attractive."

A telic society will unquestionably aim to develop individual as well as general welfare, for after all, society is but a group of individuals and the higher these are in development the better for society. Real progress, whether social or individual, depends on *achievement,* the sum total of which makes civilization. Achievement is human creative synthesis. Nature creates and man also is a creator. He synthesizes differing things into a new combination, a new unity, a creation. It may be mechanistic as in invention; it may be a newer comprehension of nature so as to utilize its energies more fully, as in scientific discovery; it may be new combinations of ideas and matter as in an artistic creation or new combinations of thoughts or spiritual insight as in philosophy or morals or religion. Social structures, the social institutions, the social order are achievements; codes of conduct, ethical or legal, anything in short that comes *de novo* into existence through human agency, are achievements. It is human energy and intelligence constructively seeking expression in material invention and in non-material creations in fields of culture.

The achievement Ward stresses is the cultural which, developed on the basis of the material, becomes that socializing spiritualizing factor that gives to mankind its greatest joy and happiness. In other words, his monism is not materialistic but finds its complete expression in the cultural, spiritual achievements of mankind.

Real achievements, however, the best achievements, are the work of the few, the original minds, the genius type, whose lives have fallen into the sort of social environment that is able to draw out potential capacity. Many minds of high caliber remain dormant, unachieving, or waste themselves in anti-social directions through lack of stimulus in their social environment. A telic society conscious of the need of larger and higher achievement would study, scientifically, potential talent and genius so as to ascertain the sort of environment best suited for the stimulation of potential genius. This argument of Ward's is best developed in *Applied Sociology*, in which inductive studies seem to indicate what aspects of a social environment are best calculated to multiply achievement by the development of potential into actual genius. Should society become telic in this matter, he shows, achievement could be accelerated and civilization advanced.

This argument of his, however, is not one applicable to the small number of geniuses only, for the same environment suited to the genius is also best for the average man who under stimulus might readily double or treble capacity, thus making a more efficient population, better able to appreciate the worth of achievement and to add to it in their degree. In this teaching one finds that strong democratic trend so manifest in Ward's sociology. Civilization and achievement are not for the enjoyment of the few only, but for the many also. All persons are entitled to life and the happiness of life, and when society telicly furnishes opportunity through a right environment, the average man will give recompense through his added efficiency and minor achievements. This teaching he would apply also to the defectives and the criminal classes; most of these, he argues, are capable of better things if rightly environed, and the expense of this would be amply met by the saving of wasted expenditures in caring for them under present conditions.

In this same discussion he raises a favorite question as to the place of women in civilization. This question interested Ward almost from the beginning of his literary career and he returned to it again and again. In his famous Chapter XIV of *Pure Sociology* he sought to work out a biological and social argument to the effect that in nature femaleness is fundamental and maleness accidental or variational. From this he reaches the conclusion that in humankind woman is at least equal and possibly superior to man in inherent worth, and that if woman were given larger opportunity and a more stimulating environment, she also would demonstrate her talent and genius and make achievement. He makes the point also that in primitive civilization woman was the great achiever in social creativeness and not the man. Hence he advocated the freedom of woman with full rights that she might take her rightful place in social progress as one capable of high achievement. This argument of his, first formally advanced in 1888, attracted wide attention and did much to give a sort of scientific basis to the demand for women's rights. His arguments in fact were widely used by women and did much to further that cause.

In this aspect one may again see Ward's democratic trend. All classes and both sexes have capacity as yet potential. Some are genius in type, others are moron, many are ordinary, but a scientifically arranged environment will tend to draw forth capacity, whether of one or many talents, and thereby aid in the elimination of the most wasteful of wastes, the waste of unutilized human energy.

This argument also he applies to the theory of racial superiority and inferiority. He is frankly skeptical as to any inherent psychic differences in races but admits that as yet (1906) no scientific decision is possible. His argument is to the effect that the hypothetical unity of the human race implied an essential agreement in quality, though differentiation in past centuries did take place through modifications due to the selective processes of varying geographic, economic and social environments. Human achievement, he thought, by annihilating distance would once again tend to unify the human race, integrating the races through the slow processes of assimilation and amalgamation. In the long run he foresaw the ultimate integration of mankind, the " long run " being not a few generations but those several millions of years during which the earth will remain suited to an advanced civilization.

In Ward's inductive study seeking to ascertain what are the important factors in a social environment suited to achievement, he concludes that the two chief factors are leisure through economic achievement, and contact with a cultural environment including education. He did not think of education as necessarily voiced by modern school systems, yet admittedly these, in theory, aim to impart to each newer generation the social heritage of the passing generation. A real curriculum, he thought, should, aside from the mental tools such as language, logic and mathematics, impart an appreciation of the universe in which we live, especially of organic nature and more especially of the psychic and social world about us. An appreciative knowledge of the universe of which we form a part and of organic and social relationships would correspond to the love for God and man considered as the essence of religion. A truly religious man is one who comprehends the unity of things and sees himself as part of whatever is. This same teaching he applied to ethics; the ethics of restraint or prohibition made no appeal to him since it savored of low civilization. True ethics is positive, monistic, constructive, so that in a sense one may sin against animal or plant or even physical nature as well as against man. In his several works he traces in a masterly manner the beginnings of ethical conduct in what he calls " the group sentiment of safety," through group morals, the rise of the individual conscience, on to the larger ethics when moral codes embodying specialized interests become merged into humanitarian ethics. In this stage human interests become harmonized, culminating in that world code when human beings appreciate fully their relationship to the universe and to all sorts and conditions of men.

Naturally such a complete harmonization of human interests is speculative and if attained at all lies in the dim distant future. Ward's stress is on present human progress, through telesis, and this is the climax of his sociological teaching. Progress is based on economic achievement, sociocratic in kind, thus affording leisure for all. Having leisure, education becomes possible and through that human capacity is enlarged for achievement, both material and cultural. Furthermore, humanity is not to be considered as a specialized class, or as the male sex, or as a superior race, but includes all classes, both sexes, and all races alike.

In working out a theory of human progress, Ward argues that there are three principles, and only three, that need be comprehended and applied in a program of social improvement. These three " dynamic principles " he labels: difference in potential, innovation, and conation. These can be simply explained, remembering that every achievement is a synthetic creation and that the multiplication of achievement implies progress. In making achievement one may (1) synthesize differences into a new creation or (2) develop a dormant capacity by a suitable environment, or (3) comprehend one's environment so well as to be able to modify it so as to suit one's wish. In illustration of these one might suggest (1) the contact and blending of differing cultures, (2) the actualizing of potential genius and (3) scientific discoveries such as the germ theory of disease. A telic society, therefore, aiming to see with some clearness the goal it desires to attain, should carefully study situations as they exist, and then should seek to work out a solution of its problems along the lines of these three principles, which embody the essential processes in social development.

In economic and political questions Ward made no special study and what he had to say grew out from his social teachings. Naturally, therefore, he turned away from the paternalism of Comte and the *laissez-faire* attitude of Spencer, and, emphasizing as he did sociocracy, the state becomes an important agency in the accomplishment of social ends. Government is not a " necessary evil " but most useful when directed for social meliorism. Likewise, economic activity is not an end in itself but rather is the necessary foundation on which must be erected a cultural civilization. Economic achievement therefore is to be encouraged, but more attention paid to " consumption," to the development of fair living standards, so that all may share in the benefits of achievement. Illiterate, poorly skilled or unskilled labor is always a handicap to civilization and the cost of education is nominal as compared with the benefits that would come to society through its elimination. Sociocracy as a form of government is not to be identified with Marxianism, to which he was opposed, but he would use government as an agency for the improvement of the conditions of the poor and for constructive social activity.

Yet in advocating this he was not partial to charity or to other palliatives. Social problems demand not charity but telesis aiming at the causes of social weaknesses. In the interim, of course, constructive charity may be necessary. All forms of social evil he considered as part of the present social system, best solved by *indirection*, which is another aspect of telesis. A broad diffusion of knowledge, social and scientific, would automatically rid society of many social evils, and skill in work, bringing larger wage returns would free workers from many of the evils attendant on lack of skill and a low wage system.

In discussing the family, Ward had more definite teachings since his stress on sex equality and women's achievement implies an upward movement in domestic morals. Marriage, he argued, is destined to pass from a physical, economic basis to one based on emotionalism (romanticism) and an intellectual appreciation of each other's qualities and hence will become more permanent in type and of course monogamous. In kinship also, he maintained, the blood bond should be supplemented by mutual appreciation, and by a broadening of the idea of kinship so as to include all humanity.

Stressing education as much as he did, Ward, like Plato, anticipated the time when the curriculum would impart that sort of knowledge needed to make citizens of character and intellect and when the educator would be the wise leader in social telesis. The crying need is not for more knowledge, but for the widest possible diffusion of the best of what is already extant. It is easy to multiply knowledge, it is hard to diffuse it broadly and among those that need it most. The problem of the broad diffusion of attractive information, stimulating to self-improvement and to achievement is the most important problem that society has before it.

In this exposition of Ward's life and teachings no attempt has been made to call attention to his errors of reasoning and defects of judgment, which he in common with other men made now and then in his argument. It would be absurd to claim that all he asserted must necessarily be true. In due time the blunders he made will pass into oblivion but the truths he taught should place him in Comte's list of the immortals. In his system of sociology it is obvious that his conclusions are not usually based on personal studies of concrete facts. In his scientific studies of some thirty years his work was almost entirely of that sort, as shown in his botanical and geological monographs. In his generation, however, comparatively few inductive studies had been made in the field of social phenomena and to some the methodology of those few seems defective in these days. Nor had he the time nor the inclination to make such studies himself. To Ward it seemed more important in his day to master the best thought of the time, including the newer scientific teachings of the nineteenth century, and then to synthesize all into a coherent whole, supplemented by his own thought-contributions wherever he found gaps or defects in this synthesizing philosophy. These contributions he was able to make because of his marvellous grasp of the several fields of science in their interrelations, a grasp much broader and deeper than that held by his immediate predecessors, Spencer and Comte, and also because of his keen, logical intellect and his deep insight into the inner unity of this monistic universe. He is the first great sociologist to indicate scientific bases for sex equality, for democracy and racial unity; the first to mark out the roads to social meliorism and progress, and the first to stress the place of psychic factors in a civilization becoming telic.

His teachings in their original form, *Dynamic Sociology*, have now been before the reading world for over forty years; they can be read in the languages of the great nations of the world and are slowly becoming familiar to the thinking public. Much that he said and taught has become common property, numerous authors have taken his ideas, often unconsciously, and elaborated them, sometimes thereby gaining credit for the thought itself. His works are a treasure house of living thought and this will survive, perhaps long after the books themselves have grown musty on neglected shelves. Yet in future years, when another generation with a larger perspective estimates the scientifically based social philosophies of the past and passing generations, Lester Frank Ward will surely be ranked high among America's masters of social science.

At his death, the *American Journal of Sociology* [12] published some appreciations of his work, of which the following are extracts.

One of his students, Dr. Charles Carroll, wrote of him:

" Every genius is a child; every child a genius." These were almost the closing words in Dr. Ward's last lecture at Brown University. In a sense they describe the man himself — a genius with the simplicity of a child — that glorious simplicity which the Saviour of the world had in mind when he said: " Unless ye shall become as little children." But in Dr. Ward it was the simplicity which comes from great knowledge, from the possession of truth; that mental calmness which must arise from a complete philosophy of life."

Several of Dr. Ward's successors to the presidency of the American Sociological Society gave fitting testimony to their appreciation of his contributions to the cause of sociology, saying in part:

" In association with Dr. Ward there was an uplift like knowing mountain or sea. Like Spencer he was a man who early conceived a disinterested life purpose and carried it through to a triumphant conclusion. His will was adamantine, and he allowed nothing to divert him from the path toward his goal. For thirty-five years he labored like a Hercules at his self-imposed task of proving the practicability of ' telic ' social progress. In early life he was severe and caustic with the champions of traditional ideas, but as the opposition began to give way and he found himself followed by a growing host of disciples, he mellowed and became very gentle with the honest holders of ancient beliefs. With sentimentalists he was patient, but he never mixed with them, for he realized that what is lacking is not the will to social progress but the way.

[12] Vol. XIX, July, 1913, pages 61–78.

" In spirit he was Spartan and he never sacrificed a stroke in order to win either money or popular applause. He was profoundly imbued with the true scientific man's reverence for truth, and faith in its beneficence. He would take no end of pains in order to verify a statement or to get a detail exactly right. His generalizations rested upon a vast knowledge of facts and nothing could induce him to use facts in a partisan way. He was indeed a worshipper of truth, and as such held himself to a high and exacting standard beside which the standards of the ordinary custodian of religion and morals seem low and loose." — EDWARD A. ROSS.

" To Sociology he gave his devotion and the best powers of his superbly equipped mind. Not counting articles, lectures, and summaries, his constructive writings in sociology fill five large, rich volumes.

" Throughout them all runs one dominating and organizing thought. Human society, as we who live now know it, is not the passive product of unconscious forces. It lies within the domain of cosmic law, but so does the mind of man; and this mind of man has knowingly, artfully, adapted and readapted its social environment, and with reflective intelligence has begun to shape it into an instrument wherewith to fulfil man's will. With forecasting wisdom man will perfect it, until it shall be at once adequate and adaptable to all its uses. This he will do not by creative impulse evolving in a void, but by constructive intelligence shaping the substantial stuff of verified scientific knowledge. Wherefore, scientific knowledge must be made the possession of mankind. Education must not merely train the mind. It must also equip and store, with knowledge.

" This great thought Dr. Ward apprehended, expressed, explained, illuminated, drove home to the mind of all who read his pages, as no other writer, ancient or modern, has ever done. It is his enduring and cogent contribution to sociology."

                              — FRANKLIN H. GIDDINGS.

" Ward's social philosophy grew naturally out of his career as a scientist and was the fruitage of wide studies in science, philosophy, and literature to which his early life was devoted. Like practically all other sociologists of the older generation, he thus came into the field of his greatest work after a preparation in other more specialized disciplines. Whether or not this kind of preparation be one which will always prove necessary for sociologists, and there is good ground for believing that it is, it remains true that it gave to his thinking a maturity and range which it could not otherwise have had. It enabled him, relatively late in life, to develop a particularly vital and organic system of social philosophy which has equal value as an instrument of education and as a manual of fundamental principles of social action." — ULYSSES G. WEATHERLY.

" Ward undertook to show that the psychic factor is the dominant one in human society; that it is the factor which must receive chief attention from sociologists; and that, through it, human progress may even be artificially controlled. Thus Ward became one of the founders of the modern psychological sociology. He found no difficulty in recognizing at their full value all the psychic or subjective elements in the social life. In his later work, even religion itself was recognized as ' the force of social gravitation which holds the social world in its orbit,' while from first to last, education was in Ward's mind the chief instrument through which social progress was to be effected. Thus Ward found a place in his sociology for all the higher spiritual values of civilization; and incidentally by doing this he did much to relieve the materialistic monism, upon which he based his sociology, of the charge that it is entirely negative in its attitude toward these higher spiritual values."

— CHARLES A. ELLWOOD.

" Comte gave sociology a place in the hierarchy of sciences. Spencer systematized ethnological and anthropological data. Schaeffle outlined a system of social structure, and de Greef combined the social structure with social activities, but Ward developed the plan on which society was evolved, discussed the principles on which it was founded, and operated and presented a program by which it could be improved. One cannot help regret that his *Pure Sociology* and his *Applied Sociology* could not have been followed by a work on social technology to complete the system. His recent writings on eugenics and practical social problems would seem to indicate that had he lived, a third volume would have been necessary to complete his system.

" Mr. Ward has been criticized for undue emphasis laid upon social forces in both dynamic and pure sociology. Yet the great lines of his argument are in the main correct. One of his characteristics was to emphasize causation, and his social forces are social causes. They were the causes which created society and held it intact and hence were more truly socializing forces than true social forces. The latter arise out of society, and are the results of social activity rather than the causes, for real social forces arise from group activity. Nevertheless his concept is a valuable one from which all sociologists have profited. Differ as we may from some of his points of view, object as we may to some of his conclusions, the facts remain that he was the first great sociologist, that his work is epoch-making for social science, and that his system is monumental. Sociology, in its synthetic processes, and in its methods will change, but for years to come all writers must recognize the great lines of his system." — FRANK W. BLACKMAR.

I have often said, and it remains my estimate, that, everything considered, I would rather have written *Dynamic Sociology* than any other book that has ever appeared in America. Not surely because it has gained more applause of men than many others. I found in 1888 that Professor Ely was the only member of the Johns Hopkins faculty who seemed to know anything about the book. In 1893 Dr. Ward told me that barely five hundred copies had been sold. It was, however, at least a generation ahead of the sociological thinking of Great Britain, and it saved American sociologists the long wandering in the wilderness of misconstrued evolutionism, from which English sociology is at this late late day working out the rudiments of its salvation. — ALBION W. SMALL.

These are the words of the leaders in American Sociology, *in memoriam*. Similar appreciations from European scholars could be added, if space permitted. But enough has been said. Ward lived his simple life, thinking and teaching great thoughts, and, having rounded out his three score years and ten, he died, bequeathing to posterity a noble example and a worthy contribution to the world's work.

CHAPTER IV

HERBERT B. ADAMS

By

JOHN MARTIN VINCENT

Professor Emeritus of European History in Johns Hopkins University

HERBERT B. ADAMS

CHAPTER IV

HERBERT B. ADAMS

These pages are concerned with the life and characteristics of a man whose labors, coming at a particular period
in the intellectual history of America, were of high importance in the development of study and research in the
domain of History and Political Science. Therefore, the
biographical details which have been selected aim to present the qualities which gave him influence and esteem
among students and investigators, rather than to furnish
a complete life history.

Herbert B. Adams began his public career with an appointment as Fellow in History in the Johns Hopkins University in 1876. He remained in that institution in the
progressive positions of Associate Professor, and Professor
until the time of his death in 1901. His base of operations,
therefore, remained fixed, but his influence extended over
the continent and it is proper that some inquiry should be
made respecting the earlier experiences which developed
his character and prepared him for leadership in historical
studies.

Born on April 16, 1850, at Shutesbury, near Amherst,
Massachusetts, Adams was descended on both sides of the
family from ancestors who had settled in that colony in
1634. Coming from this sound Puritan stock, from Henry
Adams of Braintree, and Deacon Thomas Hastings,
of Watertown, the traditions in which this youth was

brought up were thoroughly American of the New England type.

His father, Nathaniel Dickinson Adams, was for many years a lumber merchant and manufacturer in Amherst, interested in public affairs, at one time a selectman of the town and a constant and devout member of the Second Congregational Church. As described by Adams, he was

" a man of genial and quiet ways, but of great energy and un-tiring industry. . . . His chief ambition in life was to provide a liberal education for his children. He used to encourage them in their studies by offering rewards, but things won or done were never afterwards praised or spoken of by him. He only incited them, by new rewards, to new endeavors. He was fond of call-ing upon his boys to recount in the evening what they had learned or done during the day at school, and of making them declaim in the presence of the family, and of friends who chanced to be present. Though a kind husband and indulgent father, he was withal strict, and at times severe. His children always stood somewhat in awe of him. If punished at school, they were sure of being punished at home. . . . There was much of the Puritan in his character and composition. He stood up at family prayers, and religiously kept Saturday night. He was reserved with strangers, but given to hospitality and fond of social intercourse. He was plain, sometimes blunt of speech, and intolerant of deceit and everything narrow and low. In a word, he was an honest, upright, God-fearing man. He died at the age of forty-four, in the prime in his manhood and useful-ness." [1]

Adams at this time was but six years of age, and thence-forth his guide and counsellor was his elder brother, Charles Dickinson Adams. The father's wish for the de-

[1] The Thomas Adams and Thomas Hastings Families of Amherst, Massachusetts, pp. 51–53.

velopment of his sons was realized, for Charles Adams graduated at the head of his class at Amherst, studied law at Columbia and became an influential attorney in New York. Henry M. Adams, the second son, went to Troy Polytechnic Institute and thence to West Point, where he graduated number one in the class of 1866, and reached high rank in the Engineer's Corps of the United States Army.

It was in this atmosphere of piety, hard work, high ambition and stimulating example that the earlier years of Herbert Adams were passed. At the suggestion of his elder brother he entered Phillips Exeter Academy and graduated with honor in 1868. He won the Porter Prize for the best entrance examination at Amherst College in the fall of that year, and was graduated with the valedictory in 1872. The following year he taught Latin, Greek, Mathematics and Classical History at Williston Seminary, where he succeeded Dr. Charles H. Parkhurst as teacher of the middle classical class. After a year at Williston he was encouraged by his elder brother to go abroad for higher studies and sailed for Germany to take up History. This was in fulfillment of a desire first conceived at Phillips Exeter Academy and strengthened at Amherst College. Young Adams acquired his taste for history from books given him at school by his elder brother and by early privileges, obtained as a sub-freshman, of drawing books from the library of Amherst College. President Julius H. Seelye confirmed this early historical bent of mind by a single lecture on " History " in Adams' senior year, and it was President Seelye who originally gave him a written permit to use the College Library years before the boy entered the institution.

Adams said of his own life at Amherst:

" My editorial connection with *The Amherst Student* really
gave a permanent bent to my life. I learned more real useful
knowledge in that voluntary connection than in all other college
means of training, in punctuation, composition, and rhetoric.
To this day I can discern more lasting influences proceeding
from that editorial den of mine at Amherst than from any other
one college source. I have forgotten my mathematics, which I
always hated, but in which I always ranked high by reason of
my Exeter training, but I shall never forget how to revise other
people's manuscript and read proof, although I hate that too."

His private reading in college was chiefly in connection
with the subjects upon which he had to write or debate.
History was not a large part of his collegiate training and
we might be a little surprised that he afterwards devoted
his life to it. Of this he says himself: " Of history, we had
nothing at all, after the freshman year when Smith's Manuals of Greece and Rome were studied in well-chosen se-
lections." The impulse came later.

" I remember in the philosophical course by the President of
the College one remarkable lecture on the Philosophy of History. After rapidly reviewing the course of civilization, Dr.
Seelye said that history was the grandest study in the world.
That sentence decided my fate. I determined to devote myself
to that grand subject. Up to that time I had no career in mind
except journalism. I had written more or less for the *Amherst
Record* and for the New York and Boston papers when I found
a chance to do any reporting. But now my mind was quickly
made up to pursue the grandest study in the world, the recorded
experience of mankind."

Before settling down in Germany, Adams studied
French for some months at Lausanne, Switzerland, whither

he had been directed by Professor Lalande, his French tutor at Williston Seminary, and by whom he was personally introduced to Professor Thébault, of the Lycée. After Lausanne there followed a few months of study and travel in Italy, and a second brief sojourn in Paris. Here he met his elder brother, who dissuaded him from further study in France, and urged him to take up German university life at once.

In January, 1874, he proceeded to Heidelberg with many pleasant anticipations, for the place had been graphically pictured to him by an Exeter fellow student. Here he met his Amherst College friend, John B. Clark, later professor in Columbia University, and with him heard the lectures of Wilhelm Ihne on Roman history; Kuno Fischer on German literature and philosophy; and Heinrich von Treitschke on politics. At Heidelberg Adams lived in the family of the late Dr. Emil Otto, author of the well-known grammars, and with him studied and practiced German, at the same time making many acquaintances and good friends among German students. He continued also the daily practice of French conversation with Swiss students and in a Swiss family of his acquaintance. Thus passed the winter and summer of that academic year.

After a tour of North Germany and a visit to the Amherst men residing in Göttingen, Adams spent the winter semester of 1874–75 at the University of Berlin. The professors who interested him most were Ernst Curtius, who lectured on Greek art and archaeology; Hermann Grimm, who illustrated early Christian and Italian art by familiar talks in the Royal Museum; Lepsius, who, in the same museum, discoursed on Egyptology; Zeller, the historian of Greek philosophy; Droysen, who lectured on the French

Revolution; and Treitschke, who had just come, with great éclat, from Heidelberg, and whom Adams, like many other students, had really followed to Berlin.

In the summer of 1875, somewhat discouraged at the prospect of the expensive and protracted course of study necessary for the Doctor's degree in Berlin, Adams would have returned home to America and actually forwarded his books to Glasgow with that intent; but, while on a tour through Southern Germany, he received a generous letter from his elder brother, urging him to remain in Germany and finish what he had begun at Heidelberg. Accordingly, he returned there for another year and, in the summer of 1876, under the guidance of Prof. J. C. Bluntschli, completed a definite course in historical and political science. In these subjects he was examined by Bluntschli the statesman and Knies the economist, and was awarded the degree of Doctor of Philosophy by the Political Science Faculty, July 14, 1876.

In a little old diary which Adams kept during this period there are interesting entries of his reading for this examination. Great sections of Bluntschli's *Staatslehre, Volkerrecht* and *Staatsworterbuch* were consumed from day to day. While reviewing his notes a month beforehand he writes, "Headache, scared of the prospect of exam." Hence, we are prepared for the entry of July 13: "The die is cast. Studied until dinner. Am nervous — had a bad night. Loaf until 6 P.M. Examination from 6–8 P.M. *Summa cum laude!* Knies, Bluntschli, Erdmannsdörffer, Winkelmann, Stark, Ribbeck, Weil, and others present." On the 15th of July, Adams bade farewell to his professors and entered in his diary the comment: "Bluntschli a trump."

While still at Heidelberg Adams received an appointment as Fellow in the Johns Hopkins University, an opportunity which he ascribed to the letters and personal influence of Bluntschli. His return to America followed at once.

The Johns Hopkins University opened its doors for instruction in October, 1876. It had all the advantages and disadvantages of a new institution, without hampering traditions, or antiquated faculty. Its ambition was to provide advanced instruction and research in science and the humanities, and its models, if any, were to be found in Germany, but it was free to work out its objects by any method that proved feasible in America. Housed in modest quarters in old residences refitted for the purpose, the institution began by saving part of its income for future buildings, but spending generously, for that period, on the few men who started its academic career.

There were but six full professors, but all bore the marks of distinction or of promise, and represented the learning of both Europe and America. Thus B. L. Gildersleeve from the University of Virginia was already a prominent Hellenist; Ira Remsen, chemist, was of New York and Göttingen; Henry A. Rowland, already marked as a physicist, came from the Rensselaer Polytechnic Institute; H. Newell Martin, biologist, and J. J. Sylvester, famous mathematician, were drawn from Cambridge, England.

With these were twelve Associates, most of them bearing advanced degrees, who were to give minor instruction; ten distinguished lecturers from outside, and twenty Fellows whose chief business was to be the pursuit of research in various departments of knowledge. Of this first list of

Fellows, all promising, it will suffice to mention, Henry C. Adams, late distinguished economist of the University of Michigan and the Interstate Commerce Commission; Charles R. Lanman, orientalist of Harvard; Walter Hines Page, publicist and ambassador; Josiah Royce, eminent in philosophy. To these were added for the first year but sixty-nine students from various parts of the United States, divided among the various groups of study.

These meager statistics do not represent the spirit of the place, a matter which must be considered in estimating its effect upon Adams, who was now thrown into a new American environment. A group of scholars and students, for the first few years so small as to form but a family in which everybody was acquainted, created an atmosphere which was stimulating to the last degree. Men who came out of that period have repeatedly spoken of the exhilaration felt in the new opportunities of research, the close contact with the expansion of human knowledge; and the consciousness of the unique experiment in which they were engaged.

It will be seen from this that Adams was not thrown into an indifferent environment where he would have been obliged to create an interest in historical research, but rather was he transferred at once from the stimulating contacts of the German Seminar to the enthusiastic atmosphere of Baltimore; and his activities permitted to continue without loss of momentum.

The laboratory method of historical study was ready to go into operation as soon as the doors of the University opened. A seminary of American History was in charge of Austin Scott, who at that time was secretary and assistant to George Bancroft in the revision and completion of his history of the United States. Giving part time to this work he came over from Washington to meet a group of young men in the rooms of the Maryland Historical Society, where problems coming out of an actual workshop of history were set forth and discussed. Adams was actively connected with this seminary, having at first no teaching duties except voluntary meetings with one or two students. In fact, the first mention of his regular collegiate class work appeared after he had been appointed Associate on June 3, 1878. His time was evidently spent to good advantage in research, for the results appear in papers read before historical societies and eventually in print. The first of these on record grew out of Dr. Scott's seminary exercises on the Ordinance of 1787. Adams made a study of Maryland's influence upon the great western land question, showing that her insistence upon the dedication of the Northwest Territory to the Federal Government had laid the foundations of a great national commonwealth. The emphasis on this point was a distinct contribution to the history of our formative period.

In addition to the historical seminary another instrument of publicity and coöperation in research was soon formed in the organization of the " Historical and Political Science Association." This came about at the suggestion of the historical group and included members who were interested in public questions other than historical. Beginning operations in January, 1878, President Gilman was the first presiding officer and after a few sessions Herbert B. Adams became the recording secretary. The meetings were occasionally addressed by distinguished outsiders, but the important function of the society was to give opportunity to members of the seminary to present their studies for criticism or approval before a larger audience of scholars.

This association continued to exist during the remainder of Adams' life and for many years afterward until, by the multiplication of departments and seminaries, the duties for which it was founded were otherwise fulfilled. In the course of a few years the seminary and the association were practically amalgamated, and, although the society title remained, the meetings became familiarly known as " Adams' Seminary," and secretaries were chosen in rotation. These weekly gatherings upon Friday evenings formed a noteworthy factor, not only in the history of that department of the university, but in the career of its leader. The minutes of its meetings have been carefully preserved and they reveal the capacity of Adams as a manager of research, and they record the early efforts of many men who afterward became prominent in academic or public life. When former students reflect upon the influences which most affected them it is usually these gatherings and discussions to which they refer rather than to the class work of any of their professors. Seminary work has now become so common a feature in American universities that it is difficult to realize that fifty years ago only a few sporadic attempts had been made and that Adams stood at the beginning of the systematic employment of that method.

Almost at the beginning of his work in Baltimore, Adams took up the study of American local institutions. The suggestion came originally from Professor Erdmannsdörfer of Heidelberg and was doubtless fostered by studies in primitive society through the works of Sir Henry Maine, Von Maurer, and others. Returning to America he began the study of colonial organization and the institutions, either governmental or voluntary, of which the early settlers made use. This was carried out through much research in the town archives of New England, taking advantage of summer vacations, and the opportunities of a lecture course which he conducted for several spring terms at Smith College in Northampton, Massachusetts.

Coming fresh from Germanic studies he was struck by the many resemblances in names and social habits, and the titles of a series of papers which he read and eventually printed show the trend of his mind. The Germanic Origin of New England Towns; Norman Constables in America; Saxon Tithingmen in America; Village Communities in America; and articles of a similar character testify to an enthusiasm for survivals and comparisons. This tendency was further accentuated by the visit to Baltimore of Edward A. Freeman in 1881. The historian of the Norman Conquest, already noted for his constant reference to surviving institutions in England, was captivated by the similarities which he found in America, colonial and modern. Testimony to this was his essay on " The English People in their Three Homes," and his visit in America gave further heat to his enthusiasm.

This fondness for resemblances sometimes led both of these authors to assume continuities and survivals which are debatable, but the important consequence of Adams' taste for constitutional and organic questions was the foundation of a series of studies in local government which had a decidedly important effect upon the later study of American history. The seminary students undertook investigations of local institutions, not only in Maryland, Virginia, the colonies of the South as well as New England, but studies of the later western states were also included.

In order to give publicity to these researches the Johns Hopkins Studies in Historical and Political Science were started in the fall of 1882 with Herbert B. Adams as editor, and for eighteen years he continued to be the responsible director. The contents of the earlier volumes of this periodical were furnished in part by doctoral dissertations, and in part by more mature investigators outside and inside of the University, a fact which must be considered in estimating the effect in that period of the publication of these studies in American history. It was not merely an avenue of publicity for new men, but a coöperative outlet for the work of selected scholars at large. Furthermore, the reaction of cold print upon the seminary and its director was most important. Publication brought the work before the critics of two continents with resulting stimulus to diligence in research and caution in stating conclusions. The University rule that dissertations must be printed was not enacted until the publication of the historical studies had been for several years in operation and when nearly all of the seminary work was already finding its way into type.

The list of subjects published in the first ten volumes of the Studies shows how much the department was devoted to the history and description of political and social practices. The disciple of Bluntschli and Erdmannsdörfer was not only drawn into such questions by his own taste, but he also appreciated the opportunity and the importance of these inquiries at that juncture. His class lectures included the political institutions of Greece and Rome as well as those of Early England, giving his students a wide

horizon for the study of American local government. Out
of this combination of circumstances emerged two consequences of importance. First, there was laid a substratum
of monographic research of which use was made at once
by more general authors of American history. The writings of James Bryce, John Fiske and others openly acknowledge and their footnotes reveal their indebtedness
to this pioneer work of the Johns Hopkins department of
history. Second, the study of political science upon advanced university methods began at the same moment with
history. The formation of a separate department did not
occur until after his death, but in reality, the subjects were
all the time operating on parallel lines. For years the instruction and research were founded on the intimate relationship between the history through which peoples pass
and the institutions which they create. For a long time
the words " History is past politics, and politics is present
history " formed the motto printed in the Studies and
painted on the walls of the seminary. Freeman's phrase
needed much explanation to make it true, but it was a
fair description of the activities in those precincts.

Two matters of great interest to the history of the State
of Maryland and affecting the equipment of the seminary
were brought about in this early period through the alert
activity of Adams. He had been impressed by the abundance of material in the State Archives at Annapolis and
had read a paper on the subject previous to the visits of
Mr. Freeman and Mr. Bryce to Baltimore. After their ar-
rival they were taken to see some of these treasures and
each wrote a letter urging the publication of Maryland
documents. Backed by various leading citizens Adams
conducted a lively newspaper campaign which resulted in

the removal of the precious material to a fireproof vault in the Maryland Historical Society building and the beginning of the publication of the colonial records which now occupy more than forty volumes.

In 1881 occurred the death of Bluntschli and soon after that his library was offered for sale. Adams and President Gilman were much interested and were almost ready to assume personal responsibility for the purchase, when a group of German citizens of Baltimore came forward and presented the whole library as a gift to the university. This valuable collection of works on international law, political science and history was accompanied by many personal manuscripts of Bluntschli and the seminary became more than ever a shrine of memories of Heidelberg. These materials afterward led to important studies in European history, but it might be said that the transfusion of spirit was more important than the books.

In September, 1883, Dr. Adams read a paper before the American Social Science Association meeting at Saratoga, on the subject of New Methods of Study in History. This contained the ground work of his chapter on the same subject in the first volume of G. Stanley Hall's Pedagogical Library, and pointed out the advanced methods used at Harvard, Michigan and Johns Hopkins. He related also the recent experiences of American students in German seminaries and indicated the way in which the same methods could be applied on this side of the water. The article is furthermore an exhibit of the situation of history in the American educational scheme as it was at the beginning of advanced instruction in historical research in our higher educational institutions, but a result of still greater importance came out of this meeting.

Whether Adams made the first suggestion, or not, I am unable to say, but before the next gathering for social science, the idea of an American Historical Association was formed, and in September, 1884, the plan was consummated. A call had been issued in June by a provisional committee consisting of John Eaton, President, and F. B. Sanborn, Secretary, of the Social Science Association; Charles Kendall Adams; Moses Coit Tyler and Herbert B. Adams. Correspondence with prominent historians showed that the profession was ready and eager for such a society and the promoters went forward with courage.

By the time of the meeting a brief historical program had been arranged, and upon getting together an organization was formed with Herbert B. Adams as secretary. Some discussion took place as to the character of the society, but the vote was decidedly in favor of an independent body, rather than a section of the existing Social Science Association, and in that light Adams remained as an executive officer for the ensuing twenty-five years.

Only those who were in daily contact with this secretary could appreciate the amount of time and trouble he contributed to the conduct of the American Historical Association. As the center of correspondence it fell upon him for many years to prepare the programs of meetings, as well as to record and print the proceedings, and register the increasing membership. These programs grew in extent and importance with every advancing year, and after a time there was some grumbling about Adams being the whole thing, but in those early years the Historical Association would have had a rough road if some person had not shown such an individual devotion.

In this connection his proudest moment came in 1889

when the Association received a national charter at the
hands of Congress, and thereby became an auxiliary of the
Smithsonian Institution. This opened the doors to greater
public recognition and to the national printing office for
the publication of historical papers and documentary material. To be sure, the economies of government have
since narrowed somewhat the use of federal paper and ink,
but the higher standing of the Association at home and
abroad and the additional facilities in exchange of historical literature, were gratifying acquisitions, due particularly to the energy of its secretary.

In the course of time the burden of programs was shared
by committees, but with the increasing membership the
correspondence kept pace, and there remained the tedious
task of editing the papers accepted for print. Eighteen volumes of these reports testify to the unremunerated care
with which he read proof and wielded the blue pencil.

At the request of executors and members of the family
Adams undertook the publication of the papers of Jared
Sparks, and these appeared in 1893 under the title of his
Life and Writings. The extent of this task could be ex-
ternally visualized by the observant visitor to his office,
where closets and shelves were for several years crammed
to the ceiling with files and boxes of the Sparks manuscripts. This college president and historical scholar apparently never destroyed any paper addressed to him, and
invitations to dinner were filed as religiously as diplomatic
documents. Out of this mass Adams was called upon to
select the significant things and these eventually filled two
large octavo volumes.

The work was well received, but in the meantime,
through various articles which Adams printed or deliv-

ered, and on account of the attitude of a recent editor of the writings of Washington, the controversy over the methods of Jared Sparks as an editor was renewed. A brisk newspaper war took place in the *Baltimore Sun* over a paper presented before a small audience at the Maryland Historical Society, but the point of view of Adams appeared eventually in the preface of the *Life and Writings of Jared Sparks,* and in the chapter on "Editorial Duty."

It is there pointed out that Sparks as a pioneer investigator of the Washington papers found difficulties which have scarcely been overcome in later years when the collections have become more abundant. As to omissions of papers, Sparks was endeavoring to form a typical collection to be published at a moderate price while openly stating that quantities of material remained. No subsequent editor has included all that exist.

As to omissions and changes in individual papers the fact must be remembered that there are three forms in which Washington's letters can be found: a rough draft, the letter as sent, and a letter book copy. The letter sent would be changed from the draft, and the copy ran all the risks of careless copyists. Not all of the forms were available to Sparks at once and he chose the best at his command. When critics charged him with omissions, or with changing phraseology, they usually produced some other stage of the letter.

As to changes in spelling and style, Sparks declared that he never changed the meaning of a phrase, but did rectify spelling and grammar when necessary, a practice which, as Adams points out, Washington himself followed in going over his papers in his later years. In short, without assuming that Sparks was an infallible editor, he vindicates his conscientious purpose, and awards him high credit for what he actually accomplished.

The revival of a controversy which began as early as 1827 and came to life again with every editor of Washington, is not the only significant thing to be noted. Decidedly important was the fact that Adams was here confronted with an editorial task of large dimensions and was compelled to formulate his own theory and practice. The Sparks question pro and con was stated with finality, and the experience was a test which redounded to the profit of both Adams and his students.

Adams' interest in the academic teaching of history was accompanied by a similar desire to extend the privilege of learning to the public at large. This was in accord with a sentence from Senator Siegfried of France which was posted prominently in his office: " The greatest duty of democracy is the education of the people."

He was well aware of what had already been done in the older universities of the United States, as may be seen from previous articles on the subject. The pioneer work of Professor Silliman at Yale in 1808; the lecture and lyceum system which so long prevailed in the country; the popular lectures which began at once when the Johns Hopkins University opened; all of the successes and failures of these efforts were in mind when he delivered an address to the American Library Association in 1887. In this paper he urged the public libraries to become centers of popular instruction, to provide " seminary " rooms and book collections for special public courses under competent guidance. The waning value of lecture courses by successions of speakers holding forth but a single evening was evident. It was now time to provide more substantial food and cultivate the taste for it.

The first experiment was made at the Buffalo Public Library during the winter of 1887–1888, where Dr. Edward W. Bemis, a recent graduate of Johns Hopkins, conducted a course of twelve weekly lectures on Political Economy, followed by question hours and discussion. The work was a decided success and led to further appointments for Dr. Bemis. A similar class in history was conducted by Charles M. Andrews in a Baltimore church, and a rotating lecture course to workingmen by Hopkins men was started in that same year.

Having been invited to lecture at Chautauqua in 1888 Adams drew up the first plan for real " extension " work for that great organization, and this was put into print by the Chautauqua Press in the fall of that year. The term " University Extension " as understood in England now became more and more familiar in America, and when a society was formed in Philadelphia to carry out such work on a large scale, Adams gladly left to them the details of an expanding enterprise and coöperated in the development of popular study.

An important feature in Adams' career was his work with the United States Bureau of Education, a connection which gave him occupation during the last fifteen years of his life. As early as 1885 he reported upon university extension in England and later was sent over to make a personal investigation. There were also reports on the study of history in the United States and in 1887 appeared the first of a long series of Histories of Higher Education in the United States, of which he continued to be editor to the end of his activity.

Two of these studies written by himself, gave him great pleasure in the performance, for they were both interesting in themselves and brought him in contact with new material. The monograph on William and Mary College was published at a time when the finances of the institution were at the lowest ebb. Deficits had accumulated to the point where there was nothing to support a faculty. The professors had been dismissed and no one remained but the president, who maintained the charter by his presence, and upheld the semblance of a school by the annual ringing of the college bell. This pathetic condition of the college, which, after Harvard, was the oldest in the country, and which had educated so many of the founders of the Republic, appealed strongly to Adams and he made a vigorous denunciation of a Congress which refused to pay its just debts for military destruction.

Incidentally two ideas came to the front which can be put down as a part of Adams' educational creed. One was the suggestion that the situation of William and Mary would be improved if it should move to Alexandria, or better yet to Richmond. Such counsel could be offered better in 1887 than at present, but behind it lies the theory that a municipal rather than a rural environment is the place for a state institution of higher learning. The city offers a laboratory of social and political life in which the problems of society can be more effectively studied.

The other point was derived from the close connection of education and good citizenship which had made the college of William and Mary for so long a period a nursery of statesmen. Adams here takes the opportunity to expand his views upon "the application of historical and political science to American politics." Upon this text

there follows a chapter advocating the foundation in
Washington of a " Civil Academy " on lines parallel to
West Point and Annapolis for the " promotion of the
higher political education in practical ways." Like the
École Libre des Sciences Politiques in Paris such an organization would serve as a training place for administrative
officers of the government and for the diplomatic and con-
sular services abroad. That Washington would be the
place for such a school was fortified by citations from
statesmen from George Washington to the present, and by
the fact that the basic equipment was already on the
ground in various civil and scientific departments of the
Federal Government.

In reviewing his own career later in life Adams looked
upon this as the high point in his academic attainment.
No such government school has ever been established and
so far such training has been undertaken only by private
enterprise in various universities of the country, but the
matter is part of the essential record of a scholar who was
developing from a professor of history into an educational
authority whose advice began to be sought from all
quarters.

The monograph on Jefferson and the University of Virginia, which appeared in 1888, was a congenial task, as it
was the natural continuation of higher education in the
State and the product of a generation educated at William
and Mary. Adams emphasized especially the foreign influences which had affected intellectual circles in Virginia,
and the minute paternal care which Jefferson devoted to
the construction and management of the university. He
was able to illustrate Jefferson's facility in architecture by
reproductions of the drawings which the founder had made

with his own hand, and he piled up the evidence of Jefferson's acquaintance with foreign writers and teachers in order to demonstrate that out of this knowledge of things abroad he created a new institution suited to the need of the new world.

These brief histories were published in the unattractive type and paper covers of the Bureau of Education, but their influence must be measured by the great circulation which these government documents achieved. They must be counted in the great campaign for legislative support of higher education, which for some time after was taking the attention of many of the Southern States. The plan of these reports was intended to include eventually the history of higher education in all of the states of the Union, and did actually cover twenty-nine of them during Adams' editorship. Many of them were composite works, put together by numerous hands and the results were not equally good, but they served a useful purpose in demonstrating the situation of college and university education in the regions investigated.

The delicate position occupied by an editor of government publications like these was sometimes amusingly evident. When a hot-headed congressman found a criticism of conditions in his State there would ensue at once in the House a furious demand for information as to why the United States Government was engaged in maligning the people of a sovereign commonwealth. Thereupon would follow a particular onslaught upon the Bureau of Education, while the Commissioners trembled in their office chairs and appealed to the editor to see what could be done about it. Adams' innate sense of fairness did not permit sectional or religious or race prejudice to find a place in these papers, but it is not recorded that he took back any statement of fact. This was quite compatible with a keen appreciation of the necessity of preventing political animosity if reforms or advances in education were to be accomplished.

Through these various avenues of publicity Adams' name became well known in the educational world and there followed numerous calls to other institutions, where he might have become a college president, or the managing head of an historical department, under most attractive conditions, but all of these were steadily declined. One of these positions was in a newly founded university where salary and power were most alluring, but on reflection this was put aside, on the ground, as he told his friends afterward, that he had been for seventeen years building up a department of history and the change would require him to begin again at the bottom of the process. He preferred to build higher the structure he had begun and expand his editorial and literary opportunities.

This extended consideration of Adams' outside occupations in literature and the history of education should not obscure the fact that he was at the same time conducting an historical department with eminent success. For many years there was little or no competition in real graduate work, but even after opportunities were provided at other universities the reputation of the Historical Seminary in Baltimore maintained an astonishing popularity.

The reasons for this lay in the personal characteristics of Adams as well as in the program of studies offered. He was marked by a wide catholicity of interest in the varied aspects of history. Political institutions were his favorite theme, but confined to no country or restricted period. His lectures on constitutional history ranged from the ancient Israelites, through Greece and Rome to England and America. The comparative study of religions was to him a most attractive subject, and for many years he guided a class of younger students into a better understanding both of the ancient Hebrews and of the good to be found in the " heathen " prophets of religions other than their own. More than one would acknowledge his debt for this enlightenment with Professor Hollander, who dedicates a recent book on Economic Liberalism to the memory of Adams who first taught him to be a liberal.

He was a communicant in a Christian church, but in practical work his sympathies were bound by no single denomination, for he was constantly aiding the educational movements of them all. Ministers, priests, rabbis, committees from Christian associations and all sorts of workers were continually consulting him in regard to social enterprises. This attitude of mind not only gave a broad scope to his treatment of history, but it had a profound effect upon his relations with his students. His sympathy with their intellectual aspirations, his careful attention to any proposal for research, were not the product of an office, but flowed from the common instincts of his nature, so that not only in matters of a personal character but in everything that went to build up the ambition of a scholar he was a stimulating guide.

Consequently, when he died in 1901 at the early age of fifty-one there was profound sorrow in wide circles and for many reasons. Stricken with arterial trouble two years previously there was time given to his friends while he was still living to express their solicitude and their appreciation of his many services. These expressions were warm and were abundant, but the best of wishes could only lighten the burden of his passing. One-half of his allotted time had been devoted to preparation and one-half to the fulfillment of his life-work. The rewards and honors of old age were denied, but he could carry with him the consciousness of large accomplishment in the time at his command.

His contributions to learning did not cease with his life, for by his will his fortune is still at work. He left a comfortable competence, for in business affairs he had been a man of thrift, but this permitted him to be useful to others. Many a student was the recipient of temporary economic aid, loaned unostentatiously and with a confidence rarely misplaced. He bought books freely for himself and for the seminary, and before his death presented his large private library to the University. Outside of a few family bequests he devoted his whole estate to public purposes. To the town of Amherst he gave his own home, as a memorial to his parents, and to Amherst College $2,000 as a fund for the purchase of books. To the American Historical Association he left $5,000 unconditionally. To the University which he served for twenty-five years he gave the balance of his estate to form the Herbert B. Adams Fund, the income of which must be devoted to the promotion of history, politics, and education.

If it is necessary to designate the fields in which Adams was most conspicuous, it will have to be said that he was chiefly a teacher and an editor. The quantity of his own writing was not large compared to the material that he brought into the light for others. Over against some four volumes of his own studies there stand about ninety volumes from other hands to which he gave his editorial care.

His shorter contributions make a formidable bibliography, but his monument is to be found in the works which he inspired. A mere list of the distinguished men still living who pay tribute to his influence would show where his power lay and what his touch had effected.

If one asks if there were peculiar methods of work which made him singularly successful with students, the answer must be that he succeeded, not because his plans were unique, but because of the enthusiasm which went with them. One strong point was made in keeping the student in touch with historians past and present. The seminary itself, even the lecture rooms were lined with books, so that a certain familiarity could not be avoided. This historical atmosphere was further heightened by pictures of eminent historians. Every available space was occupied by some representation of an eminent writer on political science, or history, or political economy. These were not in all cases the last word in the art of portraiture, but the effect upon the student was to create a sense of friendship and acquaintance with the great figures in the profession which he was about to enter. The abundance of these portraits and the frequent references to them in his lectures gave to the otherwise decorative material the character of a family gallery or the congenial familiarity of a social club.

Living historians from Europe and America were frequently invited to address the seminary, and thus the authorities whose writings were revered by the apprentices in the craft were brought down from the clouds and made into human friends. In this practice Adams was supported by the university authorities and by the habits of all of the other departments. Thus Edward A. Freeman, James Bryce and H. von Holst in the early days met the seminary in familiar talks on historical problems, and thus came also American scholars from time to time to stimulate the ambition and broaden the horizon of the neophytes.

One might look upon this as the obvious thing to do and as a practice common to other places, but the matter took such prominence that it should not be omitted in any attempt to explain the influence which Adams and his seminary exercised over his students. Nor were those who passed out into the world of letters forgotten as soon as they left the seminary table. The news of any success was announced in class or seminary meeting. The books they published, or the experiments they were making in historical teaching were discussed about the table, and occasionally they came back in person, with the result that the student became acquainted with a growing body of his predecessors, and stood on familiar terms with many a man of great promise, or of reputation already secure.

The effect of this was highly stimulating. The eminent historians whose books were read with great respect, might well be honored, but were difficult to imitate. They were nebulous beings of a distant past, or of an unattainable prominence, but here were men who had gone through these very halls, had sat about this very seminary table, and now were out in the world, making marks in the academic and literary world. " I can do that myself," was the answer to this stimulus, and the whole atmosphere of the place supported such an impulse.

The inspiration of Adams' teaching was not due to an extraordinary profundity of thought in his lectures, which might create wonder and admiration for himself, and establish a cult or a body of disciples. His lectures were, indeed, sound and interesting, and dealt with a broad field of knowledge, but he was also continually pointing to more work to be done, more fields to be cultivated and more reputations to be made. It was his habit to preface his graduate lectures with " prolegomena " on some current topic of public or academic interest. At such times he reported the progress of the men gone out, or described some new historical enterprise in which he was himself engaged. In this rôle he sparkled with freshness and the student frequently regretted the return to the regular schedule of the day. This method was peculiarly effective in Adams' hands, but disciples who went out into the world and imitated the prolegomena were usually not so successful.

The connections made in this seminary became lifelong friendships, for Adams' counsel and interest continued without stint. He spared no pains in answering requests for advice, whether it related to academic methods or to private affairs. His numerous literary and editorial connections placed him in position to point out work to a large number of men, consequently his friendship became an ever-widening circle. The evidence of this personal attachment blazed up when his resignation on account of ill health was announced. From all sides there flowed in letters filled with gratitude for his paternal oversight and testimony to the inspiration of his teaching. These were not kindly flowers laid upon his tomb, but heartfelt praises for a man whom they hoped to see again in life with health restored. Expressions of regret from large numbers of colleagues in other institutions might be quoted, but one from Professor Albert Bushnell Hart will indicate the quality of these tributes.

" . . . It has fallen to the lot of few men in this generation, or in previous generations, to do so much to rouse their countrymen

to a sense of historical truth and to an interest in their own past.
Long after we are all gone that influence will keep at work...."

At the time of his death these tributes came in still more
abundantly. Said one of his earlier students:

" Few American teachers more clearly recognized the value
of close personal relations with his students. In Dr. Adams
the man overshadowed the professor. He did not hedge himself
about with the artificial formalities which are far too frequently
characteristic of those who direct the training of the young, but
was perfectly free and unrestrained in his relations with those
studying under him. These traits were due quite as much to
education as to inheritance, for travel and association gave him
a wide and varied acquaintance, to say nothing of the catholic,
uplifting influences he received from the faithful study of the
poets."

Woodrow Wilson, then professor in Princeton University, wrote in 1901:

"If I were to sum up my impression of Dr. Adams, I should
call him a great Captain of Industry, a captain in the field of
systematic and organized scholarship. I think all his pupils
would accord him mastery in the formulation of historical inquiry, in the suggestive stimulation of research, in the communication of methods and ideals. His head was a veritable clearing
house of ideas in the field of historical study, and no one ever
seriously studied under him who did not get, in its most service-
able form, the modern ideals of work upon the sources; and not
the ideals merely, but also a very definite principle of concrete
application in daily study. The thesis work done under him
may fairly be said to have set the pace for university work in
history throughout the United States. That is the whole thing
in a nutshell; and it makes a reputation which can never be
justly obscured."

CHAPTER V

WILLIAM ARCHIBALD DUNNING

By

CHARLES EDWARD MERRIAM

Professor of Political Science in the University of Chicago

WILLIAM ARCHIBALD DUNNING

CHAPTER V

WILLIAM ARCHIBALD DUNNING

It is difficult to realize that prior to 1880 there had been no systematic organization of research in the United States either in the field of history or of government. Men of the type of Adams, Jefferson, Hamilton, Madison, Lieber, Calhoun, had given profound thought to problems of state, both theoretical and practical, but the orderly investment of these subjects had not been undertaken. History had of course been a subject of college instruction, and the other social studies had been casually treated in connection with the study of ethics or moral philosophy, but in the main the outstanding fact was the neglect of these important subjects. Only after a hundred years of the Republic's life had passed, did systematic political inquiry begin.

In fact during the last half of the 19th century the study of politics received a great impetus in many parts of the world. The speculative philosophy of the Germans and the Austinian jurisprudence of the English were on the decline, and new forms of research in history, geography, anthropology, comparative government, and law were springing up everywhere. Maine, Spencer, Bagehot, Post, Kohler, Roscher and Ihering were organizing methods of approach to economic and political phenomena that were destined to alter radically the whole trend of political inquiry. In Germany especially there was feverish activity in almost every phase of the social sciences. In France the *École Libre des Sciences Politiques* was established after the Franco-Prussian War. In Italy Lombroso founded the School of Criminal Law and Criminology at Rome. In England Oxford and Cambridge began to turn slowly toward the social sciences and eventually the London School of Economics and Politics was founded. Outside the universities men like Booth began significant undertakings in the social fields.

In the United States a new era began in governmental research with the establishment of Johns Hopkins University and of the Columbia School of Political Science. These were the pioneers in the study of government. Other centers of research were established elsewhere and social inquiry was enthusiastically pushed forward by considerable groups of eager students.

In the Columbia School of Political Science there was assembled a notable group of students of government and society including Burgess, Giddings, Clark, Seligman, Monroe Smith, Mayo-Smith, Robinson, Osgood. These men were among the leading spirits who developed scientific inquiry in the social field. No group has done more to emphasize the importance and necessity of close study and analysis of political phenomena than did this early set of enthusiasts who pioneered the way. Chapters II, VI, VIII, and X of this volume are devoted to the work of some of these " masters." Among these, first as a student and later as a teacher, none was more widely influential than Professor Dunning, whose combined services as teacher, investigator, and editor gave to him a position of very great influence in his institution and in the community.

Professor Dunning was born in 1857 in Plainfield, New Jersey. He owed much to his father, a man of keen intellectual and artistic interests, deeply concerned with the welfare of his family. The elder Dunning was a carriage manufacturer, but he was also a critic of art and himself painted many pictures. An evidence of the unflagging interest of Professor Dunning's father in cultural matters is shown by the fact that at the age of seventy-eight he took up the study of Greek. It was from this unusual background of interest in business, art and education that the younger Dunning emerged.

The physical and mental energy of Professor Dunning was evident in the earliest periods of his life. He was enthusiastically devoted to baseball, skating and swimming, and combining scholarship with athletics at a very early age, knew almost every one's record on almost everything. At the same time he was capturing most of the prizes offered in high school and college. The dream of his boyhood and youth was that of becoming a newspaper reporter, and if Fortune had been more or less favorable, depending upon one's point of view, he might have become a great writer of editorials, or some towering figure in the journalistic world. A very practical turn was given to his early activities owing to the fact that the money set aside for his college education was lost in a financial crash at the end of his Freshman year. This made it necessary for the young student to make his own way, which he proceeded to do with such enthusiasm and vigor that by the end of his course he was financially ahead of the point where he started. Perhaps these early activities prevented him from ever devoting himself exclusively to the gods of pure political theory. There was always through his life a certain reluctance to throw his entire weight upon the side of political philosophy.

He received the degree of bachelor of arts from Columbia University in 1881; the master's degree from the same institution in 1884, and the doctorate in 1885. In Germany he had studied under the renowned Treitschke at Berlin. In Columbia he was successively a fellow, lecturer, instructor, adjunct professor and professor. From 1913 to 1922 he occupied the Francis Lieber professorship of history and political philosophy, a chair founded in honor of the first great teacher of politics in Columbia. The degree of doctor of laws was conferred upon him in 1904, and that of doctor of letters in 1916 by Dartmouth College.

Professor Dunning's work in the related fields of history and government was recognized by his long membership on the Council of the American Historical Association, and by his election to the Presidency of the Association in 1913. He was also one of the most valued advisors of the American Political Science Association from its earliest days, and was elected president in 1921. His untimely death prevented the delivery of his Presidential address in December, 1922.

My own relations with him were very intimate, since my major subject in Columbia was political philosophy. My doctoral dissertation was prepared under his supervision (and that of Professor Gierke in Berlin). He conducted a special research course in political philosophy for my benefit, and during his sabbatical year, I gave his general courses and the course in American political theory. It was also my privilege to come in contact with him on many occasions after the completion of my study at Columbia.

My first sharp impression of Professor Dunning was ob-

tained in his Seminar on Political Philosophy.   He was
assigning topics for the semester, and in reply to my statement that I could read German, he turned over to me the
six ponderous volumes of Ludwig von Haller's *Restaura-
tion der Staatswissenschaft*.   In his keen eyes there was a
humorous challenge which we both understood.   Before
the year was over, I had learned more German and much
von Haller.

   Dunning was an interesting and impressive personality.
His sharp blue eye, his ruddy beard, his bald dome, were
the externals of a man with high intellectual power and
great social charm.   Perhaps his most striking characteristics were his delightful wit and his remarkable power of
penetration and characterization.   Both his humor and his
logic were likely to be disconcerting to the unwary, or the
wary too, for that matter.   It is notable, however, that he
was never unkindly or contemptuous or sarcastic, but was
none the less effectively critical.   He was quick to detect
superficiality, limping logic, or confused expression, and
his own rare power of statement made it possible for him
to indicate significant lines of advance.   He was clear and
suggestive as a lecturer, but was at his best in smaller
seminar groups where his abilities could have full play,
unrestricted by the more formal requirements of the
lecture.

   Dunning had in high degree a certain quality of *esprit*,
an intellectual enthusiasm and grace that radiated from
him unconsciously, whether in class room, seminar, or
among his colleagues.   In the central offices of the School
of Political Science, or when he and Professor Morse
Stephens came together at the annual Association meeting,
with others of their cronies, there were always notable passages of intellectual arms.   If Burgess had all the dignity

and dogmatism of the Dean, if Seligman had vast wealth of sophistication and erudition, if Osgood had preternatural industry, or Giddings the will to shock, Professor Dunning had a unique quality of princely fellowship and Shakesperian wit.

When I last saw Professor Dunning, a few weeks before his death in 1922, his mind was as clear as ever and, more than that, his gay spirit rallied as jauntily as ever. Like a tired soldier, he came into action, but in a few moments he fell back exhausted; and I came away with an unfading picture of the great towers of his mind still standing amid the physical ruins.

The concluding chapter and especially the final paragraph of his *History of Political Theories,* gives evidence of weariness and pessimism. Especially the sentence: " In twenty-three centuries the movement of thought has but swung full circle. Such is the general lesson of the history of political theory." He once said to me that he had written this when very much discouraged, and sometimes was sorry that he had. Yet these paragraphs were not wholly uncharacteristic, for he often talked in the same vein of weariness. Mr. Coudert of New York believes that this really represented fairly his general philosophy.

Professor Dunning seemed to have had two aversions, one to contact with political affairs, and the other to the development of systematic or dogmatic political philosophy. Even the campaign of Seth Low for mayor in 1897, which drew many of the academic group into the struggle, did not move him. It was on this occasion that I made my first political speech, — a cart tail speech — on the East Side, under the general direction of James Harvey Robinson, then a militant reformer.

Nor would he be drawn into a positive theory of the state. He always maintained that he was an objective chronicler, and not a dogmatic philosopher. On one occasion I suggested that by going through his writings and observing carefully his analyses and measuring emphasis and omission, it was possible to discover his basic political ideas. For a moment he seemed a little startled, but would doubtless have been able to find discrepancies in my proposed synthetic philosophy. Yet it is indeed possible to cull from his scattered volumes a fragmentary philosophy of politics, observing his treatment of many significant doctrines, rejected and approved, emphatically or mildly.

This unwillingness to dogmatize has of course always been the despair of those who believe that historical writing consists in free interpretation of events for purposes of such local application as the writer regards as appropriate. Dunning considered his own method as a departure from personal opinion and an approach to objectivity. His " dominant reverie " was that of a purely impersonal and objective attitude.

Dunning was a liberal and painstaking critic, but he was not wont to coddle his students along. Given a topic, the student was to find his own bibliography, outline and execute his research, organize and embody it in literary form. Then began the formidable critique by the professor. The better the work, the more searching his analysis of sources, ideas and style, and the poorer it was the less he heeded it. He proceeded apparently on the principle that " Whom the Lord loveth, he chasteneth." Among his favorite devices were that of challenging the conclusion and of forcing the recapitulation of the case. Another was that of setting up a somewhat similar problem, similar yet a little different from the one immediately under discussion. Always he made very free use of the blue pencil, cutting here and slashing there, with ironical comment and constructive criticism freely intermingled.

An outstanding feature of Professor Dunning's work was his ability to interest students in research, and his great helpfulness to men under his guidance. In the one hundred volumes of the Columbia University series in History, Economics and Public Law published during his day are many acknowledgements of his aid, and cordial tributes to his fine helpfulness. Two volumes were written as tributes to him by his students, one edited by Professor Garner in 1914, *Studies in Southern History and Politics* (with fifteen collaborators), and one by Merriam, Barnes, and others (1923) on *Political Theories, Recent Times.* Both of these were labors of love on the part of grateful students. They stand as a striking recognition of the personal attachment of a group of men with widely ranging scholarly interests to an inspiring teacher. I do not know of any higher testimonial to him than this, nor any finer type of monument that could be raised to an eminent teacher.

As a lecturer Professor Dunning was interesting and suggestive. He did not present the commanding and impressive appearance of Gierke or Burgess, nor did he develop the fervor and enthusiasm of Kohler or Harnack, nor the sharp challenge of Giddings. His lectures were full of acute characterizations and of dry wit; they were well organized and were developed steadily and effectively, like the calm unrolling of a scroll. He did not undertake anything in the nature of a quiz, nor was there much interruption or discussion in his lectures. This was reserved for the seminars. As in the case of other instructors, he was somewhat at a loss how to proceed with his lectures after the publication of his manuscript, and told me at one time that he was sorry he had published anything.

The list of Professor Dunning's writings is an extended one, and includes his doctoral dissertation on *The Constitution of the United States in Civil War and Reconstruction*, (1885); *Essays on the Civil War and Reconstruction*, (1898); *Reconstruction, Political and Economic*, (1907); *The British Empire and the United States*, (1914). The first three of these volumes in the field of American history centered around the Reconstruction period, in which he was deeply interested, and constituted a significant contribution to our knowledge of this field. They were enlarged by various monographic studies of his students, many of whom were represented in the memorial volume on *Southern History and Politics*. These studies presented the period of the Reconstruction in a wholly different light from that in which it had commonly been viewed and it may be said that no one did more than Dunning to rewrite the history of the generation following the Civil War. His survey of Anglo-American relations, while the result of a less careful study, was an admirable analysis of a field which in the years immediately following the publication of this volume became a subject of profound interest to the world.

His most significant contribution to political science was his history of political theory, published in three volumes, 1909–20. This was begun by the *History of Political Theories, Ancient and Mediaeval*, (1902), followed by *From Luther to Montesquieu*, (1905), and concluded by *From Rousseau to Spencer*, (1920). These volumes dealt with the development of systematic political thought, in its various typical forms, from the classical period to modern times. The general scope of his plan is best stated in the introduction to his first volume. Here he definitely excluded the whole mass of primitive political theory on the ground that our knowledge of it is as vague as it is vast. He limited the scope of the work to the philosophy of the European Aryan peoples. He indicated the relation of political philosophy to ethical and juristic concepts and also to the general history of ideas. Nor was he unmindful of the relation between political philosophy and the current of institutional development. " The history of political theory is to be kept always in touch with the history of political fact; and, with this purpose in view, it will be indispensable at times to depart entirely from the field of literature and to derive a notion of theory from an immediate interpretation of institutions." These limitations have been and may be seriously questioned, but they define quite clearly the scope of the undertaking and leave no doubt as to the author's general conception of his field.

He brought his history to a close with the year 1880, not because that was a logical stopping point, but because " the distinctive purpose served by the chosen date is to bring history to an end while it is still history, and thus save the author from the temptation to deal with ideas that can not, in the nature of things, be seen yet in their true perspective." This is again an illustration of his effort to be strictly objective in method and attitude.

These lucid and scholarly accounts of the development of systematic political thinking superseded the earlier *Histoire de les Sciences Politiques* of Janet, and Bluntschli's *Geschichte der neueren Staatswissenchaft*. There are of course various monographic discussions of various fields and phrases of political theory, and doubtless will be many more, much more detailed and minute in nature, but none thus far covered the field so completely.

Professor Dunning's writings have sometimes been criticized as lacking adequate reference to or appreciation of the economic, social or political background of theory, but in reality an examination of his works, or familiarity with his methods, does not justify this conclusion. He was to be sure primarily interested in the development of systematic types of political thinking, but only in relation to the environment from which they sprung. He repeatedly emphasized in the strongest terms the fundamental importance of considering particular types of theory as reflections of their time, and the danger of looking upon them as purely logical formulas, devoid of interpretative significance. Both his general historical training and interests and his theory of theories made it impossible for him to ignore the background of speculation. Indeed, it would not be inaccurate to say that he himself regarded this all-round view as one of his fundamentals.

Professor Dunning was unusually successful in three fields, that of the teacher, the editor, and the scholar. In all of them his usefulness was very large. He was editor of the *Political Science Quarterly* for a period of ten years extending from 1894 to 1903. During this period the *Quarterly* shows the effect of his careful and painstaking scrutiny, and his admirable powers of discriminatory judgment. In selection, rejection and revision of material, his fine taste was highly beneficial to the readers of this very useful journal, and the indirect value of this service is difficult to evaluate properly; but it is as substantial and important for the profession, as it is arduous and time consuming for the editor. Few outside the narrow circle of editors realize the severity of the labor involved in shaping the policy and supervising the executive detail of a scientific journal. Equally few are those who appreciate the wide-reaching influence of such efforts in moulding standards of professional excellence.

In composition he was very deliberate, choosing his way with extreme caution and only after long consideration of all sides of the situation. He wrote very slowly, sometimes only a paragraph or so a day, but this was set down in a very fine hand and very little was changed thereafter. From the vigor and precision of his ordinary conversation, as well as his correspondence, one might have expected a more fluent pen and more extended production, but Professor Dunning was highly critical of his own work, and wished nothing to have his personal imprimatur which had not been fully and satisfactorily tested. This inhibited him from the development of more extended studies and in a measure from challenging comment even, in sharp contrast to his conversational discussion where he was genuinely free. However, this quality was in no sense timidity, but rather that of severe self-criticism, making him insistent upon high standards of accomplishment, both in substance and in form. He was supremely anxious in all his work to remain detached in interest and objective in method. He seemed to fear nothing so much as to be considered prejudiced, unbalanced, immature in judgment, reckless in conclusion. This attitude reflected his conception of true scholarship, and he held to it faithfully throughout his academic career.

There is to be sure wide difference of opinion upon this

position, and many there are who hold that real objectivity is impossible and hence that the scholar may properly give his own personal interpretation of human experience as he sees it. This, it is believed, gives life and color to scholarly work, and enables its influence to be felt in a pragmatic world where after all, it may be said, truth is relative to specific situations.

This diversity of attitude turns, however, not merely upon difference in conceptions of scholarship, but also upon differences in task and temperament. One type of man prefers a degree of isolation from current world events and another is interested in mingling with the stream. Without question, Professor Dunning belonged to the group that does not rejoice in struggle with the rush of affairs, but prefers retirement and observation. In this respect Dunning and Laski are quite different types, both by temperament and by training. In the broader view of human values, both the demand for gross results for the present day, and the objectivity that withholds itself from participation in particular strife must suffice their purpose. And it may be added that in all probability neither will ever understand the other.

Quite another side of Professor Dunning's life was the social, and this centered around the Century Club. This was his social headquarters, and he was chairman of the house committee for a number of years, usually to be found in his accustomed corner. Not blessed with children, he adopted the Club and became one of its leading spirits during one of its most interesting periods. Here the genial philosopher was at home, perhaps more than with students or political practitioners, and here his ready wit and affable manner were met and appreciated by the brilliant group that gathered around this noted center, where literati and savants were wont to gather at their ease, and view the world from high Olympus.

Any attempt to appraise Dunning's work is fraught with great peril. First of all the writer is one of his pupils, and therefore not wholly impartial. And after all where are the standards by which men shall be tried? Is the test what the scholar himself produces; or what he trains or inspires others to produce; or the advice and counsel he may contribute to his colleagues; or is it perhaps the radiance of a shining personality in the field of art, letters or science that gives out light and inspiration? In truth some men have been eminent in particular achievements and some have been preëminent in the net result — the final total.

But by any test, Professor Dunning was one of the notable members of the community of scholars in America during his generation. His specific accomplishments in history and government were notable; his influence as a teacher multiplied him a hundredfold; as a counsellor he aided many of his academic associates in ways that will never be known; as an editor he helped to raise the standards of judgment and taste; as a personality he inspired enthusiasm for high ideals of scholarship and scientific advance. Are not these achievements an ample crown for any life? And do they not entitle their bearer to a place among the great masters of his time?

All things considered, it seems to me that the finest quality in Dunning was his power to arouse in students sustained enthusiasm for research, and for high standards of investigation and expression. His specific contribution to our stock of knowledge was considerable, but his own effectiveness was multiplied by the number of those who were interested by him, and who became independent tillers of the soil.   All that the personal efforts of any one individual can add to the world's wisdom is very small, unless he is able to interest others to carry on the work in directions and to consequences which he could not foresee.

In evaluating a series of masters is not this the greatest work of the *magister?*   Not merely to hand on the torch of traditional knowledge, not alone the specific contribution to science, but to kindle in many minds the divine spark of enthusiasm for research without which the great intellectual adventure of mankind would close.

CHAPTER VI

ALBION WOODBURY SMALL

By

EDWARD CARY HAYES

Professor of Sociology in the University of Illinois

ALBION WOODBURY SMALL

CHAPTER VI

ALBION WOODBURY SMALL

FIFTY years hence the student who wishes to form a mental picture of the pioneer sociologist, Albion W. Small, should begin by calling up in imagination the ideal of a gentleman. He will then have made a good start toward forming a true picture of the man, both in outward seeming and in inner essence. He should think of a person somewhat below the average height but notably virile and erect, speaking in a rich voice, and bearing himself with assured dignity. He should see him as always attired with the quiet elegance of an ambassador. And when he conceives of the traits which intimate acquaintance would reveal he should think of modesty and magnanimity.

Earnest as Professor Small has been in the declaration of his ideas, he has also been ready as few scholars are to acknowledge the tentative character of his teaching, free from determination to defend a position once taken because it was identified with himself, hospitable to the ideas of others up to the very end of his active life, and generous in his appreciation of the contributions of other scholars in the field in which he has himself been a contributor.

To these traits must be added the fact that the fundamental element of his life has been always the ethical interest. He has been interested in scholarship chiefly as a means of solving life's puzzle and bringing to realization

149

the possibilities of good inherent in mankind. He is [1] of New England ancestry and tradition. His father was a distinguished clergyman. It is true that as an open-minded scholar he of necessity escaped the bonds of a narrow orthodoxy. He recounts with merriment how when he acknowledged to a friend of his early youth that he no longer believed in a personal devil his friend replied " Why Albion, then you are an Atheist! " He believes that " fundamentalism " will prove the most powerful of boomerangs, that it will return to smite its own warriors for — to leave the figure of speech — it will force men to study both science and religion. He holds that they assume a dire responsibility who drive men from Christianity by insisting that they can not be religious unless they agree to ascribe to Jehovah all the atrocities which the ancient Hebrews committed at his supposed command, and swallow whole the mythology of prescientific ages. But it is certain that the sense of responsibility for service engendered by his early training never left him. It has made life to him a crusade and not an entertainment. However much the creed of his youth may have been left behind, the desire to contribute something to human progress has never ceased to be the dominant motive of his life. Moreover, his desire to serve " humanity " never became as it does with some a substitute for generosity in personal relations. His idealism was not drawn from mysticism, nor metaphysics, but from contemplation of the realities of human experience viewed always as part and parcel of the realm of cause and effect.

Early in his scholastic career he became convinced of

[1] The tenses used correspond to the fact that this was written just before the decease of Professor Small.

the inadequacy of the old methods of attacking the problem: how are we to progress toward the realization of the good that remains unfulfilled? This conviction became associated in his mind with another, namely: that we can understand social life only *as a whole* and that each part can be understood only by its relationships. It became the prime mission of his intellectual life to insist upon a better realization of this necessity than the older social sciences had displayed. And until the present climax of his career as teacher and author he has regarded his own work as bearing whatever permanent significance it possesses as part of the progress in developing this realization. However, with catholicity of judgment he has realized that the sociologists are not the only scientists nor the sociological method of approach the only method by which in his generation this realization has been promoted. Instead he holds, with truth, that the recent changes in the attitude of the older social sciences exhibit the timeliness of the sociological movement.

" Sociology " is one name for an intellectual movement which has increasingly pervaded the social sciences since the time of Auguste Comte. This movement includes the growth of certain realizations and their adoption as rules of method in the social sciences. The chief of these realizations are four in number. Some of these realizations have been more emphasized by some writers and others have been more emphasized by others. But the growth of them all is unmistakable. They can be briefly stated as follows:

First, the realization that all social life (and all distinctively human life is *social* life) is a part of the realm of cause and effect. The "makers of history" are not a score of men nor even a score of millions of men. The great man is far more a product than a creator. The steps of progress are short and made possible by the journey already traversed. The content of human activity is the product, not of arbitrary fiats of human volition, but of intelligible causation. Human volition itself is not arbitrary and uncaused. "One man is no man." Except as a member of society no man, however biologically endowed, would be human in the distinctive sense. An infant Aristotle, isolated from birth, would be less developed in culture and in life than is any savage tribe. Distinctively human life is participation in the social life, a product of the causes by which the social life is molded. The study of causation extends to the whole of man's social experience and achievement.

Second the realization that customs and institutions in their most essential aspect are states of mind, complexes of ideas and sentiments, a streaming process of psychic activity, now regular and relatively constant and again disturbed and changing. However, this process of activity, though in its primary aspect psychic, has at the same time an overt aspect in the visible behavior of men, and determines their acquisition of the traits which human beings possess as products of social evolution.

Third is the realization of the unity of the social life, that is, the interdependence of all types of social activity, of diverse social groups and of human individuals, and that all distinctively human activities have certain characteristics in common and are explicable in their main outlines by reference to common tendencies and the same types of causal conditions.

The fourth element in the sociological movement is the

realization that ethical judgments and sentiments have not been derived by intuition of a metaphysical absolute but by actual experience of weal and woe, that good and evil, the ultimate values of life, are realities and like other realities are dependent upon causes, that chief among the causal conditions on which they depend are human activities, that knowledge of the relation between human activities and the values they effect is matter-of-fact knowledge, that human life can not be adequately or truthfully described so long as such knowledge is omitted from the description, that, in the phraseology of Comte, the study of ethics, that is of the method of the realization of values in experience, is passing and must pass entirely from the theological and metaphysical to the positive stage. The varying conscience codes of different societies are results of their imperfectly interpreted experience as to the method of success in the experiment of living together, as these results of experience have become embodied in conventionality and sentiment. The difficult threefold problem in proportion (1) between present and future satisfactions, (2) between conflicting desires of the same individual, and (3) between the effects of conduct on the actor and on others, is the supreme practical matter-of-fact problem. It pervades all departments of human action and is therefore part of the *general* study of social life.

Such is the intellectual movement in which Professor Small has participated. The order in which I have named its four chief elements corresponds to the increasing degrees in which he has contributed to them, the third and the fourth having been chiefly emphasized by him.

More than any other American sociologist, Professor Small has mediated to us the results of European scholarship. The intellectual world is now one society. No nation would have had its present scientific development without the collaboration of the scientists of different nations. Indeed, science as a national phenomenon is unthinkable. It is a part of the life of " the great society."

In order to understand the development of the intellectual attitudes that have characterized the life-work of Professor Small, and how he came to be so important a mediator between the scholarship of Europe and America, it is necessary at this point to sketch briefly some of the events of his career.

Born May 11, 1854, at Buckfield, Maine, he was graduated from Colby College in 1876. Already as a student he showed the fondness for telling phrases and the gift for constructing them which has always characterized his speech and writing. There is a tradition that when in the senior class in Moral Philosophy he was asked to draw the distinction between morality and religion he rose and said: " Morality is religion in her working clothes and religion is morality robed for the altar." If he sometimes swathed his thoughts in purple clouds he could also have been a great inventor of crisp slogans. And if he has sometimes used a rhetorical locomotive unnecessarily he has often given to weighty ideas the momentum of an express train.

For the three years ending in 1879 he was a student at Newton Theological Seminary. The next two years he spent in study abroad, one year at the University of Berlin and one at the University of Leipzig. He had taken to Berlin letters which introduced him to the family of von Massow, where there was a charming daughter, and where with an American friend he was a frequent visitor. The two months of the summer vacation were spent by the von Massow family at Weimar, and at their invitation by the two Americans also. Before the summer was ended a relation was established which resulted in the coming of Fraulein Valeria von Massow to America as Mrs. Small, an event which more or less facilitated the life-long intimacy of her husband with German life and thought. If it made an American of Mrs. Small it was far from making a German of her husband. And while his life-long appreciation of the noble elements in German traditions and German science was deeply sympathetic, his intimacy with German junkerdom made him a severe and discriminating critic of its faults.

After his return to America he was made professor of history and economics at Colby. In 1888–89, he took a sabbatical year which was spent at Johns Hopkins University, an institution of a type then new in this country, pervaded as is well known by a fine scholarly idealism, and at which there had been gathered a group of extraordinary teachers and of students who became notable in the intellectual development of our country. While pursuing his own studies at Johns Hopkins he taught a graduate course in American Constitutional History with a class that included F. J. Turner, later professor at Wisconsin and Harvard, and J. A. Woodburn, later professor at the State University of Indiana.

During these years he was becoming increasingly impressed by the fact, now recognized far more generally than then, that in much of their research historians were not really finding out what mattered most, but were largely occupied with trivialities that would be gossip if they pertained to yesterday or the day before. He was disturbed by the inconclusiveness and relative futility of the results attained by much painstaking research. He realized that the permanent tendencies in human affairs, the inner methods of causation that determine the destinies of men and nations were not being revealed. He believed that such casual principles existed and that the search for them was the supreme intellectual task. He hoped to find a clue by the study of comparative constitutional history. And he became moreover an indefatigable but disappointed reader of the " philosophy of history."

On returning from Johns Hopkins to Colby he was elected President of the latter institution and remained in that office for the three years that terminated in 1892, with his call to the University of Chicago.

His administrative duties as President of Colby allowed some time for teaching and he proceeded to substitute in place of Noah Porter's Moral Philosophy a course in Sociology. This course was first offered in the third or spring term of 1890. That same year a course in Sociology was opened at the University of Kansas by Professor F. W. Blackmar, who had been a fellow student with Professor Small at Johns Hopkins. Previous to that year the only course in sociology at any American institution had been the one given by Professor William Graham Sumner at Yale.

For use in connection with this course he prepared a printed syllabus and source book in Sociology, " with special reference to the works of Comte, Spencer, Schäffle, Bluntschli, Lieber, Lotze, H. C. Adams, Mulford and Ward."

When William Rainey Harper was told that John D. Rockefeller proposed to give a million dollars to revive the Baptist institution that had existed under the name of Chicago University, and was asked whether he would accept the presidency, Professor Harper replied in the negative, but added that if Mr. Rockefeller cared to give fifteen millions for the purpose of founding a really great university then he would willingly undertake its presidency. Mr. Rockefeller recognized the calibre of the man who made such a proposition, as well as the character of the project, and responded in the way now well known. Since then we have grown accustomed to large figures, and figures that then seemed monstrous now seem moderate. And when President Harper, in order to assemble a faculty of the highest eminence, offered to the heads of departments in the new institution annual salaries of seven thousand dollars each, the figure was unprecedented in this country. Among the heads of departments thus assembled from England, Germany and the United States, was Professor Small, head of the first department of Sociology ever established in any institution in the world.

The creation of such a department was a bold stroke on the part of President Harper. And to accept the responsibility for conducting such a department was a pioneering venture on the part of Professor Small. But both men were pioneers and crusaders. The difficult situation was made still more difficult by the attitude of the head of the related department of Economics. And it is a testimonial to the qualities of Professor Small that among a faculty composed of men so highly distinguished in the more thoroughly established sciences as those who gradually were brought together at Chicago, in 1905, he was made Dean of the Graduate School of Arts and Literature.

Whatever may have been the attitude of teachers of the

other social sciences, there was no lack of able graduate students in the new department of Sociology, and the faculty of the department was augmented by the addition of Professors Charles R. Henderson, George E. Vincent, and William I. Thomas.

Meanwhile Professor Small was taking deep interest in the approaches toward the sociological point of view on the part of many of the most gifted students of the older social sciences, by historians like Guizot, Taine, Lamprecht, and Laurent of Belgium, by political scientists like Bagehot, Bluntschli, and Stein — forerunners of Wallas, Kohler and Max Weber of Heidelberg, by economists like Schmoller, Wagner, Dietzel, Brentano, Boehm-Bawerk, Phillippowicz, Alfred Marshall, and John Stuart Mill, and by philosophers like Wundt, Simmel, Durkheim, and later Dewey and Hobhouse. For a time it seemed as though the contributions toward the developing movement that has taken the name of sociology which were being made by German social scientists were at least as notable as the hostility toward it that was common among social scientists in our own country.

This hostility in the case of some of them was apparently due to the fact that they were individualists of the old fashioned sort, while sociology as developed by men like Ward and Giddings and Small and Ross was largely a protest against individualism of the type suggested by the phrases "laissez faire" and "every man for himself." It has been said that the meeting of the American Economic Association held in Philadelphia in 1917, including a joint session with the American Sociological Society, celebrated the funeral obsequies of the doctrine of laissez faire. But it would hardly be too much to say that during the first decades of Professor Small's connection with the University of Chicago that doctrine was the summary and conclusion of economic teaching as presented by the majority of its professors in the United States.

There is a sense — but quite a different sense — in which sociology is as individualistic as economics ever was, for sociology holds that the values experienced by every individual count at par; that though the values experienced by different individuals are not all equal they are all equally real, and as realities are not to be disregarded; that, in the phraseology of Kant, " no human being is to be treated as a means only but as an end in himself "; that there is no *social* value, of the ultimate sort which is an end in itself and to which all other values are means only, save the aggregate of individual values; and that if social value is more to be regarded than individual values it is because the sum is greater than any of its parts.

Within two years after Professor Small came to Chicago, there appeared in 1894 an " Introduction to the Study of Sociology," the first textbook in Sociology ever published, which he had prepared in collaboration with his pupil and colleague, George E. Vincent.

Before another year had passed the American Journal of Sociology was founded as one of the publications of the University of Chicago Press, and Professor Small became its editor-in-chief, a position which he held for over thirty years. The importance of the part played by this journal under his discriminating editorship in affording an avenue of publication and of communication between sociologists during the period of development that has intervened since its first appearance in 1895, can hardly be overestimated. It has been true to a scientific ideal and has achieved an enviable reputation, not only in this country but in other nations as well.

Professor Small was one of the three vice-presidents of the Louisiana Purchase Exposition held in St. Louis in 1904, director of its Department of Arts and Sciences, and so in charge of arranging the World's Congress of Arts and Sciences held in connection with the exposition, and editor of the report of that congress.

He was one of the chief actors in the organization (in 1905) of the American Sociological Society, and in 1911 he became its president, holding that office for two consecutive terms.[2]   In 1913, he was elected a member of the International Institute of Sociology which has its seat in Paris.

In 1905, Professor Small published his *General Sociology*, a work of more than 700 pages which must still be regarded as his *magnum opus*.

The *General Sociology* opens with the declaration that it is to be an elaboration of the concept of " the social process." The phrase " the social process " is used by different sociologists to stand for two distinct concepts which should not be confused: First, the socially conditioned activities and changes in these activities, and second the " process of social causation " or " inter-stimulation and response " which, when critically viewed, is seen to be a multitude of cause-and-effect relations between the activities that make up the social process as first defined, such causal relations as those between the English speaking of a mother and of a child who learns the language, between the activity of a teacher and of those taught, between the

[2] Lester F. Ward, William Graham Sumner and Franklin H. Giddings were his predecessors.

activities of the members of a crowd, between the activities
of immigrants and the activities already prevailing in the
group which they join, or between the activities of com-
petitors in business. Professor Small did not keep clear
the distinction between the two essential concepts: first,
social activities and changes in such activities, second,
causal relations between social activities.

Culture or the life-process of society is what sociology
seeks to explain, in so far as that process in its wide outlines is capable of a general explanation that applies to all
of its subdivisions, economic, political, linguistic, ethical,
religious, etc. If the scientific explanation of any facts
is a description of those facts so extended as to include reference to all the other facts by which they are directly conditioned, in the absence of which the facts to be explained
would not appear, and by the modification of which they
would be modified, then the most important element in the
explanation of social activities is their relation to other
social activities. Social relations are the main factors in
the explanation of culture, or the social life-process. However, they are not the only factors in the explanation.
Social activities are conditioned also by the inherited or
acquired psycho-physical traits of the actors and by their
material environment. Professor Lester F. Ward emphasized the physical environment, particularly the artificial
physical environment, as conditioning social activity so far
as to say that " matter alone is dynamic." [3] And no one
has argued more eloquently than Professor Small for recognition of the natural material conditions, or geographic
factors.

Both Ward and Small clearly recognized the importance

[3] Ward, *Pure Sociology*, p. 32, ch. 3 passim. Also pp. 254 and 255.

of conditioning factors external to the social process. But neither of them observed clearly enough the fact that causal relations between social activities themselves are the chief factors in sociological explanation. Therefore both were led to seek the chief factors in the motives or desires by which social activities are prompted, and refer to these desires as " the social forces." But there is a marked difference in the meaning which these two writers put into the phrase " social forces." To Professor Ward the social forces are the universal tendencies of human nature. It is of course true that the proclivities of man's psycho-physical nature are conditions which universally affect his social activity. But because of their universality they can not explain the differences between the activities of savage and of civilized societies, and all the wide range of diversity and change that characterizes social activities in different places, and at different stages in the development of the same society. The impossibility of their affording an explanation of these differences and changes — which is precisely what is sought by sociology — demonstrates the futility of conceiving of sociological explanation as mainly reference to universal human desires considered as " the social forces." Professor Small escapes this difficulty by taking as his explanatory " forces " not universal and inherent traits of human nature but the specific desires of men.

These desires he classifies under six heads, which he symbolizes by six words: *health,* or all physical desires including the desire for beefsteak, football, and a mate; *wealth,* or the desire for houses and automobiles and all material goods, particularly the desire to make them; *sociability,* including the desire to be boss of the gang or governor of the state, for which group of wants Small in later years substituted the term prestige; *knowledge,* including the desire to attend the meeting of the American Sociological Society; *beauty,* including the desire to paint a picture or to wear well-cut clothes; *rightness,* including the desire to speak the truth, to support the church, and all ethical aspiration. (Given to his classes in 1893.)

Such desires are specific activities rather than forces causing activity. Every specific human desire is an activity or rather an element in activity. Human activity is an organic unit. Its psychic essence (having ideas, desires, satisfactions) and its overt or muscular manifestation are parts, or aspects, of a single complex reaction. It is the activity as a whole that we want to explain. Indeed, it is more important to fix our attention on the opinions and desires of men as the objects of our explanation, than to fix it upon their overt conduct, for it is only by explaining the former that we can explain the latter, and it is only a knowledge of the explanation of the former that can be practically applied in controlling either the psychic or the overt muscular aspect of human activity. Accordingly, both the scientific and the practical tasks of sociology require us to explain the specific desires that prevail among men, and that are an essential element in the activities that make up the social process. Therefore a classification of the desires or interests of culture men such as Professor Small has made does not constitute an enumeration of " forces " which explain human activity, (as he originally maintained). Nevertheless such a classification of human desires does furnish a set of descriptive categories for the social activities to be explained, identified by one of their inherent elements.

Moreover, it furnishes a classification of " social values."
" Wealth " stands for certain secondary or derivative
values, that is *means* to ends which have value; and the
other five categories can be so interpreted as to include
and classify all the primary or ultimate values, that is the
ends or elements of worth in experience.

Half of the General Sociology was presented as " an interpretation of Spencer, Schaeffle, and Ratzenhofer, and
has been the principal medium through which the two German writers have become familiar to readers in the United
States. Small's " interpretation " of the three authors just
named is by no means a slavish adoption of their ideas, it
is a critical discussion which gives full credit for what is
taken over, intermingled with Professor Small's own conceptions.

Ratzenhofer has a classification of "the interests "
somewhat different from that which Professor Small had
independently worked out. Ratzenhofer's list is (1) The
desire to continue the species represented by the sex and
parental instincts. (2) The desire to continue individual
life, represented by the instincts to acquire and consume
food. (3) The desire to develop a definite and significant
individuality and to play a large rôle. (4) The social desire to establish satisfactory relations and promote the
well-being of associates. (5) The transcendental desire or
the yearning for a satisfying sense of relationship, not only
with our human associates but also with the Great Whole
of Being, which finds expression in varying forms all the
way from the crude mysticism of savages to philosophic
pantheism.

A study of the struggle of interests, when by interests
one means specific cultural activities, is a study of one part

of that network of interrelations between social activities which when viewed in its completeness is the chief type of causal relation by which the content of the rich diversity of the social process is conditioned. It is a study of the relations of conflict and competition. And such a study is illuminatingly presented by Small and Ratzenhofer. Their discussion may in part be paraphrased as follows:

The fundamental urgencies of human nature appear in the cultural interests. And groups in which divergent cultural [4] interests are aroused struggle one with another. What we call " parties " are in reality alliances of particular interest groups. They do not necessarily proclaim the interests for which they are really struggling, but often others that they think will win popular support or at least tolerance. Majorities shift when some interest groups become inactive or others are aroused; or some shift their allegiance to a new alliance. The fighting strength of an interest group does not depend chiefly upon its numbers. Majorities do not rule. Majorities are made. Those who make majorities rule. The fighting strength of a group depends in part on numbers but also on wealth, facility of organization, and the possession of a fighting nucleus. There are vicarious interest groups which will struggle for the welfare of others and for justice. But they are likely to be relatively supine in comparison with groups that are struggling for their own vital interest. The struggle of interest groups, when free, results in a compromise that is the nearest practicable approach to justice, and the struggle is somewhat modified by the presence of social and transcendental interests in men.

[4] Any socially conditioned interest is " cultural " in the technical sense.

There is perhaps no better discussion of the underlying activities that find political expression than that contained in the combination of the ideas of Ratzenhofer and of Small, presented in *General Sociology*.

Two years after the publication of *General Sociology* appeared *Adam Smith and Modern Sociology*. In this book Professor Small emphasized the idea of a desirable synthesis of all the social sciences. He said " Sterility must be the fate of every celibate social science," and "cross-fertilization of the social sciences occurs in spite of the most obstinate programs of non-intercourse." His zeal carried him somewhat further than his later judgment approved and he even asserted that " an objective economics without an objective sociology is as impossible as grammar without language."

Following the suggestions of Adam Smith he would have the whole modern progress of the social sciences interpreted as " an enlargement and enrichment " of the field of moral philosophy (p. viii), and " sociology in its largest scope and on its methodological side," he says, " is merely a moral philosophy conscious of its task and systematically pursuing knowledge of cause and effect within this process of moral evolution." (p. 22.)

This seems a far cry from the assertion of Ward (*Pure Sociology*, p. 4) that pure sociology must be utterly divorced from all ethical considerations, and the insistence of Max Weber and von Wiese that sociology must be " *wertfrei*." However, a definition of terms is possible that would remove the apparent divergence. To be " *wertfrei*," to the recent German sociologists, means primarily to refrain from attempting to give debatable policies the weight of professorial authority. To be divorced from ethics, means to Ward to be objective, and free from merely speculative notions as to the intuitive and absolute. In Ward's day ethical understanding by most people was thought to be derivable only from metaphysical speculation. But none of the writers named escaped or would desire to escape from ethical considerations if we mean by ethical considerations the recognition of cause and effect relations in which human experience is the reality affected. To recognize cause and effect relations is the supreme business of science. Those cause and effect relations in which the distinctively human activities are the realities affected are the characteristic objects of sociological research. Distinctly human activities are experiences. The description of experiences contains the element of value (pleasure and pain) as the description of a rose or a rainbow contains the element of color. To be able to say that certain compounds in the sap determine the color of the rose would be purely and typically scientific knowledge. To be able to say that specific conduct in general has specified effects on subsequent experience either of the actor or of others would be equally so. And ethical judgments, in the sense in which they are in place in sociology, are precisely such statements of fact concerning the conditions that affect distinctively human activity (which is human experience). Description of the causation, or conditioning, of human activity-experience is in this sense the declaration of ethical judgment. The formation of painstaking and objective judgments as to the conditions that affect human activity is the business of sociology. The most important conditions affecting human activity are other human activities. Perception of the effects of human activity upon other human activity is the prime business of sociology and is also scientific ethics. And Professor Small early pointed out that existing ethical codes, though attributed to intuition or to revelation, have in fact originated by the method of trial and error in contact with reality as all primitive practical arts originate. And a study of the development of the varying conscious codes in which different societies have embodied and sentimentalized the imperfectly learned lessons of experience is one branch in the study of social evolution, for conscious codes, like languages or political institutions, are products of social evolution.

This view of ethical judgments as simply declaration of the objective and observed causal relation between human activity and other human activity, either of the original actor or of another, as that causal relation has been witnessed in the past and as it is therefore foreseen for the future, is in harmony with the fundamental teachings of Adam Smith that " our moral judgments with respect to our own conduct are only applications to ourselves of decisions which we have already passed on the conduct of our neighbor."

After another interval of two years, in 1909, appeared " The Cameralists." This book is an important achievement of scholarship in a field not elsewhere adequately treated in English.

The Cameralists undertook to supply the wisdom necessary to guide the government of states. The " *Kammer* " was the council chamber and the " state " was the German principality, little or great, as German principalities existed from the middle of the sixteenth to the end of the eighteenth century, long before their union under Bismarck into the German Empire. The wisdom necessary for the government of states is largely fiscal, so that cameralistics was a mixture of political science as developed under absolute princelings, princes and kings, with economics studied with particular reference to taxation and full coffers for the state. But it was not oblivious to the welfare of the subjects, though strictly subordinate to that of the state; or as Machiavelli would have put it more frankly, of the prince. And it paid heed to all matters that affected the strength and glory of the political unit, including population increase and the intelligence, morals and religion of the people. Cameralistics therefore developed as a composite study of the life of a particular type of social unit with special reference to a definite practical purpose largely symbolized by the strong box of the prince.

Here were worked out the maxims of a prudence, both comprehensive and detailed, in striking contrast, as Professor Small remarks, with the " slovenly, improvident, and reckless " management of natural resources and opportunities by unregulated democratic individualism in America.

Cameralistics had two pronounced similarities to sociology as Professor Small conceived of sociology: First, it was a comprehensive or synthetic study of the life of a people regardful of the interrelation of the different components of their social activity. Second, it conducted this synthetic study under the guidance of a practical aim, though that aim was an absolutistic one and not the democratic aim of realizing values in the individual experience of the members of society. With reference to its practical aim cameralistics was not so nearly identical with sociology, as Professor Small conceived it, as was the " System of Moral Philosophy " of which Adam Smith's *Wealth of*

Nations, according to the intention of its author, was a fragment.

Among the important statements which Professor Small makes about the cameralists are these:

They assumed as normal a stratified society, each stratum having a standard of living proper to it, and while recognizing the necessity of maintaining their several standards of living in the different classes of the population, regarded it as the aim of public policy to have as large a surplus as possible for the treasury of the state.

Their state policy was paternalistic, but this was necessary in the infantile condition of popular intelligence and of the country's industries and resulted in undeniable efficiency.

They were mercantilists; but their doctrines were not formulated as abstract economic principles universally valid, but as practical policies adapted to existing exigencies. They wanted money in the treasury, but they recognized that money was a tool for measuring and handling wealth and not the substance of the wealth of the nation. They recognized the importance of extractive industry as truly as the physiocrats, and treated their country as a great farming estate. They believed that Germany would gain by increase of population, but recognized, as clearly as Malthus, that such increase could go too far.

Only a year after the publication of *The Cameralists* there came from the pen of Professor Small a book entitled *The Meaning of Social Science.* It was made up of a series of lectures that had been delivered to a company of graduate students drawn from all the social science departments of the University of Chicago.

The primary proposition in these lectures is that the

separate social sciences, although they realize its truth, are too little guided by the principle that " knowledge of human experience can not at last be many; in the degree in which it approaches reality it must be one knowledge." It may take a million words to describe the San Francisco earthquake, but it was one occurrence. And the seeming divisibility of our description merely exhibits its clumsiness and the contrast between our " symbolism of representation " and the unity of the objective reality.

There is an obvious connection between this principle and the interest which Professor Small felt in cameralism as a study of the organization of society as a unit, and in the " moral philosophy " of Adam Smith as one system of thought including an investigation of all the divisions of man's life.

The second thesis of the book is that social sciences will discover their unity by realizing that they are studies of men, that no abstraction from the life of man, however essential in subdividing the work of detailed comprehension, whether that abstraction be " government," or " wealth " or " society," must be allowed to obscure the fact that specific researches into these abstractions have *their meaning* as contributions to the study of men, of men acting in pursuit of purposes in ways conditioned by a material environment, and by the activities of other men, and the men themselves in so doing becoming something other than they were.

The third main proposition is that knowing includes evaluation. That in our study of the life of man and all that affects it evaluation can not be escaped. Evaluation begins with perception itself. It is essentially involved in our reaction to reality. The question is whether evaluation shall be made with the benefit of as adequate contact with reality as is possible to the coöperative endeavor of competent investigators. The very declaration that social science ought to abstain from valuations is itself a valuation and an imperative, but a mistaken because an impracticable one. A consensus of the competent as to values may not be final or absolute. With absolutes human intelligence has neither concern nor competence. But evaluation we can not escape, and it may be superficial and ignorant or in varying degrees scientific; that is to say based upon knowledge of the realities of human experience and of the conditions by which they are affected.

Since this is a study of a man as well as of his works, and because in the following passage, besides revealing himself, Professor Small deals with one of the most vital problems of our time, it is permissible to quote:

" I do not say and I do not think that social science can ever be a substitute for religion. It is getting plainer and plainer, however, that social science, in the sense in which I have used the term in these lectures, is the only rational body for religion.

" No man has lived his life to the full who is not at last, in one preserve of his personality, a mystic. It is a grub's life not to feel out after the connections of what we can know with what we can not know; after the fulfillment of what we have been or might have been in what we may be. From first to last religions have been men's more or less conscious attempts to give finite life its infinite rating. Science can never be an enemy of religion. Stop the stress and strain, the rush and roar, the fuss and bluff of modern life long enough for the deeply human in us to have its chance, and the more science we have the more are we

awed and lured by the mystery beyond our ken; the more
do the unsatisfied longings in us yearn for larger interpretation.

" And this is the heart of religion. It is the investment
of such values as we have along with the best labor within
our power to make them productive. We have no other
scope for this work but in our intercourse with our fellow-
men. In this view social science carried into the creative
stage is the only conceivable body in which religion can be
vital.

" Theological religions have always been ungenuine because they have made the mystical the key to the real.
The religion of social science will make the real the key
to the mystical. While men are bound to achieve this in-
version in proportion as they become sophisticated, while
men are bound in proportion as they conquer ignorance
and banish terrors of their own invention to find the meaning of life less in escaping unknown evils than in realizing
known goods, it does not follow that they are bound to
limit the meaning of their lives to the measure of experience. On the contrary, the more we compare the span of
experience with the sweep of mystery within which we are
inclosed the more certainly will our known life borrow
some of its value from our thought of the infinite unknown.

" This again is merely a modern way of expressing a
reality of religion which in some degree the most spiritually minded men of all faiths have held in common.

" In all seriousness then, and with careful weighing of
my words, I register my belief that social science is the
holiest sacrament open to men. It is the holiest because
it is the wholest career within the terms of human life.
Restraining myself from prediction, and holding strictly

to confession, I am able to foresee no other development for religion than the progressive sloughing off of its ritualistic attachments and corresponding enrichment of its realistic content. The whole circumference of social science is the indicated field for those " works " without which the apostle of " salvation by faith " declared that faith is dead." [5]

In 1913, a book of Professor Small's appeared which is quite different in character from any of his other published works. It is fiction in the form of conversation. And the conversation is social philosophizing. Four hundred and thirty pages of undeniably clever conversation, often too clever to be easy reading for the many, always carrying a heavy load of social philosophy with a slender thread of incident and characterization. The book is entitled *Between Eras* with a sub-title *From Capitalism to Democracy*. It is a penetrating attack upon the supposed right of individuals to hold and to bequeath to their heirs all that the present organization of business allows the organizers to accumulate in their own possession and an argument for such governmental supervision and control and for the development of such social sentiments as would promote the transfer of ambition, of reward and of applause from acquisition to production and administrative service. It is not only an argument but a prophecy of progress toward greater justice, better economy of human and national resources and larger productivity of real values.

Professor Small's most recent book, now just off the press, is entitled *Origins of Sociology*. Its contents have appeared as a series of articles in *The American Journal of*

[5] *The Meaning of Social Science*, p. 275.

Sociology. Its preface tells us that it is supplementary to
the author's "Fifty Years of Sociology in the United
States," which appeared in the *American Journal of Sociology* in May, 1916, and that among his unpublished manuscripts is one entitled *The Development of Sociological
Consciousness in the United States.*

While we are speaking in detail only of his books it
should not be forgotten that the articles which he has
published from time to time in the journal just mentioned,
during the long period of his editorship, are a significant
part of his work.

The "origins of sociology" which are traced in this
latest volume follow a line of descent which runs mainly
through the writings of the German historians, economists
and political scientists. It is thus a complement to *The
Cameralists,* dealing with the more recent German authors,
but beginning with Thibaut, Eichhorn, Niebuhr and
Ranke, dealing with the "historic" and "Austrian"
schools of political economy, and "the restoration of ethics
in economic theory," as well as with representative political thought, and culminating in the group of German writers of whom Gustav Schmoller is representative, and ending with "the Emergence of Sociology in the United
States."

It is important to observe that in this latest book, representing its author's maturest judgment, Professor Small
reasserts at the outset the view that "the indicated task
for social science" (not of sociology alone) "is to interpret the meaning of human experience, and to find out how
human experience may be directed in the future toward a
larger output of life's values." This assertion may easily
be misunderstood to indicate an excess of emphasis upon

the practical and ethical, and some lack of regard for the scientific approach. But the one subject oftenest stressed by Professor Small is methodology. And on that subject the one idea above all others which he intones is the necessity of objectivity. He evidently believes that the motive to provide guidance for life may reinforce, and not inhibit, the motive of pure intellectual interest, and also that the double motive need not distort the method. The practical and the scientific motive may combine, as joy in workmanship combines with desire to produce or to earn wages to make a better carpenter than either motive alone would produce.

Again he insists upon the unity of social science. " Just as theorists of innumerable sorts have mangled and shredded the Bible so as to make it teach the most incongruous and contradictory counterfeits of wisdom; just as believing and unbelieving students of the Bible alike have abstracted phrases from it, and constructed those abstractions into systems of positive or negative faith, more or less distantly related to the substantial contents of the Bible when comprehended in its genetic relations, so the different exponents of social science tore human experience to pieces, and reconstructed the shreds and patches which particularly interested them into so many competing interpretations of human experience." [6] " In fact, human experience is one volume. It must be read as a whole. Each part must give meaning to every other part. It may and must be analyzed into its elements. It can be understood only by synthesis of its elements." [7] " The totality of human experience is too big, too complicated, too unexplorable to be exhibited by the human mind as a complete

[6] *Origin of Sociology*, p. 9.   [7] *Ibid*, p. 10.

and inclusive system of functioning parts, with each event throughout the length and breadth of human experience, bearing its actual relation to all other events. . . . Our ideal at present is discovery of typical, qualitative relationships of antecedents and consequent, of cause and effect, of harmony and disharmony, of stability and instability, of constructiveness and destructiveness in human groups." [8]

"The immediate purpose " (of this book) " is to show that sociology was not created by the fiat of a few individuals who had no attachments to previous and contemporary scientific growth. On the contrary, sociology is merely the latest differentiation of scientific procedure within a containing movement which must be understood in general in order properly to understand the functions of sociology." [9] " The differentiation of sociology was one of the incidents of this evolution. This has not been the conception of their specialty which American sociologists as a rule have held. This book then is primarily an attempt to show the vital connection between sociology and the whole modern unfolding of social science. In other words it should make plain that the movement of thought in the United States which is known by the name sociology is not an isolated phenomenon. It is not a freak. It is not something that has an existence by itself, independent of and unrelated to the rest of the thinking of mankind. It should show that the precise contrary is the case." [10] " In other words, between 1800 and 1880 everything that we now call social science went through a change which may be likened to the passing of an individual from babyhood to

[8] *Ibid*, p. 62.   [9] *Ibid*, p. 10.
[10] *Origin of Sociology*, p. 13.

adolescence. The sociologists have not generally appreciated the fact that their specialty came into existence as an organic part of this maturing social science as a whole. . . . It would be possible to make a dramatic exhibit of the smuggling into conventional social science, not to speak of popular thought, of processes of sociological analysis and construction that have been carried on in all the social sciences, during the last two decades in particular, by men who mostly have denied with scorn and often with curses that they have anything in common with sociology." [11]

The major principle of Savigny, to whom Professor Small gives prominence, in the early part of this work, was that of " historical continuity," the doctrine that a nation can not break with its past, as Frenchmen of the revolutionary period had thought to do, nor create institutions as sheer inventions, but that " influences propagate themselves from generation to generation, and from age to age," according to principles of social causation.

Savigny exaggerated the application of the principle in making it the ground of opposition to progressive changes, as a physicist would do who inferred from the law of gravitation the impossibility of building skyscrapers. Yet the principle he employed is as true as the law of gravitation, and the perception of that principle was the motive of the " historical school " of political science.

While Savigny can by no means be regarded as the discoverer of the principle of historical continuity, he is instructive as a representative of that principle, and was the first to carry out its application on a great scale in the exposition of the lasting influence of Roman law.

[11] *Ibid.*, p. 15.

Professor Small selects Eichhorn as the exemplar of a second fundamental perception, namely, that the causation of social situations is not merely a temporal sequence of similar activities, ideas, customs or institutions, but that each social activity is conditioned by a multiplicity of diverse factors. His " Constitutional and Legal History of Germany " accounts for legal development in terms of the soil inhabited, the language spoken, class distinctions, marriage customs, relations to neighboring states, and the general social conditions of the German people.

The recognition of " historic continuity " and of the " multiplicity and complexity " of the conditions affecting the customs and institutions of a people are important steps in the direction of sociological interpretation. Further progress in that direction was made by the German " historical school " of economics on the initiative of Roscher. This school adopted the two principles above enunciated and added to them the principle of the comparative method: the study of given types of social activity not only at different stages in the progress of the same people but also as they have existed among different peoples, in order to discover the typical and recurrent forms of activity and of causation. Such comparative study discovers also the " principle of relativity," that is it shows, in contrast to certain hard and fast dogmas of classical economics, that what is true under one set of conditions is untrue under another and what is practically wise under one set of conditions under others may be folly. This method was not proposed as invalidating the results of the classical economists, but as supplementing them.

The Austrian School of Economists, headed by such men as Böhm-Bawerk and Menger, adopted another principle which is prominently included in the technique of sociology, namely, that of psychological interpretation. They held it to be essential for the economist (social scientist) to keep in mind the fact that economic (social) phenomena are essentially mental phenomena (desires, interests, opinions, inventions). This perception 'that human activity in one of its essential aspects is desire, and that the specific desires of culture men are part and parcel of their socially evolved activities, is the truth that was emphasized in that earlier connection where Professor Small's theory of " the interests " was discussed. The Austrian economists pointed out that while social activity is conditioned by the traits of human beings, it is unthinkable that a human being should pass from one state of activity to another except as subject to the law of causality, that is, as affected also by changing conditions not included in the universal and permanent traits of human nature.

The perception that human activity, at least in one essential aspect, is a " mental phenomenon," and includes desire, was made use of by these economists primarily in constructing a theory of value. Human activity because it is desire, or wants, is worth making. Value whether " for use " or " in exchange," as they pointed out, means primarily that some thing of some service is wanted. And such " wanting " is a part of the social activity of the time and place, to be explained in terms of the various conditioning factors affecting it.

The next idea presented by Professor Small in this book was injected into German economics by writers of whom Knies is representative. It is the idea that "political economy can not be conclusive until it consciously and deliberately recognizes itself as moral science." This recognition had of course been clear in the mind of Adam Smith, and of late has been clear in the minds of some of the leading American economists.

It might be pointed out that the psychological point of view leads naturally to the ethical, for the activities of " real men influenced at one and the same time by various motives " are *experiences*. As these activities in respect to one essential element are wants, so also in another element they are satisfactions or pains, and this fact is an equally essential part of their description.

After recognizing that Knies was the Isaiah, Professor Small adds that Adolph Wagner was the John the Baptist of the ethical point of view in German economics. Few purely intellectual incidents are more dramatic than the address of this eminent Berlin professor before the general assembly of the Prussian church in which he declared (in the paraphrase of Dr. Small) that " in economic transactions between persons the relation of man to man must come into its own, and that the proper policy of the state is neither pacivity nor indiscriminate intervention, but constant watchfulness and throwing of its weight from case to case against injustice." [12]

Presently Schmoller, also a professor at the University of Berlin, came to the side of Wagner and for a generation the two chief economists of Germany stood for this ethical point of view. " The guiding motive and standard of judgment in all his (Schmoller's) writings at that turning point is indicated by the phrase ' the ethical aim in civilization ' (der ethiche Kulturzweck)." [13]

The *Verein fur Socialpolitik* which resulted largely from the influence of these two men " became the most influ-

[12] *Origins of Sociology*, p. 236.   [13] *Ibid.*, p. 244.

ential organization of academic men that has ever been organized."

Another German economist, the discussion of whose work by Professor Small can not be omitted here, is Schäffle. He will be thought of by most readers of this article as a sociologist, but he was first the author of works in economics. His sociology was the offspring of dissatisfaction with the system of economics in which he had been schooled and of a conviction that " we must first get an insight into the inter-connections of human phenomena in general before we can have the standing ground from which to explain the phases of human phenomena which we label ' economic,' " [14] Schäffle was not the first to exhibit this conviction which has become the dominant motive of some of the contemporary economists. He also transferred the focus of his interest from impersonal wealth to concrete human reality and regarded economic activity and organization as the effort " at minimum cost to obtain a maximum of utility and thus to secure the amplest possible provision for the entire personal life." With Schäffle goods are no longer ends but means. He teaches " that consciously purposeful or morally useful effort which emerges in the realm of individual and of group socialization has accordingly as its bearers and as its goals, richly articulated moral organisms, *i.e.*, particular persons and whole communities of persons." [15]

All this is from Schäffle the economist. As is well known, when later, in his *Bau und Leben des socialen Körpers* he attempted to correlate economic activity with the whole nexus of social life, he did so, like Lilienfeld, under the form of the biological analogy.

[14] *Ibid.*, p. 297.   [15] *Origins of Sociology*, p. 331.

Turning now to the German political scientists, Professor Small sketches the contribution of von Mohl and Ahrens as promoters of "the movement to develop a distinct science of society, parallel with the science of the state." Professor Small points out that the defect of their movement was a kind of mystical concept of society akin to the German concept of the state as a vast entity over, above and outside of the people. And he adds that the earlier American sociologists certainly started with a conception of society, if not identical with, at least closely related to that of the Ahrens-von Mohl group. Mohl proposes the study of vocational groups, parishes, economic associations, nobility, clergy, artisans, peasants, land-owners, castes, races, creedal groups, the intelligentia, the family, etc.

Professor Small concludes this book, to which, because it is so new and of so great interest, I have given what would otherwise be disproportionate space, with a chapter on "The Emergence of Sociology in the United States." He protests against the common practice of calling anything and everything sociology if only it deals with society and is not otherwise classified. And he reiterates his statement that sociology is a definite technique of investigation, that its chief methodological tool is the concept of "the group" and that its primary procedure consists in identifying and explaining types of behavior that are made possible by group relations. He clearly recognizes that to many sociologists this "group concept" seems vague and inadequate as a symbol for the sociological technique, but insists that for his mind it serves that purpose well.

At this point it may be permissible to quote a personal

letter of Professor Small, because it gives a glimpse of the man truer than mere description.

"If you consent to tell the world anything about me, do not mince matters at all in telling the plain blunt truth that I spent my life insisting that there *is* something at the far end of the sociological rainbow, and at the same time altering my view of *what* that something will turn out to be, with every year's accounting of stock.

"The one impulse that has remained constant in spirit, with developing details of content, has been the conviction that experience will never let itself be interpreted as an affair of aggregated monads, but that somehow we live, move and have our being as members one of another. Some day that will be the unquestioned *a priori* of everybody. If my name is anywhere extant at that time, I hope it will have a tag attached with the memorandum 'he had something to do with laying the individualistic superstition.' "

Professor Small is a man of distinct personality. Of all his traits the most fundamental is that he is in earnest about life. He does not take life jestingly nor cynically but seriously and hopefully. This is the reason why he is a sociologist. Sociology he regards as a study of life with a view to understanding it in order that its values may be realized by men. His interest is primarily ethical; that is, it is an interest in the values of human experience and the method of their realization. He became and remained a sociologist because he believed that this realization of values could be promoted by understanding. He realized that the values of life are not mere incidents of life but that they are of its essence. It can not be truthfully conceived or described if the fact that it is weal and woe is omitted from the conception or the description. His dissatisfaction with the older social sciences was due to the fact that their perspective seemed to him to be distorted by their omission of this central fact. To restore this fact to its central position gives to social science a new perspective and a new orientation. The fact of value in experience pervades life in all its subdivisions. This fact gives to all life unity and coherence as an object of study.

The writer is impelled to remark that this point of view does not destroy the " objective " character of sociology if only we make clear a distinction which our language is imperfectly prepared to express. It would be well expressed by contrasting " the good " and " the right," if these words were defined thus: Good is the value which an activity (experience [16]) has *for the actor* when the activity (experience) is regarded *as an end in itself without regard to consequences*. Good (or bad) is then a reality that is known to the actor, and that can be intelligibly described to all who have had similar experience. There are various kinds of good: physical, intellectual, æsthetic, social and personal, the last inherent in *self-*consciousness. THE GOOD is the sum and harmony of all these goods. If good (or bad) in any given instance can not be accurately measured, yet it can be compared with other instances so as to get judgments, in many instances unmistakable judgments, of better and worse. Good (and bad), thus defined, is reality that is known to man if any is. Right, on the other hand, is the quality of an act fit to be approved *for its consequences*. It is the way to the better and away from the worse as above de-

[16] All experience is activity whether it issues in overt behavior or not.

fined. There are right ways to graft a tree, right ways to train a singer, and there are right ways to promote physical, intellectual, æsthetic, social and personal good. What is right? in the given case or class of cases; is a purely objective, matter of fact, question. Definition of the word " moral " is also needed in this connection. Moral may be defined as meaning, approved by the mores. The mores, while perhaps among every people better than no guide, may embody mistaken judgments as to what is right.

Our knowledge of what is good, however imperfect, is wholly a matter of experience, not of metaphysics in the old bad sense. And in many instances weal and woe are so outstanding that we know clearly what is better and what worse in the strictly limited sense above defined, and so what right should aim toward and away from. What is right we can discover only by experiment and open-minded investigation. In regard to morality there is the scientific task of describing the mores of different groups, and of explaining how they have come to be what they are, which is a typical problem in social evolution and, like the problem " what is right " is a purely objective inquiry. What greater obstacle to progress than the old notion which denies that the question " what is right? " is wholly an empirical, matter of fact, problem and assumes instead that the question is settled by the mores or by a metaphysics that is merely a rationalization of the existing mores?

Besides the fact that social life in all its subdivisions is pervaded by the reality of value, of weal and woe, of good and evil as just defined, and by the problem of the right, that is of cause-and-effect relations between human activities and the values which they affect, there is another essential fact namely the unity of human life, economic, political, moral, and in all the various subdivisions of " culture," by virtue of which all these parts are not only interdependent, but in their broad outlines explicable by the same principles of causation.

Adequate recognition of these two facts (the fact that social life is pervaded by *ethical* realities and problems and the fact of the *unitary* character of social life) constitutes, in the main, the sociological point of view as it is held by Professor Small. The specific insights which this point of view makes possible are numerous, and their completeness increases with the passage of the years and with the labor of many minds. They are at first mere glimpses, so incomplete as often to be replaced with growing knowledge. But the growth of knowledge serves to increase the clearness with which these two central facts are perceived and with which their importance as guides to understanding is realized. To see their full import and clearly to comprehend the task of sociology implies as well the two other realizations which, near the outset, were defined as characteristic of the sociological movement, and which, as has been shown, Professor Small by no means ignored. Posterity will find his monument, not in his sketch, but in his works. But while his works will perpetuate his contributions to sociology, and many without knowing its source will feel the momentum which he has done so much to impart to the sociological movement, his works can not convey to his successors an adequate understanding of the character of the man which causes his contemporaries to regard him not only with lasting honor but also with deep affection.

CHAPTER VII

FRANKLIN HENRY GIDDINGS

By

JOHN L. GILLIN

Professor of Sociology in the University of Wisconsin

FRANKLIN HENRY GIDDINGS

CHAPTER VII

FRANKLIN HENRY GIDDINGS

Auguste Comte, the inventor of the word sociology, delivered his lectures on positive philosophy between 1830 and 1842. His *System of Positive Politics* was published between 1851 and 1854. Harriet Martineau published a condensed translation of Comte's positive philosophy in 1853. The second edition came out in 1875 and a new edition in three volumes in 1896.

Herbert Spencer had published his Prospectus of a System of Philosophy in 1860 and as the first volume of the series *First Principles* appeared in 1862. His *Study of Sociology* was published in 1873 and in 1874 appeared the first volume of his *Principles of Sociology*. From that time on until the whole work was completed the remaining parts appeared from time to time, many chapters of which were published in magazine form in the United States.

In 1869 appeared Bagehot's *Physics and Politics*. It was published in the United States in 1898 in Youmans' International Scientific Series. Doubtless there were some students of the social sciences in America who had become familiar with the English editions.

These three men, then, Comte, Spencer and Bagehot, the one a Frenchman and the others two Englishmen, whose writings were available in English, furnish one group of influences which explain the origin of sociology in the United States. That the measure of their influence was great, especially that of the first two, is evidenced by the writings of almost every one of our early American sociologists.

However, another and perhaps a more important historical inspiration for American scholars interested in the social sciences was the work of a large number of German historians, political scientists, and political economists in the German universities to which large numbers of American students went, especially in the last quarter of the nineteenth century. Professor Small of the University of Chicago readily remembered fifteen important scholars of the United States who studied in the German universities in the 70's. These returned to the United States inspired by a new spirit and by the methods of their German teachers. These men and men trained under them in the universities of this country gave new direction to and inspired fresh interest in such social studies as history, political science and economics. Even the casual list recalled by Professor Small suggests some of the most important leaders in the development of social studies in the United States. The spirit of German scholarship had made its mark on the thought of these young Americans who had returned from Europe and were leading the new educational adventures in our growing American universities.[1]

Consider only a few of the epoch-making names in the development of the social studies in this country who had taken their graduate work in Germany. William Graham Sumner had studied in Germany in the 60's and on his return was teaching at Yale, announced a course in sociology in 1876. Another, Herbert B. Adams had been made

[1] Small, *Origins of Sociology*, pp. 325–326.

head of the Department of History and Politics at the
newly established The Johns Hopkins University. Associated with him from 1881 to 1892 was Dr. Richard T.
Ely who had received his Ph. D. degree at Heidelberg in
1879. President Gilman had drawn thither a galaxy of
these German-trained professors when he organized the
university. Albion W. Small, who in 1893 became head of
the Department of Sociology at the newly organized University of Chicago, in 1881 had become Professor of History and Political Economy at Colby University. In 1888
and 1889 he spent a year as reader in history at The Johns
Hopkins University with Herbert B. Adams. He went
back to Colby University as President, and in 1889 conducted a class in sociology for his seniors. There was Professor John W. Burgess who had been at Leipzig and Berlin from 1871 to 1873. On his return he was called upon
to organize the Faculty of Political Science at Columbia
University. Besides these leaders the roll should include
Henry W. Farnum of Yale, Frank J. Goodnow of Columbia, now president of The Johns Hopkins, Arthur T. Hadley, now president emeritus of Yale, George E. Howard,
until recently head of the Department of Political Science
and Sociology at the University of Nebraska, Edmund J.
James of the University of Pennsylvania, Professor Simon
N. Patten of the same university until his death, Professor
E. R. A. Seligman of Columbia University, Professor William M. Sloane of Columbia and Professor Frank W.
Taussig of Harvard.

With that situation in the intellectual atmosphere of the
United States is it to be wondered at that there was an
awakening of interest in the study of man's social relationships? In addition do not forget that the ten or fifteen

years following the close of the Civil War presented a series of problems political, economic and social which challenged the best thought of the time. We who are living in the days since the World War can readily understand that unrest. The thoughtful people of that day were no longer content with the old methods of education and with the old solutions offered for problems which had followed the war. They demanded a new consideration of those social problems. In these circumstances the ideas of Comte and Spencer on the one hand, and of the German teachers on the other, could not fail to find fruitful soil in these young American scholars.

With this background consider the developments of sociology in the United States from the standpoint both of the writers of books and of the courses in the universities.

Lester F. Ward published his *Dynamic Sociology* in 1883. A paleobotanist in the Government service at Washington, Ward shows the influence of Comte and Spencer. Until the last years of his life he was not a teacher of sociology. His *Dynamic Sociology,* however, had a great influence upon thoughtful scholars in the social sciences in the United States. In 1884 he wrote a review of Sumner's *What Social Classes Owe to Each Other,* which book, he said, was a good illustration of what sociology is not. His widely ranging mind got into contact with the economists and political scientists who had been trained in Germany. In 1888 he delivered an address before the American Economic Association entitled " Social and Economic Paradoxes." In this address he showed the psychological trend of his thought which got complete expression in his *Psychic Factors of Civilization* in 1892. He gave further expression to his emphasis upon psychology in social relationships in an address entitled " The Psychologic Basis of Social Economics " in 1893.

I have already noticed that Sumner had returned from Germany and was giving a course in Yale University called Sociology in 1876. In 1873 he published *What Social Classes Owe to Each Other*. Doubtless his course at Yale was the first course in Sociology in any American university. In this course he used as a text Spencer's *Study of Sociology* which had appeared in 1873.

Andrew D. White, president of Cornell who had moved in an atmosphere of European thought on university education was dissatisfied with the elements of the curriculum in American universities, and in the early eighties had been making plans to introduce a course at Cornell which would acquaint students with the practical social problems of that day. In 1885 he got Frank B. Sanborn of Massachusetts to give such a course at Cornell for the first time.

Professor Frank W. Blackmar of Kansas was one of that large group of men who were attracted to The Johns Hopkins to study with Herbert Adams and with Dr. Ely. He returned to Kansas in 1889 as head of the Department of History and Political Science and began giving a course in sociology.[2]

In addition to these men just cited other leading educators were feeling the necessity of introducing a new spirit and new methods into university education, as was manifested by President Angell at Michigan and a few other important leaders. It was in this atmosphere of unrest and seeking for new outlets for their thoughts on social problems and for a new method in the study of social affairs that Giddings moved when he succeeded Woodrow

[2] *American Journal of Sociology*, May, 1916, p. 760.

Wilson at Bryn Mawr in 1888. Let us now turn to examine the intellectual development of Mr. Giddings up to that time.

Franklin H. Giddings, born at Sherman, Connecticut, March 23, 1855, had as ancestors on both sides New England Puritans of the strictest type. He came from a sturdy and hard-working stock. His father was a Congregational minister of evangelical and orthodox tendencies who threw around his children a strict Puritan atmosphere. The hours devoted by the household to religious services were many, and created a spirit which in contrast to the life outside the home gave a semblance of uncanny unreality to that portion of young Giddings' life. These religious devotions not only were boresome but depressing. Giddings found a great deal more enjoyment in doing the tasks about the farm on which his father lived than in the religious devotions. It is reported that " the ache that his back took on from weeding onions he found preferable to the sensation experienced from activities supposedly spiritual." The chores about the farm and on the farm of his grandfather, who lived nearby, gave to him a sense of reality which the religious devotions lacked. He assisted his grandfather in surveying and the latter gave him instruction in mechanical drawing and in the rudiments of farm work and management.

In spite of, or perhaps even as a relief from, the religious seriousness of the home Giddings spent his youth in the usual diversions of boyhood. He was a lover of outdoor sports and in the wintertime would often get up at four o'clock in the morning and skate until school time in order to satisfy his love for this sport. Another grandfather owned a tannery, and Giddings found diversion in puttering around the place interested in all the processes, and in a shop where stationary engines were built. He became interested in some of the practical mechanical aspects of economic life and these experiences were an important part of his early education.

In the schools which he attended he found little of interest. Not until he chanced upon Scott's *Marmion* did he learn to know the joy of the printed page. It happened, however, that a certain Harry H. Scott was one of his teachers. This man had the unusual ability to interest this young boy in intellectual pursuits and provided him intellectual comradeship. Scott introduced him to the new and provocative group of writings which were just coming from the pens of Spencer, Huxley, Darwin and others of that group of English scientists and philosophers. He read Darwin and Spencer with great avidity. Giddings himself has described this period. He says, " My interest in sociology, as I have on various occasions told, began while I was yet a youth, when accidentally a copy of the first number of the *Popular Science Monthly* fell into my hands a few days after its publication, and I read the first chapter of Spencer's *The Study of Sociology*. Before I entered college I had read a lot of Darwin, Tyndall, and Huxley, and nearly half of what Spencer had then printed. At college, and during ten subsequent years of newspaper work, I kept up my interest and my reading in sociology and was ready to improve the first chance that offered to teach it after I went to Bryn Mawr." [3]

He entered Union College at Schenectady, New York, taking the studies which he thought would prepare him for the profession of civil engineer to which he was then look-

[3] *American Journal of Sociology*, May, 1916, p. 762.

ing forward. He failed to find the stimulating leadership
at college which he had with Scott in his school work at
home and after two years at Union left college for a time
and taught school in Massachusetts and Connecticut.   In
1877, however, he received his A.B. degree from Union
College and went into newspaper work at Winsted, Connecticut, where he worked on *The Herald*.   From there he
went to the *Springfield Republican,* then under the editorship of the younger Samuel Bowles.   Giddings' study at
Union had given him that love for precise knowledge which
appears to such a remarkable degree in his later writings.
Under Bowles and the other remarkable men of that time
on the editorial staff of the *Springfield Republican* Giddings received an invaluable training in the expression of
his ideas.   From the *Republican* he went, after an interval, to the *Springfield Union* with which he was connected
for a longer time.   Ten years in all was given to newspaper
work and provided Mr. Giddings with a remarkable knowledge of men and world events, trained him in clear and
vivid expression, and together with his reading in sociology, which he had carried on from his pre-college days,
gave him an interest in the subject which all unconsciously
prepared him for his great career.

This interest in social questions had led Giddings to
write articles for the *Political Science Quarterly* then being published at Columbia and for the Massachusetts
Bureau of Statistics of Labor.   His special interest so far
as it is revealed in these early articles was in the social aspect of economic problems and economic theory.

These articles had attracted the attention of men in the
university world and therefore, when Woodrow Wilson,
Associate Professor of History and Political Science at

Bryn Mawr, went to Wesleyan University in 1888 Giddings was invited to Bryn Mawr as Lecturer on Politics. By rapid promotion he was advanced to the full professorship of Politics. He began by teaching four subjects by lectures and seminar, (1) Development of Political Institutions (2) Political Economy, including Economic Theory and Economic History (3) Methods and Principles of Administration and (4) Methods and Principles of Charity and Correction. In 1890 he introduced a graduate course entitled Modern Theories of Sociology. In his catalogue statement concerning this course he said, " Fellows and graduate students expecting to do advanced work in this course must have, besides their equipment in history and political economy, at least a general knowledge of philosophy and some acquaintance with modern biology and empirical psychology." Among the preliminary readings suggested were Galton's *Natural Inheritance* and Richmond Mayo-Smith's *Statistics and Sociology*.

His interest in sociology was given a further chance to develop when in 1891 he was asked to give lectures on sociology in Columbia University during the absence of Professor Mayo-Smith. These he continued for three years while still teaching at Bryn Mawr. In 1894 a new chair of sociology was established at Columbia University and Professor Giddings was invited to occupy it. There he has been ever since stimulating generation after generation of graduate students who are now scattered to the ends of the earth doing yeoman service in this field.[4]

[4] Small, " Fifty Years of Sociology in the United States," *American Journal of Sociology*, May, 1916, pp. 721–864; See also Frank L. Tolman, " The Study of Sociology in Institutions of Learning in the United States," *The American Journal of Sociology*, Vol. 7, 1901–1902, pp. 797–838 continued in subsequent numbers; Bernard,

Let us now turn to the consideration of the development of Professor Giddings' sociological thought during the more than forty years in which he has been writing upon this subject. It is impossible in the limits of our space to do more than note the salient points in that development. Professor Small has remarked that Ward's sociology was fully formed when he wrote his *Dynamic Sociology* in 1876 and that all his subsequent writings were only slight changes and elaborations of the points which he had made in that work. Not so with Professor Giddings. One who reads carefully his early articles devoted chiefly to political economy and political science can clearly see that for a number of years his mind was working away at the problems which his wide reading and observation had created for him. Having become interested in these problems it was inevitable that he should endeavor to apply to their solution the results of his wide reading in the English speculative political philosophy and natural science, and his knowledge of Comte, Spencer and Ward.

Reference has been made to his articles in the early numbers of the *Political Science Quarterly*, the publications of the Bureau of Statistics of Labor of Massachusetts, and to the publications of the American Economic Association. Let us now endeavor to trace the development of his fundamental sociological concepts in these articles and addresses which found summary but complete statement in the first part of his *Principles of Sociology*.

While still editor of the *Springfield Union* Giddings had

" The Teaching of Sociology in the United States," *American Journal of Sociology*, Vol. 16, p. 164; Clow, " Sociology in Normal Schools," *Ibid*, Vol. 16, p. 253.

undertaken a study of profit-sharing, especially in Massachusetts. This is cited in the first volume of the *Publications of the American Economic Association* as having been made in 1885 and published in the *Report of the Massachusetts Bureau of Labor* in 1886, and is described as so ably done that no further attempt at investigation of the subject has been made.[5] In the winter of 1885 he read before a Springfield scientific society a paper on " Sociology," in which he contended that the distinctive and characteristic phenomenon of human society is simultaneous like activity in a common situation or under identical circumstances. He was an early member of the American Economic Association formed in 1885.

Giddings' interest in the American Economic Association is shown by the fact that he was an officer in 1887 of the Connecticut Valley branch of that association, which had been organized by Dr. Edward W. Bemis, and his active participation in the discussion at the annual meetings of the national organization.[6] He began to appear before the annual meetings of the American Economic Association. In 1888 he read a paper entitled " The Sociological Character of Political Economy." This clearly revealed that from the first his economic writings had a sociological flavor. In this paper he pointed out that economics consists of four parts (1) economic physics, in which mathematics will be the method used (2) descriptive economics (3) economic politics (4) economic biology and psychology. In this connection he said, " Political economy, then, as the science of wealth, is necessarily the science of the

[5] *Publications, American Economic Association*, Vol. 1, pp. 44, 408.
[6] *Publications, American Economic Association*, Vol. 2, 1887–1888, pp. 211–212.

reciprocal relations of wealth and the social organism." [7]
It was at this time that the long and intimate friendship
began with Professor John B. Clark, then professor of
Political Economy at Smith College. During 1887–1888,
at Clark's suggestion, Giddings contributed articles to the
Political Science Quarterly, of Columbia University on
various economic topics. Two of these articles entitled
"The Persistence of Competition" and "The Natural
Rate of Wages" were published with two essays by Pro-
fessor Clark under the title of *The Modern Distributive
Process.*

In the autumn of this year Mr. Giddings went to Bryn
Mawr and there began his academic career. Here his
writings began in real earnest, first on economics but always with an emphasis upon its social relationships. He
was active in the affairs of the American Economic Association and while here became the editor of its publications for a time. While here he also became interested
with Professor James, Professor Patten and others of the
University of Pennsylvania in founding the *Annals of the
American Academy of Political and Social Science*, and for
a time was one of its editors. However, by 1890 his special interest in sociology appears in an article on "The
Province of Sociology" which appeared in the *Annals of
the American Academy of Political and Social Science,*
Vol. 1, No. 1, July, 1890. His wide readings in European
sociological writings as well as his extended acquaintance
with the evolutionary philosophy and with certain writers
in psychology here appeared. He cites Mills' *Logic;*
Lewes' *Problems of Life and Mind,* first series; Sedgwick

[7] *Publications, American Economic Association,* Vol. 3, No. 1,
March, 1888.

and Wilson's *Biology;* Ward's *Dynamic Sociology;* Spencer's *Principles of Sociology;* Schäffle's *Bau und Leben;* de Greef's *Introduction a la Sociologie;* Gayau's *L'art au Point de Vue Sociologique,* and also his *Education et Hereditie, etude sociologique;* Gumplowicz's *Der Rassemkampf,* Combes de Lestrade's *Elements de Sociologie;* the works of Darwin and Haeckel; and de Roberty's, *La Sociologie.*

In this article he blocks out in a general way for the first time his conception of the scope of sociology. Here he argues that in trying to delimit the province of sociology it must be clearly understood that it is a general social science similar to biology in the physical sciences. He says, " An analysis from the general characteristics of social phenomena with a formulation of the general laws of social evolution must be made the basis of special study in all departments of social science. It is upon just this work that sociologists are concentrating their efforts and for their results there can be no other name than sociology." Here he contends that no sociologist he knows has clearly differentiated sociology from psychology. This he attempts to do in this paper. He says, " Psychology is concerned with the associations and disassociations of the elements of conscious personality. How sensations are associated and disassociated in perception; how perceptions are associated and disassociated in imagination and in thought; how thought, feeling and impulse are coördinated in the marvelous composite, the individual personality, are problems for psychology to state, and if it can, to solve. But the phenomenà of conscious associations do not end with the appearance of the individual personality. They are then only engendered. Individual personalities as units become the elements of that vastly more extensive and intricate association of man with man and group with group which creates the varied relations of social life. A society is, therefore, on its conscious side, a super-physical product just as on its physical side it is super-organic and a product of tertiary aggregation." [8]

It was also in this article that he proposed what no other previous writer had attempted, " to interpret social evolution by the operation of natural selection upon human personality." [9]

These early articles of Professor Giddings' began to attract a great deal of attention and to excite controversy. His reaction against the narrower political economy of the late classicists, his emphasis upon the social factors in explaining economic concepts, and his clear and forceful statement of his ideas, called forth the criticism of some of his colleagues. From this time on for many years the discussion of his ideas at meetings of the scholars in economics, politics and sociology forced him to think through clearly his fundamental sociological theories.

As we have seen, sociology was being taught in a number of the colleges and universities of the country at this time. But the question had been raised as to whether sociology could be a university subject. To this problem Giddings addressed himself in an article entitled " Sociology as a University Study " in 1891. It is evident that he was struggling to clear up the relationships of sociology to the other social sciences. In this article he says, " The central scientific problem of sociology lies now before us. The questioning scientific mind of this age cannot longer rest

[8] " The Province of Sociology," *Annals of the American Academy of Political and Social Science,* Vol. 1, No. 1, July, 1890, pp. 66–70.
[9] *Ibid.,* p. 69.

content in the vague and merely general assumption, that it has been association that has brought into existence the desires that have built up empires and created religion. How has association done this, is the question that a rigorous scientific spirit must ask and the conditions of the answer are such that the resulting body of knowledge will be sociology and not as some have imagined a division of psychology." Here also he takes the first step toward a definition of sociology. He says, "The object of sociology is to learn all that can be learned about the creation of the social man." [10] It is also in this paper that he first divides the problems of sociology into three coördinate groups, (1) Problems of Social Structure and Growth, (2) Problems of Volitional Association, (3) Problems of Social Progress. [11] We shall see that this statement becomes clearer as time goes on. Under the fire of criticism and in reaction against the interpretation of some economists and some sociologists, Giddings points out that many have misunderstood Spencer because they have not clearly seen that Spencer's underlying foundations for sociology are to be found, not in his *Principles of Sociology,* but in his *First Principles.* Not knowing the *First Principles,* they have failed to understand his *Principles of Sociology.*

During this same year Giddings attempted to carry over into economics his sociological thinking in an article entitled, "The Concepts of Utility, Value and Cost." In the meeting of the American Economic Association at which this was read, his remarks on other papers which appeared upon the program are not important except his discussion of Professor Folwell's paper in which he called attention

[10] *Political Science Quarterly,* Vol. 6, No. 4, Dec., 1891, pp. 642–643.

[11] *Ibid.,* p. 645.

to the narrowing of political economy from Adam Smith down to Ricardo and others whereby "a vast amount was left out of the scheme of economic instruction, which in earlier days, had been included in it." [12]   This article excited the attention of Professor Patten between whom and Professor Giddings there was a lively discussion in which Giddings contended that marginal utility could not arise until after association had been set up between individuals. Into the merits of the discussion it is not our province to go. It is not without interest, however, to notice how his synthetic mind could not rest content until his sociological conceptions had worked themselves out into neighboring fields, especially those fields in which he had been interested.

In an article published the next year entitled "The Nature and Conduct of Political Majorities" Giddings first worked out his "Law of Social Choices." It is characteristic that his keen analytical mind found here in the field of politics the material from which to forge his interesting sociological generalization.[13]   This law was reiterated in his monograph, "The Theory of Sociology."

In 1893 Giddings contributed a chapter to the book called, *Philanthropy and Social Progress* in which he first worked out his theory that poverty, dependency and crime are costs of progress. This article was later included in his *Democracy and Empire* and later still in his *Studies in the Theory of Human Society.* Giddings has been criticized for the attitude taken in this article because it was said the logic of it was so Spencerian as to discourage all effort at improving these social classes. As a matter of

[12] *Publications, American Economic Association*, Vol. 6, 1891, pp. 41, 97.
[13] *Political Science Quarterly*, Vol. 7, No. 1, March, 1892.

fact, however, to anyone acquainted with the earlier writings it is apparent that Giddings does not intend that this idea convey the notion that society should not attempt to help those who are the victims of circumstances, but that it is impossible for society to expect as much from those deficient by nature as from those who have been richly endowed. These deficients are certainly incapable of spontaneously adjusting themselves to the increasingly complex conditions of society which progress brings about.

In this same year Giddings had returned to his task of attempting to broaden the economic theory of his day with an address before the American Economic Association entitled, " The Idea and Definition of Value." The main point of this address is stated as follows, " A definition that identifies subjective value with subjective utility is cardinally defective. It leaves out one whole order of mental processes " — judgment about an anticipated or foreseen feeling.[14]

The time had now come for Professor Giddings to unite in one logically organized statement his sociological theories developed up to this time. He did this in a monograph issued as a supplement to the *Annals of the American Academy of Political and Social Science*, July, 1894, entitled " The Theory of Sociology." This monograph had six chapters as follows. 1. The Sociological Idea. 2. The Province of Sociology. 3. The Problems of Sociology. 4. The Primary Problem: Social Growth and Structure. 5. The Secondary Problem: Social Process, Law and Cause. 6. The Method of Sociology. To anyone acquainted with Professor Giddings' more recently pub-

[14] *Publications, American Economic Association*, Vol. 8, 1893, pp. 87, 88.

lished works it is clear that here at last he has combined
in one coherent statement the thoughts which had been
germinating in his mind in the previous ten or twelve years.
Here is the outline of his later sociological theories. Here
in quintessence without illustrative material is the logical
development of his sociological theory. He himself indicated that it was but the skeleton of a work which he had
in mind, and which appeared as his *Principles of Sociology*
in 1896. However, that his mind was not concerned
merely with the skeleton is indicated by the title of the
commencement address which he gave at Bryn Mawr that
same year entitled, " The Relation of Social Democracy
to Higher Education." [15] In this monograph appear practically all the terms made familiar to us by his *Principles
of Sociology* such as " social composition," " social constitution," " aggregation," " association," " zoögenic stage of
society," " anthropogenic," " ethnogenic," " physical
causes of aggregation," " congregate association," " genetic association," " demotic composition," " society not
merely an organism but an organization," and here is the
idea that society is for the purpose of creating a social
personality. The criminal is anti-social but the pauper is
unsocial which later became pseudo-social. Here was the
Principles of Sociology in embryo.

In this monograph Giddings was approaching his final
analysis of the fundamental factor in the making of society, namely " consciousness of kind," but has not yet
reached it. He writes, " But now at length individual
social nature begins to react on society. Conscious that
their social relations are their most important means of
defense, succor, pleasure, and development, individuals

[15] *Democracy and Empire,* New York, 1900, Chapter 13.

endeavor to conserve and perfect them.   Society becomes
a consciously cherished thing and to an increasing extent
a product of conscious planning." [16]   In developing his
theory of " Social Mind " he analyzes the idea somewhat
further.   At this time to Giddings the social mind was the
second great stage of social evolution as social population
was the first.   He says, " In its social consciousness, a
community has a logical bond of union.   The mutual aid
and protection of individuals operating in an unconscious
way are no longer the only means that preserve social cohesion.   The community feels and perceives its unity." [17]
Out of this struggle to express the fundamental factor
which makes society was to come that happy phrase,
" consciousness of kind " — but not yet.

Furthermore, in this paper he works out still further the
implications of his definitions of sociology written in 1890.
In this definition he had said, " It is an attempt to account
for the origin, growth, structure and activities of human
society by the operation of physical, vital and practical
causes working together in a process of evolution."   The
implications of this definition in 1894 are made more clear
and explicit.   He said, " The sociologist has three main
quests.   First, he must try to discover the conditions that
determine mere aggregation and concourse.   Secondly, he
must try to discover the law that governs social choices,
the law, that is, of subjective process.   Thirdly, he must
try to discover the law that governs the natural selection
and survival of choices, the law, that is, of the objective
process." [18]   It is in connection with his discussion of the

[16] *Democracy and Empire*, p. 35.
[17] *Ibid.*, p. 37.
[18] " The Theory of Sociology," *Annals of the American Academy
of Political and Social Science*, supplement, July, 1894.

law of choices or the subjective aspect of evolution, that he introduces some of the results of his discussion with Professor Patten over the relations of association to utility. Here you find the concepts, "concourse," "suggestion," "imitation," "conflict," "toleration," "alliance," —concepts destined to much greater development in his *Principles*.[19] In the same year he published a paper in the *Journal of Social Science* entitled "The Relation of Sociology to Other Scientific Studies" in which he took another step in clarifying his concept of the province of sociology. This was a short article and contained only a brief statement of his general theory. Here he first proposed a diagram of the sciences not in a linear arrangement such as Comte proposed, but one in which the concrete sciences were indicated on one side of a right angled triangle and the abstract sciences on the other side so that if the lines were extended the abstract and the concrete sciences cut across each other.[20] The purpose of this diagram, which was worked out much more fully later, was to show the fundamental nature of sociology to the other social sciences.

His mind continued to play upon economic theory and in the publications of the American Economic Association in discussing Hadley's paper "The Relation Between Interest and Profit" Professor Giddings called attention to the sociological origin of risk which is paid for by an amount added to commercial interest. He contended that interest is economic in its origin while risk is sociological. He asks "In economic theory ought we not to distinguish

---

[19] "The Theory of Sociology," *Ibid.*, pp. 24-33.
[20] *Journal of Social Science*, Vol. V, No. 3, July, 1894.

carefully between the economic elements and the sociological elements? " [21]

At the annual meeting in 1894 of the American Economic Association Professor Small of the University of Chicago read a paper on the " Relation of Sociology to Economics." A long discussion ensued between Patten, Giddings and Ward. In this discussion Professor Giddings once more outlines more fully his triangle showing the relationship between the concrete and the abstract sciences for the purpose of demonstrating that sociology is a fundamental science to economics and politics and is also a coördinating science. Here, also, for the first time I find the expression " the social mind." [22]   The debate did not end with this meeting. In Volume V of the *Annals of the American Academy of Political and Social Science* Professor Giddings answered Professor Patten's paper, " Relation of Economics to Sociology," which had appeared in the January number. Here he outlined in final form his classification of the concrete and abstract sciences and here for the first time appears that expression which he had anticipated for a number of years, " the consciousness of kind." It occurs in the course of his reply to Patten's charge that Giddings had used the word " social " and " association " with a meaning opposed to all usage. Giddings replied, " I have never thought or spoken of mere physical contact, hostile or friendly, as constituting association or a society. It is *association only if accompanied by a consciousness on the part of each of the creatures im-*

[21] *Publications, American Economic Association,* Vol. IX, 1894, pp. 61, 62.

[22] *Publications, American Economic Association,* Vol. X, 1895, pp. 110–113.

plicated that the creatures with which it comes in contact are like itself. This *consciousness of kind* (italics mine) is the elementary, the generic social fact; it is sympathy, fellow-feeling in the literal as distinguished from the popular sense of the word."

Professor Giddings now felt that his thought had crystallized sufficiently to be worked out in a complete system. In 1896 appeared the fruition of his labors of many years in the book which gave him his great reputation, *Principles of Sociology.* Whatever we may think of the book after the lapse of so many years there is no question that in it Professor Giddings reconciled in a consistent system as no one before him had done with anything like his thoroughness the theory of the physical factors of social evolution and the theory of the subjective or volitional factors. In his system each has its place equally emphasized and vitally coördinated. It was this attempt to reconcile the theory of the influence of these two sets of factors which had led Professor Giddings to his "consciousness of kind principle." [23] Nothing can better set forth his view of this process than his own words, "It might be thought that sociology could meet this criticism by surrendering all subjective explanations to other sciences, and by confining itself to an elaboration of the objective explanation. But this would be to abandon entirely the claim to the unity of social phenomena. The volitional process is obviously essential. If there is no unity here, there is none anywhere in society; apparent unity is a circumstance of the physical basis only. Plainly, a true sociology must combine the subjective and the objective interpretations. It must reduce each to its lowest terms, and must consistently trace

Principles of Sociology, pp. 9, 10.

the fundamental principles of each through all social relations. Then it must unite them, in no merely artificial way, but logically, as complementary doctrines, and show how they condition each other at every step." [24]

Let us turn now to see the growth of Professor Giddings' thought from its comprehensive statement in his *Principles of Sociology* as it is revealed in his succeeding sociological works. From this point on we need not concern ourselves so much with his articles and addresses. Professor Giddings continued to follow the practice which we have seen in his *Principles of Sociology* of compressing into a book the results of his further studies and thought which appeared in the articles intervening between the publication of one book and the next.[25]

In 1898 Professor Giddings published his *Elements of Sociology*. Even though it is an elementary book intended for the use of classes in schools and colleges, this book shows certain developments in his thought since the publication of his *Principles* in 1896. For example, his definition of society in the two years had increased in definiteness and precision. While in 1896 he defines a society as " a naturally developing group of conscious beings, in which converse passes into definite relationships, that in

[24] *Ibid.*, p. 13.

[25] I have not endeavored to set forth in this paper an exposition of Professor Giddings' theories any more than was necessary to show the development of his thought. For such an exposition see Northcott, " The Sociological Theories of Franklin H. Giddings," *The American Journal of Sociology*, July, 1918, Vol. XXIV, No. 1. Nor will space permit any attention to the criticisms which have been made of his theory. These may all be found in the sociological publications of the years since 1896. For a brief list of reviews of some of Giddings' important books see Small, " Evolution of Sociological Consciousness in the United States," *American Journal of Sociology*, September, 1921, Vol. XXVII, No. 2.

the course of time, are wrought into a complex and enduring organization," in 1898 " a society is a number of like-
minded individuals — socii — who know and enjoy their
like-mindedness, and are therefore able to work together
for common ends." [26] Again in the *Elements* Giddings for
the first time describes the unit of sociological investigation
as the " socius." [27] While Professor Giddings in his *Principles* had traced out the chief inter-relations of physical
environment to the aggregation of a population, in the
Elements he works out in much more detail the varieties
of physical environment in the United States and in some
of the European countries.[28] In 1896 Professor Giddings
in his *Principles of Sociology* had devoted seventeen pages
to the subject of " association." In the *Elements* he develops this in considerable detail from a somewhat new
point of view in his Chapter V entitled " Practical Activities of Socii," elaborating still further his analysis in
the *Principles*. Chapter VI in the *Elements* entitled
" Socialization " is entirely new seemingly due to the
stimulation of Professor Giddings' thought by the
publication of Baldwin's, *Social and Ethical Interpretations.*[29]

While Professor Giddings had dealt rather extensively
in his *Principles* with coöperation, Chapter VIII in his
Elements is an extensive elaboration of that subject in his
Principles, p. 114 ff. His discussion on page 100 of the
Elements of the qualities of the social nature seems to be
entirely new. Chapter XI of the *Elements* entitled " The

---

[26] *Cf. Elements of Sociology*, p. 6 with *Principles of Sociology*,
p. 51.
[27] *Ibid.*, p. 51.
[28] *Elements of Sociology*, Chapter II.
[29] See Professor Giddings', *Democracy and Empire*, p. 32.

Preëminent Social Class " is a further development of his discussion of the social classes in his *Principles* p. 124.

In Chapters XII to XV of the *Elements* we have a much more complete analysis of the social mind than is to be found in the *Principles*. In Chapters XX to XXIV of the *Elements*, Professor Giddings' thought has further developed his treatment of the stages of civilization in his *Principles*.

In 1900 appeared Professor Giddings' *Democracy and Empire*. This was made up of a series of previously published magazine articles and unpublished addresses, together with certain new material intended to give a unified treatment of the relations of democracy and empire.

In this we get a glimpse into Professor Giddings' workshop. It reveals in a remarkable way the technique of Professor Giddings' sociological craftsmanship. As one reviews these essays keeping in mind what he had written before and what writings followed them, we clearly see that these essays served three purposes. They reveal (1) that Professor Giddings was accustomed further to develop in essays and addresses rudimentary concepts found earlier in his papers and books. Take for example the chapter entitled " The Psychology of Society." Since the writing of his *Principles*, Professor Giddings had read and carefully studied Baldwin's *Social and Ethical Interpretations*. This book gave a new impetus to Professor Giddings' thought on social psychology. Certain parts of Baldwin's presentation he rejects. Other parts of it fit into his scheme, while still other parts he elaborates in line with his previous thinking.[30] (2) In some of these essays we find first drafts of new sociological ideas which later

[30] *Democracy and Empire*, Chapter III.

found their way into his system of thought. For example the one on " Industrial Democracy " and the one on " The Costs of Progress " are essays which appeared before his *Principles* and which were later worked into that book. (3) In others of them we find more detailed application of his sociological principles to specific social problems. Illustrations are " The Mind of the Many," " Democratic Empire," " The Railroads and the State," and " The Trusts and the Public."

They also reveal the wide range of Professor Giddings' mental interests. Nothing that belonged to the spirit of man was foreign to him. Philosophy, politics, economics, international relations, art, literature, culture, all provide grist for his mill which is ground into the fine flour of sociological thought.

Professor Giddings' first published writings manifested an interest in the statistical measurements of social and economic phenomena. His association, however, with Professor Mayo-Smith at Columbia seems to have greatly intensified this interest. In his *Inductive Sociology* published in 1901 we find the first record of his attempt to stimulate among his students the quantitative measurement of social facts. Limited to only a half of the field of general sociology, omitting entirely studies in historical evolution of society and of the deeper problems of causation, it sets forth certain tentative social categories, and suggested a methodology for the collection and treatment of facts under these categories. It was, however, not merely the schematic analysis of the first part of his *Principles* or of his *The Theory of Socialization* published in 1897. Much new material on theory was worked out in this book. For example, Chapter III on " The Inductive Method " was entirely new. Here he attempts to set forth a method of studying phenomena in which exact measurement is possible. Here we find the anticipation, later developed in an address before the American Sociological Society, of the measurement of social phenomena in terms of more or less differences, that is, an algebraic rather than an arithmetical statistical treatment of social phenomena.[31] In this volume also he makes further analysis of " Demotic Composition " and " Demotic Unity." His analysis of what he earlier calls " the social mind " and its various results appears in what he now for the first time called " concerted volition." Under this category he analyzes in a much more detailed way, many things which in his *Principles* and *Elements* are not so well integrated. Moreover " social organization " is very much developed in this book. In addition to " social composition " and " social constitution " Professor Giddings analyzes organizations further into " private and public," " the unauthorized and the authorized," " the unincorporated and the incorporated," thus giving five classes of organization instead of two.[32] Part IV entitled " The Social Welfare " represents a decided elaboration of certain earlier conceptions. For example he devotes a whole chapter to " Public Utilities," under which he discusses security, equity, economy and culture, and in the last two chapters on " Social Personality " and the " Interaction of Society and Personality " respectively, much earlier material is somewhat reorganized and new ideas are introduced.

Professor Giddings' next important book was entitled

[31] For the detailed treatment of this matter see his " A Social Marking System," *Publications, American Sociological Society,* Vol. IV, p. 42.

[32] *Inductive Sociology,* p. 183.

Readings in Descriptive and Historical Sociology. He himself has well stated the additions to his thought which this book represents. " New theoretical matter, that is not to be found in my *Principles, Elements,* or *Inductive Sociology,* includes the following sections, namely — The analysis of kinds of societies; the theories of social causation which is carried throughout the book, and especially the application made of the laws of increasing and diminishing return; the analysis of interstimulation and response; the new analysis of sovereignty and government, and the account of the great social policies; the hypothesis concerning the genesis of the various forms of the family, and the interpretation of the curious double process seen in the evolution of social organization whereby as a society expands and complicates, the unitary group is divided and subdivided, until finally the individual is set free as the true unit in the highest social order." [33]   The significance of these developments for Professor Giddings' social theory lies chiefly in the more penetrating analysis of his former fundamental conceptions of " consciousness of kind " which now appears to be a somewhat culminating point rather than the beginning of his analysis.   The process begins with the response of sensitive matter to a stimulus.   However, Professor Giddings recognizes that the unequal response of different organisms to the same stimulus or the subjection of the similar individuals to different stimuli, produces the infinite variation in human activity which accounts not only for coöperation but also for conflict, toleration, the foundation of classes, etc.   This development necessitates a somewhat different definition of society.   Now he is able to say, " Summarizing our anal-

[33] *Descriptive and Historical Sociology,* p. vii.

ysis to this point, we may say that we conceive of society as any plural number of sentient creatures more or less continuously subjected to common stimuli, to differing stimuli, and to inter-stimulation, and responding thereto in like behavior, concerted activity, or coöperation, as well as in unlike, or competitive activity; and becoming, therefore, with developing intelligence, coherent through a dominating consciousness of kind, while always sufficiently conscious of difference to insure a measure of individual liberty." [34]

In his discussion of the physical basis of society Professor Giddings incorporates the essence of his " A Theory of Social Causation," a paper read before the New Orleans meeting of the American Economic Association in December, 1903. " Inter-stimulation and Response " now appeared for the first time in his books. The final chapter of this book is a new one entitled " Contributions to Humanity." On the whole with the exception of the developments noted this is a book of readings illustrating the points brought out in his *Inductive Sociology.*[35]

From 1906, when Professor Giddings published his *Readings in Descriptive and Historical Sociology,* to 1922, when appeared his *Studies in the Theory of Human Society* is a long period in the intellectual life of such a man. In these sixteen years Professor Giddings' mind was not quiescent. In 1914 appeared his *Pagan Poems.* In 1915 his *The Western Hemisphere in the World of Tomorrow* and a number of other more or less important addresses

[34] *Descriptive and Historical Sociology,* pp. 8, 9.
[35] In addition to his " A Theory of Social Causation " for the new developments found in this book see " The Concepts and Methods of Sociology," *American Journal of Sociology,* Vol. X, No. 2, Sept., 1904, p. 161 and *Science,* N. S. Vol. XX, No. 515, p. 624 ff.

and papers, and in 1918 he delivered the Colver Lectures at Brown University under the title of *The Responsible State,* lectures called out by the World War. In this he further worked out the sociological implications of sovereignty as expressed in the State. Only one contribution of these years demands our attention in this survey of the development of Professor Giddings' sociological theories. This was a rather long article entitled " Pluralistic Behavior: A Brief of Sociological Theory Restated " published in the *American Journal of Sociology* for January 1920. During the years since the publication of the *Readings in Descriptive and Historical Sociology* a new psychology had commanded public attention. William James' *A Pluralistic Universe* and Woodworth's *Dynamic Psychology* besides many other important psychological works had appeared. Always aware of significant new books Professor Giddings shows the influence of this new development of psychology in his writings. The very title " Pluralistic Behavior " shows the deep impression the new psychology had made upon his thought. This term " pluralistic behavior " is used to designate what he had already described in his *Principles* — the fact that in any aggregation of human beings some respond to a stimulus more rapidly, more persistently and with greater intensity than others. This phenomenon which hitherto he had described as different response to stimulus now becomes pluralistic behavior. Moreover a new term appears in this paper, " Circumstantial pressure." With this category he now gathers together all that he has had to say on the influence of physical environment upon the formation and the differentiation of society, but enlarges the concept to include the mental media through which the environment acts — annoyance, hardship, danger and adversities which nature produces and which generates aggregation, which in turn generates social pressure. In this way his analysis is extended and groups of facts separately treated are brought together into relation. Furthermore, in the meantime William Graham Sumner's *Folkways* had appeared and Miss Harrison's *Themis* had come to his attention. Both of these important books he lays under tribute in his discussion of " social pressure." The *mores*, and the *themistes* are the means whereby social pressure is distributed and applied in a consciously concerted pressure and in this way pluralistic behavior is traditionalized. In the *Responsible State* Professor Giddings had used the term protocracy by which he meant the leadership and subjection growing out of unequal response to stimulation in early aggregates of population. In *Pluralistic Behavior* it appears worked out in the scheme of sociology as restated. Again, in this paper, he makes certain further analysis of groups into closed groups, selectively open groups, and indiscriminately open groups.[36]

Thus frankly Professor Giddings attempts to use the new knowledge to reorganize his theory in the light of further developments and a fresh analysis which the new psychology had stimulated. We may expect the results to appear in a revised edition of his *Principles*. This article appears entire in Chapter XV of his *Studies in the Theory of Human Society*.

The adumbration of this pluralistic behavior concept appears in his definition of society in 1904. Then he said, " Society is any plural number of sentient creatures more or less continuously subjected to common stimuli, to dif-

[36] *American Journal of Sociology*, Jan. 1920, p. 545.

fering stimuli, and to inter-stimulation, and responding thereto in like behavior, concerted activity, or coöperation, as well as in unlike, or competitive activity; and becoming therefore, with developing intelligence, coherent through a dominating consciousness of kind, while always sufficiently conscious of difference to insure a measure of individual liberty." [37] In 1922 Professor Giddings published his *Studies in the Theory of Human Society*. This consisted partly of new material and of material which had been published as magazine articles and partly certain chapters from *Democracy and Empire*, a book which had long been out of print. Like everything which comes from Professor Giddings' pen the material is clearly analyzed and logically related.

In this book he sums up, so far as he has one, his scheme of sociology. This is stated in Chapter XVI as follows:

" 1. A situation or stimulus is reacted to by more than one individual; there is pluralistic as well as singularistic behavior. Pluralistic behavior develops into rivalries, competitions, and conflicts, and also, into agreements, contracts, and collective enterprises. Therefore social phenomena are products of two variables, namely situation (in the psychologist's definition of the word) and pluralistic behavior.

" 2. When the individuals who participate in pluralistic behavior have become differentiated into behavioristic kinds or types, a consciousness of kind, liking and disliking, approving or disapproving one kind after another, converts gregariousness into a consciously discriminative association, herd habit into society; and society, by a so-

---

[37] "The Concepts and Methods of Sociology," *American Journal of Sociology*, Vol. X, No. 2, Sept., 1904.

cial pressure which sometimes is conscious but more often, perhaps, is unconscious, makes life relatively hard for kinds of character and conduct that are disapproved.

" 3. Society organizes itself for collective endeavor and achievement, if fundamental similarities of behavior and an awareness of them are extensive enough to maintain social cohesion, while differences of behavior and awareness of them in matters of detail are sufficient to create a division of labor.

" 4. In the long run organized society by its approvals and disapprovals, its pressures and achievements, selects and perpetuates the types of mind and character that are relatively intelligent, tolerant, and helpful, that exhibit initiative, that bear their share of responsibility and that effectively play their part in collective enterprise. It selects and perpetuates the adequate." [38]

In 1924 Professor Giddings published his *Scientific Study of Human Society*. Parts of this had appeared in the *Journal of Social Forces* and portions of Chapter XII were printed in the publications of the *American Statistical Association*. This book represents Professor Giddings' summation of his thought for many years on the use of scientific methods in the study of sociology. Its earlier expression was found in his *Inductive Sociology* over which this book is a distinct advance. While some new terms here appear, such as " societal patterns ," " societal variables," " societal experimentation," and certain restatements of sociological theory, the main emphasis is upon methods in social research. There are three fundamental types of patterns as we perceive them (1) a form pattern (2) an action pattern (3) a factoral pattern. The

[38] *Studies in the Theory of Human Society*, pp. 291–292.

form patterns give us social structure, and action patterns give us human behavior in social groups. By factoral patterns Professor Giddings means certain factors which are combined in specific ways or ratios to constitute given products, and are of three kinds, component, constituent, dynamic and conditional. By societal variables Professor Giddings means those factors which one by one or in combination are subject to change. In society these must be understood by careful study before we can understand the various social manifestations in groups, customs, traditions, organizations, etc. The remainder of the book is a plea for the application of scientific method and standards to the study of social facts. The book has illustrative material to show how this may be done with due regard for scientific method. He applies this method not only to the facts found in statistical reports but also to cases, and makes an important contribution as to how cases from social agencies may be used in a scientific way. He has a very interesting chapter on how to learn from various social experiments that are being carried on with full recognition that social experiments are very much more difficult to control than physical experiments. Valuable suggestions are made as to the application of scientific method in social exploration and the use of the survey method in a scientific study of human society. Valuable suggestions are also made as to the scientific methods of studying societical energies and trends. The book closes with a very good chapter on methods of measurement.

On the whole the book is a real contribution to the application of scientific methods to the study of society. The examples given of efforts by Professor Giddings and his students are suggestive of new methods in the study of society, and social science will benefit from it for many years to come.

This long survey of Professor Giddings' more important writings is interesting if for nothing else than to show how a trained mind has reacted upon the complex phenomena of social life. It is a mind with great curiosity, persistence, and insight, a mind of logical order which insists on seeing things in their relationships and wholeness. We have seen how, beginning with his rather elementary "Theory of Sociology," his thought has developed through the thirty years since that first systematic attempt at the presentation of sociology. The restless mind, ever open to new knowledge, has not been content till that knowledge has worked into his scheme of things. Modification has been made in accordance with new truth. Some points have been very materially enriched by his further thought and study. Thirty years of contemplation, analysis and criticism of his own work has clarified many things which early were somewhat vague. Continually he was struggling to simplify as much as possible by reducing the great mass of material to certain fundamental concepts. Ceaselessly Professor Giddings has hammered away at his system to make it coherent, inclusive of all facts which have a bearing, and as closely interrelated as the complex processes and interactions of social life make possible. Here is a fine example of the human mind "accepting the universe." However he not only accepts it in good faith; he endeavors to understand it.

I have now finished the task of tracing, albeit inadequately, the growth of Professor Giddings' sociological theories. To do justice to the task a volume would be required. In his writings he has literally crammed the re-

sults of his wide reading, and of his reflection and keen observation. Each portion in his scheme of sociology is
greatly compressed in statement to make room for the
many points he sees in the marvelously complex thing,
society. The breadth of his view of society is widened
by that fact. He sees it whole, and that whole is so great,
and has so many aspects that to describe its structure, its
growth, its processes and results requires the most concise
statement on each point. That requirement accounts for
the compression. However, that his mind can illustrate
and elaborate as well as analyze and summarize is shown
in articles and addresses in which he has opportunity to
develop his rich and varied thought. Looking back over
twenty years since I saw him in his lecture room I see now
that elaboration was the function of his lectures. No wonder that the student who assiduously studied his books,
and who often was left feeling that he had been given a
formula or a brief generalization, found in his lecture room
that elucidation through example and illustration which
was the complement to his books. The number of items
in his analysis, all logically arranged in a system, challenged one's admiration. His broad knowledge, his logical
analysis, his synthesis of materials from many fields, and
his power of generalization commanded immediate attention. His lectures amazed one at his power of exposition
and illustration. The comprehensiveness of his scheme
challenged thought. No one who heard him lecture could
ever be narrow in his outlook.

It should not be inferred from long discussion of Professor Giddings' sociological thought that he has led by
any means a cloistered life. In addition to the goodly
number of books which have come from his pen, in addi-

tion to his busy life as a class-room lecturer and a director
of research with his graduate students, he has found time
for many practical activities among his fellow men. For
more than twenty years he was a member of the editorial
staff of the *New York Independent* and contributed almost weekly to the editorial pages. He has served as a
trustee of his alma mater, Union College, and of the Al-
bany Medical College. As we have seen he was one of
the founders of the American Academy of Political and
Social Science and served on the editorial staff of the
journal of that society during its earlier years. For three
years he edited the publications of the American Economic
Association. He was twice President of the American Sociological Society and once of the *Institut Internationale
de Sociologie*. Twice he has served on Citizens' Committees which have preceded reform administrations in New
York City. He was a member of the Board of Education
of New York City during the administration of Mayor
Mitchell. During the War he took an active interest in
America's part in that great conflict, was a member of
the American Rights League, and spent the greater part
of a winter speaking in support of American participation in the war in the Gulf states of the South. He was one
of the founders of the League to Enforce Peace and
drafted the preamble which constitutes a statement of the
objects of the movement. He was one of the speakers at
the Washington meeting of the League at which President
Wilson first intimated his purpose to work for a League of
Nations. He was one of the speakers at the Carnegie Hall
meeting of the first anniversary of the sinking of the Lusi-
tania when the municipal authorities tried to prevent the
meeting for fear of riot. That through his long academic

and intellectual career he has been alive to the practical issues in social life in America is shown by his writings and by his practical activities. Professor Giddings is a splendid illustration of the usefulness of the sociological theorist in practical life.

CHAPTER VIII

THORSTEIN VEBLEN

PAUL T. HOMAN

*Assistant Professor of Economics in the University
of California*

THORSTEIN VEBLEN

CHAPTER VIII

THORSTEIN VEBLEN

A CURIOUS place in the development of economic theory in the United States is occupied by Mr. Thorstein Veblen. His extraordinary fate has been to become within his own lifetime an almost apocryphal and legendary character over whose oracular utterances economists disagree with a truly religious warmth. The present study is of a man who has compelled a whole generation of economists to search their hearts lest the truth be not in them.

Veblen came upon the scene at a particularly controversial period in the history of economic thought. During most of the nineteenth century what passed as " orthodox " political economy carried an explicit or implicit defence of the existing economic order. The fact that it carried such a defence may, indeed, account for the fact that it was regarded as orthodox. It arose out of the intellectual and economic life of its times and spoke in terms that commended themselves to the more influential classes of the community. In England the Ricardian political economy was converted into a series of political precepts which purported to base a policy of *laissez faire* upon established economic laws. The same individualistic bias which obtained in England was present in even greater degree in the United States, although the peculiar circumstances of the century did not permit it to flower into the logical policy of free trade. Among the intellectual classes economic thought was firmly grounded in the philosophy of Utilitarianism.

Those who ranked as dissenters to currently acceptable systems of economic theory were therefore, on the whole, persons who were not impressed by the beneficence of the economic order. Dissenting economic theory was generically related to discontent with existing economic arrangements, and was almost universally accompanied by some scheme of social reform designed to remake the world closer to the heart's desire.

The novitiate of Veblen in economic studies came during the decade of the 'eighties just when Ricardianism had lost its position of supremacy. One need not here go into the causes of that decline. In England it was associated on the practical side with the realization that modern industry created problems of welfare for which *laissez faire* offered no remedy. On the more strictly intellectual side it was associated with the rise of the influence of the German historical school, with the rise of marginal utility analysis as introduced by Jevons, and with the increasing consciousness of the hypothetical character of economic logic in its relation to the workaday affairs of the world. Moreover, the revolutionary uses to which Marx put the doctrines of Ricardo hastened the search of economists for new grounds of validity for their science. Twenty years of controversy over methodology in England were stilled somewhat by the appearance of Alfred Marshall's *Principles* in 1890, wherein his eclectic view appeased the contending parties.

The controversy over economic theory ran on somewhat different grounds in the United States, but it was similar in that it had to do particularly with methodology.

At first it was between the deductive and inductive methods, a phase sharpened by the return to America of a group
of able young men trained under Knies and Schmoller in
Germany. Many American economists, however, gradually fell in a marked degree under the influence of the
marginal utility type of economic analysis, and interest
came to centre in the somewhat abstract problem of the
proper method of arriving at laws of value and distribution. Economists for the most part trailed in the wake of
the Austrian psychological school and J. B. Clark on the
one hand or of Alfred Marshall on the other, in so far as
their interest lay in theory. Their concrete studies of
economic life were rather divorced from their theoretical
positions, and went by the name of " applied economics."
By the time that Veblen came to take an active hand in the
game, economic theory had reached this later phase. It
was almost exclusively concerned with the search for the
laws of value and distribution which would obtain under
a hypothetical competitive situation.

This abstract character made it a thing apart in contemporary thought. Business men were frankly contemptuous except in so far as theory in the hands of some economists lent a degree of moral approval to the existing order.
Social reformers went their way devising schemes for the
renovation of society undeterred and unaided by schemes
of thought which seemed to them entirely divorced from
the really important and pressing problems of economic
life. The other social sciences pursued their own problems
under their own disciplines, little interested in the course
of economic thought.

Such was the situation when, in the late 'nineties, Veblen stormily entered the arena of economic theory. He

came in the guise of a dissenter, but his dissent was of a
different sort from that of earlier nineteenth century dissi-
dents. Like them he was a critic of the economic organization as he found it. But he bore in his hand no alternative form of economic organization designed to remove
the world's ills and woes. Philosophically minded and
armed with a mighty erudition, he proceeded with a heavy
hand to demolish the customary forms of economic analysis and to impugn the terms in which economists were
wont to explain the functioning of the economic organization. This he did, so he stated, in the name of science.
His avowed purpose was to subject the economic system,
its origins and processes, to an objective, scientific scrutiny, free from the preconceptions which had led other
economists to misinterpret it. How well this purpose was
carried out and how far it was a screen to quite different
ends it will be necessary to inquire at a later point.

One may usually secure a better understanding of an
economist's views by investigating the influences that
shaped his thinking in the formative period of his youth.
In the case of Veblen, unfortunately, so little of recorded
history exists that one cannot get very far with such a
plan. The very fact, however, that so little information is
available concerning his life and particularly concerning
his intellectual development is characteristic of the man.
Of a peculiarly reticent temperament, he has consistently
shrunk from any publicity other than that which his books
afford. Even toward his more intimate associates his relations have been marked by a reserve which has left him
in their eyes an unexplored and enigmatic personality.

Veblen's youth during the 'sixties and 'seventies was
spent in a pioneer rural community in Minnesota. His

parents were Scandinavian immigrants, and nothing more
can be said of his early years than that they were spent
under the harsh conditions that characterized bucolic life
during the early period of the settlement of the Northwest.
He was graduated in 1880 from Carleton College, Minnesota, where he was first introduced to economic studies
by John Bates Clark. A few contemporary anecdotes
indicate that at that period he had already a definite independence of judgment and a habit of looking at people
and things in a curiously objective fashion. It may be
supposed that Veblen's peculiar independence of outlook
began to take definite form at that time, when a curious mind digging about in the scientific and religious
controversies of the period might be expected to react
against the narrowness of the ideas circulated in the pious
atmosphere of a small denominational college in the Northwest.

With a mind as yet uncentred but intent upon further
exploring the world of ideas, he passed from Carleton to
Johns Hopkins University. Not finding it the scholar's
paradise which his imagination and current repute had
conjured, he repaired to Yale, where in 1884 he took his
doctor's degree in philosophy under the tutelage of Noah
Porter, with a doctoral dissertation upon Kant. His interest in economic studies at this early date is attested by
the winning of a university prize at Yale for a study of the
panic of 1837. Having for years pursued the gleam of
knowledge under distressing conditions of poverty, he was
compelled for a number of years after leaving Yale to with-
draw from any active work because of ill health.

Turning up from somewhere at Cornell in 1891, un-
kempt and penniless, Veblen impressed Professor J. Lau-

rence Laughlin with a sense of intellectual ability hidden under an unpromising exterior, and was granted a teaching fellowship. Even at that early date he exhibited evidence of his appetite for those curiously varied fields of learning upon which he later drew in forming his economic views — a trait illustrated by his authoritative knowledge of Norse literature and Cretan and Icelandic archeology. When Professor Laughlin removed to the newly established University of Chicago in 1892, Veblen was taken with him, and there he remained until 1906.

The early years at Chicago were undoubtedly of great importance in fertilizing Veblen's thinking. Arriving with an esoteric knowledge of philosophy and economic speculation and with scattered information upon a considerable range of scientific and cultural matters, he was thrown into an atmosphere designed to stimulate him to effective intellectual work and to furnish him with new information and ideas. The new university had gathered a distinguished group of men in the natural and social sciences, men not too much bound by traditional methods and most sincerely concerned with advancing the boundaries of knowledge. And with them were associated a group of very able younger men, who were later to establish their competence in their various fields.

Association with a competent faculty of economics strengthened Veblen's grasp upon an understanding of the economic order, and the intellectual freedom existing permitted his native originality to function freely. In his own department his mind rubbed daily against those of such different men as J. L. Laughlin, H. J. Davenport, and R. F. Hoxie, not to mention others, each striving in his distinctive way to perfect a scientific technique for economic analysis. Among his associates in other departments one judges that he owed most to John Dewey and Jacques Loeb, to mention no others. Loeb undoubtedly gave him something general in his apprehension of the meaning of science and something specific through the investigations into the physiology of the mind, which bore upon Veblen's nascent problem of the relation of human psychology to economic theory. But Dewey in particular must be supposed to have influenced him, since one finds their ideas so frequently running parallel. In his efforts to bring philosophy into a state of harmony with the modern scientific point of view and to bring a realistic psychology to bear upon the problems of human activity, Dewey was forging instruments for Veblen's hand.

One must not, however, make the mistake of interpreting Veblen in the light of this or that particular influence. He has passed through his mind a curiously varied mass of information and ideas. Sorted and combined in its passage by the reaction of his striking intellectual processes, this raw material has emerged as the characteristic outlook on economic life and interpretation of it which are describable only as Veblenian.

Veblen passed from Chicago to Leland Stanford University in 1906 and from there was called to the University of Missouri at the instance of his former Chicago associate, Professor Davenport. More recently he has been a lecturer at the New School for Social Research at New York. He has not during his lifetime displayed any high regard for the conventional usages and amenities which rule in university circles, nor for the dignity of those in high places, nor for " middle-class morality " in general. He has consequently tended to be something of a thorn in the side of the powers-that-be and his changes of base have not always been of a voluntary sort. This unfitness of his temperament for American university environment and the occasional unpleasant episodes to which it has led may be surmised to have fostered the satirical spirit which has increasingly marked his writings.

As a teacher Veblen was hardly a success with undergraduates, not being gifted with the patience necessary to cope with the average stupidity of American college students. Among those who took their advanced work with him, however, one finds him regarded, not with love, hardly with friendliness, but with a certain awe at the sweep and power of his mind, and with gratitude for his fertile and stimulating suggestions. And without exception they display in their own work the influence of their master.

From any external view Veblen has scarcely any history at all. His history is almost exclusively the history of the thoughts that have germinated within his mind as it played over the field of intellectual speculation, over the panorama of history, and over the scene of American life. And it may seem history enough for one man; for those thoughts have been of sufficient force essentially to modify the views of the entire rising generation of American economists. In England economic theory remains predominantly in bondage to the categories of Marshall; whereas in the United States the recently strong grip of Clark, Marshall, and the Austrians has been loosened, and the whole subject is in a state of ferment, marked by the tentative pursuit of new and promising constructive leads. One might list a considerable number of reasons for the situation, but so far as one man can be held accountable it can hardly be denied that Veblen has been the arch-disturber of the economist's academic peace of mind.

It is not the least interesting aspect of his history that three economists of quite orthodox lineage should have intervened at crucial moments to put the feet of this modern iconoclast of conventional views upon the highroad of achievement. J. B. Clark introduced him to the study of economics. J. Laurence Laughlin rescued him from poverty and obscurity and opened the doors of opportunity. H. J. Davenport extricated him from an unpleasant situation which might suddenly have cut off his career. And it is such as they who are the targets for his most deadly critical shafts.

In proceeding to an exposition of Veblen's work one has necessarily to protect himself with a word of warning. It is at times very difficult to break through his curious rhetoric into the true import of his meaning. He is, for one thing, addicted to the use of words and phrases in senses far removed from their customary uses. In particular, expressions that almost universally carry a derogatory connotation are used with the avowed intention of imputing neither praise nor blame. But one cannot trust his avowed intentions. Moreover, though casting himself in the rôle of scientific observer, he is essentially a satirist, much impressed with the comic or futile aspects of human life. An aloof Olympian humor possesses him. From behind a pose of objective analysis he launches his shafts of humorous exposure or indignant protest against the absurdities, short-comings, and vices of human nature and human institutions. He is, again, an inveterate and brilliant phrasemaker, and rather continuously sacrifices the objective character of his analysis to the exigencies of striking, even flamboyant, diction. And finally, he attempts to consolidate some rather weak positions by taking a great deal for granted, blandly adopting a position of the shadiest scientific authenticity and arguing from it as though it were not open to question.

One has ever to be on guard against being taken either by storm or by guile. Veblen may not be read without the necessity of discounting satire, pose, terminology, and scientific assumptions. What lies beneath must be pursued with as much perspicuity as is available to the task. Through the mere fact of being himself, Veblen was under the necessity of making his impressive contribution to economic thought in his own peculiar personal way. The idiosyncracies themselves, enlivening each page as they do, are hardly to be accounted defects. And it is worth some little trouble to arrive at an accurate comprehension of the fertile range of ideas which are imbedded in his curious prose.

Veblen's relation to economic theory is not, as has sometimes been alleged, that of a critic only. Since, however, his early reputation was founded upon his capacity as a critic, it will be convenient to examine first the grounds upon which he dissents from all systems of theory which have achieved any wide degree of acceptance.[1]

Economic science has been, in Veblen's view, "a body of logically consistent propositions." He is willing to admit that economists, from Adam Smith down, have been passably good logicians, and that, "if the test of theoretical truth is the congruence of the system with its prem-

---

[1] The main body of Veblen's critical position is to be found in a series of essays published periodically between 1898 and 1908, and republished as essays III to XV inclusive in *The Place of Science in Modern Civilization and Other Essays* (1919).

ises," little can be said in criticism of them, early or late.
Since, however, any system of deductive logic is based
upon its premises, the test of the system as a scientific explanation of current facts lies not in its internal congruence but in the relation of its premises to the facts of the
external world which it purports to explain. Veblen's test,
it will be seen, is the same as that which John Dewey sets
up for philosophical systems. The critical examination of
any system of economic thought consequently becomes an
examination of the premises upon which it is based. But
what shall serve as premises to an inquiry into human
affairs, Veblen conceives to turn ultimately upon some generally acceptable canons of knowledge, mainly metaphysical in character, which serve as the preconceptions from
which the inquiry starts.

Classical political economy Veblen found to start from a
a few preconceptions of this sort, including (1) a hedonistic view of human psychology, (2) a belief in Natural Law
and Natural Liberty, and (3) a conviction that there is a
meliorative trend in the course of events. Hedonistic psychology permitted human nature to be eliminated from the
economist's problem, since activity could be regarded as
the automatic attempt to achieve pleasurable sensations
and to avoid painful ones. In the economic sphere this
meant a balancing of the pleasures of consumption against
the painful exertions of labor.

In its earlier aspect the scientific belief in immutable
laws of nature and the belief in the meliorative trend, of
theological origin, were closely associated. Utilitarianism,
however, emphasized hedonism and in its formulas natural
law in the human sphere came to be merely whatever actions flowed out of man's hedonistic nature. On this basis

was built the system of ethical determinism whereby whatever happens is inevitable and, by a process of interpretation, whatever is inevitable, being the working out of natural law, is right and good. The belief in natural melioration, though thus attenuated, persists.

The classical economists had only to complete their premises by adding to these purely metaphysical preconceptions a statement of the institutions through which the economic system functions. Competition, or individual freedom of enterprise, being the most marked feature of contemporary economic organization, served this purpose, and it was accepted as the " natural " or " normal " form, well buttressed by the philosophy of Locke as developed by eighteenth century thinkers. The natural equity of private property is taken for granted.

Classical economic science, in Veblen's view, thus turns out to be only a series of logical deductions from the premises of perfect competition and hedonistic human nature. By the nature of their preconceptions, " the classical economists knew that the consummation to which, in the nature of things, all things tend, is the frictionless and beneficent competitive system." [2] This competitive ideal became the " normal " from the point of view of which all economic phenomena are tested. Normality thus corresponds not to any causal relationship of concrete facts, but to an imaginary ideal.

When abstractions had been made of human nature and of institutions, economic science became merely a theory of value. Money entered into the case merely as a common measure for the " hedonistic magnitudes " which entered into the process of valuation. The acquisition of

[2] *The Place of Science in Modern Civilization*, p. 145.

money was identified with the production of goods, and individual gains in terms of money were regarded as equal to social gain in terms of goods. Under the premises of the system, the competitive system was supposed to promote the maximum production of goods, to produce the maximum satisfaction of wants, and therefore to be ethically defensible as the ideally best system.

Upon some such analysis of classical economics Veblen bases his criticism of later systems of economic theory. While admitting that they have for the most part escaped the peculiarly crude metaphysical preconceptions of earlier theory, he thinks that they are still much under the sway of the conceptions, and particularly of the methods of the classical system. The particular point of criticism is that they without exception construct their bodies of theory in terms of a quiescent normal situation. Normality is a concept entirely anathema to Veblen. It can, he thinks, in the nature of the case mean no more than logical congruence with the postulates. And the postulates of all latter-day offshoots of the classical line are in some degree out of harmony with external reality.

His categorical criticism of recent types of theory centres about five points, (1) that all involve a hedonistic psychology, (2) that they contain an attenuated belief in a teleological end and a meliorative trend, (3) that they identify acquisition and production, (4) that they cling to the philosophy of Natural Rights and Natural Law, and (5) that their view of normality involves a conception of economic life and institutions out of harmony with the external facts. His criticism thus centres upon those aspects of recent economic theory in which its relationship to classical theory is most direct and marked.

A similar kind of criticism is turned against other types of theory. The historical school so far as it had theoretical aims is pictured as having been built upon a foundation of Hegelian metaphysics which are no longer tenable. And Marx is demolished as a mere logician, arguing from untenable premises derived from a materialistic Hegelianism and from the English system of Natural Rights.

Enough has been said to indicate that Veblen is out of step with all types of economic theory that have flowered into systematic expression, and to reveal the technique of his offensive strategy. He does not combat logic with logic. There is no tactical turning of flanks. The main fortress is taken at the start by discrediting the preconceptions and postulates upon which the body of logic rests. The method is infinitely disconcerting. For it knocks out the underpinnings of whole systems of thought, and places at an overwhelming disadvantage those who are not equipped to meet Veblen on his own ground. Bringing into action a wide erudition in philosophy, natural science, psychology, and cultural history not common to economists, he proceeds with deadly effect to put the exponents of logically systematic theory upon the defensive.

Veblen's view of what economic science should be is based upon a definite conception of the nature and method of scientific inquiry. His view is, he insists, that of modern science. Modern science is regarded as inquiry into the unfolding processes of changing and developing life. It is, in short, post-Darwinian evolutionary science, impersonal and matter-of-fact, and concerned only with the run of the facts. Its primary tenet is the changefulness of all things, and its task is to trace the process through which change expresses itself. Each stage of the process arises

out of that just preceding it, and all eventualities are regarded as the equally " natural " results of the exfoliation
of the cumulative life-process. There is no place in such a
conception for the artificial classification of phenomena
into categories of " normal " and " abnormal." The pre-
Darwinian scientific method which ran to classifications,
natural laws, specific causation, and a general conception
that phenomena tended toward a state of equilibrium is
considered obsolescent and inadequate to deal with the
phenomena of a changeful life-process.

In the light of this conception of science, a scientific inquiry into the life-process of human society necessitates a
realistic view of the forces at work. This means that the
social scientist must be equipped, on the one hand, with an
adequate knowledge of human psychology in order to understand the motivation of human activity, and on the
other hand, with a knowledge of the institutional forms
through which human activity expresses itself. Veblen
thus centres attention upon those aspects of life which
economic theory has customarily eliminated from the
problem by abstracting human nature into hedonistic rationalism and economic institutions into free competition.

For his psychology Veblen draws upon recent investigators in that field, particularly upon William James, William McDougall, Jacques Loeb, and John Dewey. For
his purposes the essential facts are that, fundamentally, the
ends of life are set by man's instinctive propensities and
that the instincts are relatively stable and enduring. Overt
activity emerges as the result of concessive adjustments
between the more or less conflicting urges of the instinctive
proclivities. The equipment of instincts undergoes only
gradual modification as the result of the selective adapta-

tion of groups to their environment. Intelligence, or rationality, enters into the situation by way of assisting in the provision of ways and means for accomplishing the ends, not rationally, but instinctively set.

The discipline of daily life, representing fundamentally group-action dictated by the instincts, takes on the consistency of habit and custom. Habits of thought and action widely current in social groups solidify into established institutions, which come to have a prescriptive force in limiting the activity of individuals, whose ends must be achieved through these socially sanctioned channels. The support and perpetuation of their institutions become, in the outcome, the proximate end of groups whose actions have been disciplined by their existence.

The study of institutions thus comes, in Veblen's mind, to occupy a position of peculiar importance. For, while human nature remains relatively fixed and stable, institutions are notably transient and changeful. Institutions at any given time constitute the prevailing culture, and as such are an important factor in the process of the selective adaptation of human beings to their environment. In the complicated institutional situation in advanced civilizations they are, indeed, perhaps of greater importance in this regard than the material circumstances enforced by nature.

One may then clearly apprehend Veblen's conception of the nature of human activity as the outgrowth of desires which are " the products of his hereditary traits and his past experience, cumulatively wrought out under a given body of traditions, conventionalities, and material circumstances." [3] Underneath the constraining force of institu-

[3] *The Place of Science in Modern Civilization*, p. 74.

tions, by which the group guides or limits the activity
of individuals, there continues the pressure of those propensities native to mankind.   And the weight of this
constraint may at times bear down too hardly upon the
underlying human nature, as has often happened
historically when "imbecile institutions" have set
the scene for the violent shifting of the institutional
scheme.

It is in the light of such general ideas as these that Veblen proceeds to his task. Enough has been said to indicate
that his work is "cultural analysis," the investigation of
the origin and nature of the institutions through which the
economic side of the life-process of society functions. It
thus lies largely outside the recognized field of economic
theory. He insists, however, that it is economic theory,
the theory of the process through which economic activity
takes place. And he presses the point further, by holding
that what is ordinarily included in economic theory, systems of logic and schemes of normality, are no more than
obsolescent aspects of a bygone habit of scientific thought.
Obviously, he proposes to rebuild economic theory within
a framework of ideas borrowed from biology, psychology,
and anthropology.

In planning what he calls a "genetic" study of economic institutions, Veblen has in mind something quite
different from a mere tracing of historical sequences. Regarding the development of social life as a process of cumulative causation, he hopes sufficiently to disentangle the
skein of causation to explain *why* men in the modern world
act as they do and think as they do in their economic relations. The question naturally arises in one's mind
whether, in attempting genetic studies in the unfolding

life-process of society, he is binding himself to an organismic theory of society. The point is one upon which he never has deigned to express himself, and it is perhaps of little importance whether his biological terminology be taken literally or metaphorically. For his real interest lies elsewhere.

Having, however, insisted upon the idea of the life-process, he is faced with a certain methodological difficulty. This lies in the necessity of separating from the life-process certain portions which can be specifically labeled " economic," and which can be studied in isolation. It is much like the problem would be of studying the evolution of man's digestive tract without reference to that of the respiratory and nervous systems. Veblen accomplishes this feat of prestidigitation heroically and a little cavalierly by defining economic as having to do with provision of the material means of life for the group, and by tacitly assuming that the rest of the life-process can be shelved while the human traits and institutions bearing upon this problem are separately examined.

To examine at all adequately his more or less plausible interpretation of past economic institutions is impossible within any brief limits of space. It is based upon a categorical classification of instincts and institutions into two groups, (1) those that serve the " generically human " ends of life, that is to say, promote the fullest provision for the group's material needs, and (2) those " contaminating " ones that hinder such provision. These categories are run vertically across the scene of history as divided into four periods rather arbitrarily arrived at. Institutions at one period and another are then examined to discover the extent to which they offer adequate scope for the expression of the generically human traits and the extent to which they hinder such expression.[4]

Along the lines of this classification runs whatever may be found of moral judgment. Veblen disclaims all intention of judging the process which he purports to describe objectively. Nevertheless, the force of his caustic satire is forever turned against those contaminating institutions and habits of thought which hinder the working out of the generically human ends of life. These ends, which, if not " good," are at least advantageous to group-survival, are, it should be noted, always expressed in terms of technological proficiency, of bulk of output in weight and tale. He refuses to discuss the justice of distribution and neglects all spiritual traits not bearing upon the production of goods. He has, in consequence, no line of demarcation between instincts and institutions except their effect upon the volume of output.

The part of Veblen's work in which he attempts to construct an organon of thought for the evolutionary interpretation of history in economic terms is perhaps the least convincing and least valuable aspect of it. It has seemed necessary, however, to display it briefly, since the mechanism runs somewhat through all his writing. The attempt to establish this organon calls attention to the fact that one must distinguish rather carefully between the general evolutionary viewpoint from which Veblen starts on the one hand and the specific manner in which he attempts to apply it on the other.

From the economist's point of view, probably the most interesting part of Veblen's constructive work is his inter-

---

[4] This aspect of Veblen's thought is best displayed in *The Instinct of Workmanship* (1914).

pretation of contemporary economic life.[5]   The antitheti-
cal principles about which we have seen his whole interpretation of economic life to be centred are displayed in
modern life as " business " and " industry," between which
there is deemed to be a necessary disconsonance.   Industry, in his view, represents the organization of the technological ways and means by which the material wants of
mankind are cared for, while business represents the efforts of individuals to acquire for themselves as large a
money income as the circumstances permit.

The modern age he characterizes as " the era of the machine process," which grew out of the preceding " handicraft period " as the result of a series of revolutionary
technological changes.   The task which he sets himself is
to explain the functioning of the economic organization in
terms of habits of thought and action which men have had
imposed upon them by the machine process, as modified
by other norms of validity carried over from a previous
stage of economic development.

Veblen pictures the machine as giving the scope and
method for modern industry.   The pace is set for the rest
of the industrial system by the machine industries; " the
scope of the process is larger than the machine."   The
machine process makes of the industrial system a highly
complicated, completely integrated mechanism.   Physical
production has become an endless sequence of processes,
which are linked by a continuing series of interstitial adjustments and which demand accuracy and quantitative

[5] The best example of Veblen's analysis of current economic institutions is to be found in *The Theory of Business Enterprise*
(1904).   The views there expressed are extended or amended in *The
Vested Interests* (1919), *The Engineers and the Price System* (1921),
and *Absentee Ownership* (1923).

precision for their effective functioning. From the point of view of the material welfare of the race, the function of this system is to supply goods in abundance, and in the present high state of development of the industrial arts this function could be adequately fulfilled.

It happens, however, that in the operation of the system discretion lies in the hands of business men. The motive of business enterprise is not maximum production of useful goods. It is pecuniary gain. And the pecuniary interests of business men are not necessarily best served by the unbroken maintenance of the industrial processes upon a high and efficient productive level. The business man's opportunity for profit arises out of the interdependence of all the parts of the industrial system. The adjustment between the parts takes place through the agency of the price-system, and at the points of adjustment involving purchase and sale the great gains of business enterprise are made.

The origin of profits gives Veblen no trouble, for he entertains no theory that competition is ubiquitously active, reducing or tending to reduce profits everywhere to some normal minimum. On the contrary, the business world is to him an affair of widespread collusion where great corporations, trusts, and all manner of semi-monopolistic enterprises and practices are matters of course, not mere occasional excrescences upon the pure surface of a competitive order. The principle of price-making is "what the traffic will bear," and business profits typically arise from the exploitation of some differential bargaining advantage, from some power to interrupt the free flow of materials from one part of the industrial system to another. This relation of business to industry may be shortly described

as " sabotage," or " conscientious withdrawal of efficiency." Veblen thus examines business enterprise from
the point of view of the dissociation, or conflict, of interests between the community and business men.

Not only does he assume a high degree of collusive control of industry; he attempts to demonstrate the impossibility of free competition under the conditions of machine industry. When technological improvement reached
the point where markets could no longer be expanded rapidly enough to carry off the increased product profitably,
he conceives that a situation had arisen which foretold the
death of active competition. Under the exigencies of business enterprise, as set by the price system, this situation
inevitably led to a movement toward combination and collusion designed to insure profits through a restriction of
output. The trouble with the modern industrial system,
from the point of view of business men, is that it has
become " inordinately productive," so that the prime element of business success is the exact opposite of what it
had been under the earlier handicraft situation, when " un-
sophisticated productive efficiency " was the avenue to
profits.

Veblen, following out his " genetic " idea, is mainly interested in the cultural dualism which has sprung out of
these two dominant aspects of modern economic life, business and industry. The business groups, concerned with
pecuniary gain, are engaged in transactions running almost
wholly in terms of money measurements. Their power is
based upon the differential advantage arising out of large
property holdings, and their whole manner of thinking is
shaped by their pecuniary preoccupations. The institution of property, around which their interests centre,

" dominates the affairs of civilized peoples more freely and widely than any other single ground of action." The current views as to the proper limits, rights, and responsibilities of ownership are " the outgrowth of the traditions, experiences, and speculations of past generations," as embodied in the philosophy of Natural Rights at a time when, under the handicraft regime, property and productive work were more generically related. The natural right of ownership is still the prevailing view of the business community and is firmly embedded in the law, which, as it stands, is primarily designed for the protection of property rights, and conspires to make easy the way for pecuniary manipulation and profit.

On the other hand, a large proportion of the populace are exposed in only a secondary way to the discipline of pecuniary habits of thought. These are the ones whose daily work brings them under the standardizing, materialistic sway of the machine, — industrial workers, engineers, technical experts, and the like. And with them are associated the students of the material sciences and all those who are " required to administer the laws of causal sequence that run through material phenomena." The habits, induced by their preoccupations, of apprehending and explaining facts in terms of material cause and effect engenders habits of thought that are " sceptical, matter-of-fact . . . , unmoral, unpatriotic, undevout." Such habits of thought traverse the conventional eighteenth century truths upon which the institution of property rests, and are weakening the sense of allegiance toward the received institutions. The groups which are being disciplined in these habits of thought are, " however crudely and blindly, endeavoring, under the compulsion of the machine process, to construct an institutional scheme on the lines imposed by the new exigencies imposed by the machine process."

The present cultural situation is, then, displayed somewhat dramatically by Veblen as a clash between two cultures. One, grounded in matter-of-fact habits of thought, runs to the view that the industrial system should be directed to the provision of a plentiful supply of goods for the benefit of the community. The other, grounded in law and an obsolete philosophy, is designed to protect the differential advantages incident to ownership, and to protect business men in their practices of deriving gain from a sabotage upon the industrial system. Out of this clash of interests the next phase of the economic process will arise. " Such wear and tear of institutions is unavoidable where circumstances change; and it is through the altered personal equation of those elements of the population which are most directly exposed to the changing circumstances that the wear and tear of institutions may be expected to take effect. To these untidy creatures of the New Order common honesty appears to mean vaguely something else, perhaps something more exacting, than What was ' nominated in the bond ' at the time when the free bargain and self-help were written into the moral constitution of Christendom by the handicraft industry and the petty trade. And why should it not? " [6]

It will be impossible here to indicate the infinite detail with which Veblen embroiders the argument. Yet in the luxuriant exfoliation from his central ideas are best displayed the extraordinary fertility and originality of his mind. The skeleton of ideas that has been here presented he clothes with an amazing array of comments upon the

[6] Concluding passage of *The Vested Interests* p. 183.

varied scene of modern life. And, in so doing, he loses contact with his scientific pretensions, and becomes the satirist and critic. Adroitly and wittily, he exposes to view
the deficiencies of the law, the imbecility of our thinking,
the futility of our habits of consumption, and the amazing
ineptitude of our economic institutions. Overtly maintaining the pose of following out an objective analysis of
the process of cumulative institutional change, unrelated
to any norms of ethical validity, he is in reality telling the
world exactly what Veblen thinks of it.

Very much of Veblen's best work has consisted in an
examination of business enterprise as it manifests itself
in the machine era under modern forms of ownership.
The collusive control of the industrial system by the " key
industries " and the great banking enterprises holds the
centre of his interest. The effects of this collusion, combined with the disappearance of price-competition and
with the growth of selling-costs in the secondary fields of
merchandising and manufacturing, are interpreted as a
progressive diversion of the benefits of industrial advancement into the hands of the fortunately placed persons
whose control of property entitles them to the usufruct of
the community's stock of technological knowledge, to the
damage of " the underlying population," — the farmers
and industrial workers.

The current manifestations of credit represent to Veblen one of the most fascinating aspects of the situation.
As collusively controlled, it permits the maintenance of
profits through the progressive inflation of values. And it
works out, under the devices of corporation finance, to the
curious result that the discretionary control of the industrial system has come to be vested in the owners of intan-

gible assets, representing nothing more substantial than the capitalized value of assured income arising out of differential or monopolistic business advantages. This latest development in the field of credit appears as the final absurdity of permitting the industrial system to be controlled by and for business, on the basis of a set of obsolete notions concerning property held over from the eighteenth century.

In the outcome Veblen's analysis runs to a very incisive and biting criticism of the control of the industrial system by absentee owners whose object is profit. He sees an industrial system amply able to supply material abundance curbed and disabled by the struggle for pecuniary acquisition. And one feels at times that the point of the massive argument is that western civilization is headed straight for the abyss.

In the attempt to cling to the central aspects of Veblen's thinking, it has been impossible to do justice to the sweep of his mind as it plays over the modern scene. With brilliant, if unsupported, generalizations, he comments upon the economic position of farmers, wage-earners, merchants, manufacturers, and bankers; upon the economic effects of advertising, salesmanship, monopoly, and the control of credit; and upon the allocation of economic power. He examines the field of international politics, in *The Nature of Peace,* and traces statesmanship, patriotism, and competitive nationalism back to the institution of property and to the principles of business enterprise. He looks into current standards of consumption in *The Theory of the Leisure Class* and lumps them largely into the category of " conspicuous waste," based upon invidious distinctions in point of property. And in *The Higher*

Learning in America the control of education by men of property is pungently characterized.

Always and everywhere the analysis comes back to the institution of property, to its origins, to the habits of thought by which it is supported, to its submersion of the " generically human " ends of life, and to the dissension and distress to which, under modern conditions, it inevitably leads. And always there rise in opposition the habits of thought inculcated by the machine process, involving with ironical certainty the necessity that mankind shall pass through a period of institutional adjustment by stormy paths to one knows not what *dénouement*.

What direction change *ought* to take Veblen is usually careful not to hazard. His picture is of a world buffeted by the blows of powerful forces. He does not speak of " progress," but only of " cumulative change." The mantle of the reformer is not his characteristic garment. His analysis of current economic life is, nevertheless, decidedly an exposé of the deficiencies of business control. And, since he presumes to cast himself as the spokesman of modern evolutionary science which he traces to the matter-of-fact apprehension of phenomena induced by the machine process, it is not unfair to say that he is in a sense the spokesman of industry, as against business.

He is, in effect, arguing for some revised form of control by which the potential productiveness of the industrial system may be relieved of the incubus of the present debilitating business control for pecuniary ends. He goes some distance, in *The Engineers and the Price System*, in outlining rather vaguely a desirable form of economic control. And there creeps into *The Vested Interests*, written under the emotional stress of the war period, a suggestion that mankind can, by taking thought, intelligently control its environment for humanly useful ends. For the most part, however, he consistently clings to the portrayal of a deterministic process, whereby man's instinctive traits, his material environment, and his cumulatively wrought-out institutions induce habits of thought and action which lead to the inexplicable fate of the human race.

Enough has perhaps been said of Veblen's general scheme of thought to permit some estimate of his contribution to economic thought. Many questions linger in the mind after reading Veblen. His primary preconception that scientific studies must proceed from the evolutionary point of view is highly questionable. Taken literally, it would read much of our physics and chemistry, mechanics and astronomy, botany and zoölogy, out of the scientific fold. Nor is it demonstrable that scientific social studies must proceed by a method analogous to that of biology. Veblen is at no pains to defend his approach. He merely blandly assumes it to be indisputable. He assumes for his purpose that the life of society is comparable to that of a biological organism, and contends that living and growing types of organic life are not amenable to explanation in the terms used for explaining inert matter. The mere device of adopting the evolutionary approach tends at the very beginning to cast doubt upon the " static " and " dynamic " analysis of orthodox economic theory.

It would appear to be hardly open to question that, in introducing the evolutionary approach, Veblen claimed too much for it. It may reasonably be supposed that much important scientific investigation is possible in the social field from quite other viewpoints. His approach, nevertheless, has leavened the whole lump of contemporary economic thinking, and has set many of the economist's problems in a light where they may be approached by methods not available to those using the classical technique.

If the general framework of Veblen's thought may be described as an exaggerated insistence upon the evolutionary viewpoint, the specific method by which he attempts to develop the theory of the growth of economic institutions is open to more serious objections. Were he to follow out rigidly his conception of the cumulative life-process of society, he would be committed to some scheme of analysis as grandiose as Comte's. To make a scientific study of the evolution of society would require a knowledge of cultural history amounting to nothing less than omniscience, and would entail an encyclopedic presentation of the factors that have entered into the process of " cumulative causation."

To escape this difficulty he has made abstractions of most of man's mental traits and of many of his institutional arrangements. He has given attention only to such phenomena as could be crowded into two rigid categories, constructed to include, respectively, such phenomena as promote and such as hinder the adequate provision of the material means of life to the group. And with equal readiness in the art of classification, he has divided the eternity of past time into four quite arbitrary eras, on the basis of certain putative relationships between the technological and pecuniary aspects of the prevailing culture. Veblen, in short, is somewhat the master of the use of the " taxonomy " which in others he so sarcastically criticises.

Insisting upon a realistic use of psychology in economics, Veblen is nevertheless led by the nature of his analysis into taking certain liberties with that sister science, and he invents an "instinct of workmanship" and a "bent to idle curiosity," unknown to more professional psychologists, which, in combination with a reconstructed "parental bent," constitute the psychological underpinnings of much of his analysis.

The nature of his two controlling categories commits him, moreover, to an uncritical acceptance of Mill's " economic principle " that the greater material gain is preferable to the lesser, with its corollary that the most desirable form of economic organization is that which will maximize material output. In short, he knows no canon of welfare except maximum output of material goods, certainly a very narrow interpretation of the " generically human " ends of life.

And his scheme for attaining welfare is as dubitable as his idea of the content of welfare. With no more concrete suggestion than a vague plan for the supervision of the economic system by a hierarchy of technical experts, he merely succeeds in evading the problem of economic guidance and the problems of value and distribution, which lie within the sweep of the price-system. He thinks the " mutual defeat " inherent in the present economic order should be escaped in the interest of material welfare and of race survival. But no intelligible theory of social ends, no adequate account of social forces, and no tenable scheme of social control are anywhere advanced.

One often has the feeling that, in proceeding to his constructive work, Veblen never left out of mind the distasteful doctrines and methods of orthodox economic theory, which he wished to discredit. With a certain conscious and deliberate contrariety, he has gone out of his way to dig up and expose to view every real or putative fact which would operate to their confusion. Exhaustively and brilliantly he has provided the antithesis to every economic thesis. It might at times be almost thought that his sole ambition was to demonstrate that a more plausible case might be made out in terms running directly contrary to the generally acceptable canons of truth, whether in economic theory or in the practical phases of economic life. But if, in pushing his antitheses to extremes, he reduces himself occasionally to absurdity and fails to come to grips with many problems, it cannot be denied that the delightful play of his skepticism is infinitely enlightening and stimulating.

On a large view, it is obvious that Veblen cannot be rated very high as a scientist. His task is carried out with none of the cold objectivity which, in his own view, distinguishes the scientific spirit. With consummate skill in selecting and coloring his facts, he has succeeded in building up his central antithesis between business and industry, between obstructive and invidious acquisition on the one hand and humanly useful production on the other. With his tongue in his cheek and under cover of a sophistical scientific pose he has accomplished a covert ethical damnation of the dominant modern economic institutions. It is the eye of a philosopher that he casts over the mundane scene, — an eye trying to see as clearly as may be into the heart of modern economic life, as it arose out of the muddled course of history. Much that he sees appears futile and ignoble and imbecile, nor does his somewhat jaundiced sight lend any temptation to gild the scene. Regarded in this light as some composite form of cosmic philosopher, shrewd observer, and bitter critic, Veblen still retains the signs of undoubted genius — not, indeed, of the man of science, but of some more humane gift of impressionistic art, strongly expressing a brilliant and baffling personality.

Though so many questions and so many strictures spring into the mind concerning Veblen's work, his importance and significance in the field of economic theory is not to be denied.

The force of his critical attack upon established systems of theory has been sufficiently noted. Its disintegrating effect has been enormous. Anyone familiar with the theorizing of the past generation will know that the search was primarily for the controlling laws of the normal case, which would explain prices and distributive shares subject to minor corrections. The method was chiefly that of deductive logic, and such controversy as existed was chiefly confined to the amending of postulates and the defining of concepts. In the minds of many economists Veblen has thoroughly discredited the usefulness or the scientific validity of that type of analysis. He has attacked the concept of normality as a metaphysical hold-over, scientifically untenable. He has riddled the hedonistic implications of economic theory and demonstrated the insufficiency of a normalized competitive institutional situation as a postulate of theory. He has denied the coincidence of acquisition and production; developed a capital concept in which capital is merely capitalized earning-capacity but little related to industrial plant; and riddled the connection between utility and consumption.

Having thus summarily disposed of the postulates and preconceptions, Veblen is in a position to relegate to footnotes or parentheses, as obsolete or absurd, the normative systems of value and distribution with which economic theorists have been mainly concerned. No one can read him and retain quite so simple an acceptance of any systematized economic faith. It is by the deadly character of this critical attack that he has thrown the whole subject of economic theory into such utter confusion in the United States. If one accepts the idea that institutional change is "normal," then all forms of normality postulated upon the fixity of institutions disappear, and the whole character of one's social theory must depart from the customary types of economic speculation.

The Veblenian idea that economic life is part of an evolutionary process, and that an important function of economic theory is to throw light upon the process, has been widely accepted among the younger generation of economists. On one side, his work has points of resemblance with that of Sombart, Ashley, and the Webbs. But he differs from them strikingly in his insistence upon "genetic" studies and in his use of psychology. He is less the historian than the biologist of human institutions. This characteristic turn also differentiates him sharply from Marx, to whom his thought is without doubt deeply indebted. Unlike Marx, he insists that knowledge of the process is to be gained only from a knowledge of the run of the facts, and cannot be achieved by logical processes.

Like his evolutionary point of view, Veblen's unique use of psychology in analyzing the social process has been widely influential. His influence in this field may be compared to that of Graham Wallas in popularizing psychological analysis for purposes of political theory. Economic life appears to him primarily an exhibition of the play of human motives. Learning from the psychologist that human nature is relatively stable, he is permitted to use the data of anthropology and history and of his observation of contemporary life, in the attempt to explain those habitual modes of thought which have given direction to human activity, past and present. While, therefore, the study of institutions comes to occupy the centre of Veblen's attention, this interest arises out of, and is integrally related to, his view of human nature.

In his anxiety to escape the bounds of customary types of economic thinking, Veblen appeals to many sources of knowledge for light upon the problems of human activity with which economic theory is concerned. And it is this undoubtedly that has made him " a light, set upon a hilltop," guiding the thought of many who were wondering, however vaguely, whether the methods of economic science were not somehow out of step with the progress of knowledge in other fields.

The outstanding characteristic of his novel and arresting approach is its power to raise new questions and problems. The economist is stimulated to inform himself concerning the canons of scientific knowledge and concerning the bearing of psychology upon his problems. He needs to know more of the origins of the conventional practices which constitute the institutional arrangements through which economic activity expresses itself. Above all, he needs an accurate apprehension of just how economic activity is carried on, and that is only possible through a thorough study of contemporary institutions. He must ask how these institutions affect the welfare of the community, and whether the process of institutional change is amenable to intelligent control, and what are the origin and nature of the conceptions of welfare for purposes of which control would be desirable.

Such questions and innumerable others lie inherent in

the evolutionary, psychological, institutional approach to economic theory. They carry the economist beyond all the conventional frontiers of his field of labor. They defeat all attempts to carve out a specifically " economic " sphere within which he can work in isolation; or, if he be limited in his field of endeavor, they form a framework of problems toward the solution of which his particular problem is an item in a large coöperative intellectual enterprise.

New questions of this sort Veblen has set for economists. He has also attempted to answer a good many of them. Any careful estimate of his work demands that a sharp distinction be made between the approach which he devised and the questions he has raised on the one hand, and the methods he has used and the conclusions he has reached on the other hand. The obvious criticisms, of the sort that have been recounted, refer primarily to the latter aspects of his work. He is there stimulating and enlightening, but, also, one would say, often far-fetched and prejudiced, and at times merely absurd.

If his method of analysis has had some influence, and his specific conclusions more, upon contemporary economic thinking, one must still go back to his general approach and to the questions he has raised to find the dominant source of his influence. That human activity may be most profitably approached from the angle of an evolutionary process; that economic studies must deal with real human beings, not with a rationalized human nature; that institutions are decisive factors in shaping human behavior; that to study the run of the facts, not to normalize them, is the function of the economist — these ideas form the framework within which increasing numbers of economists are defining their problems. And the idea that the pecuniary and technological aspects of economic life must be strictly distinguished from each other has come to be regarded by many as an indispensable instrument of economic analysis.

These ideas attract men whose methods are as the opposite pole to Veblen's methods; whose work is as restricted, painstaking, and scientifically accurate as his is sweeping, universal, and impressionistic. They represent a formula sufficiently broad to include the most varied types of economic investigation, at the same time that they suggest an array of attractive intellectual problems. To such facts must be credited the spread of Veblen's influence and the outcropping of Veblenian notions in the most unlikely quarters, not only among economists but among the devotees of the social sciences at large.

There is nowhere among American economists a very homogeneous Veblen cult. People do not swallow him entire, but they secure from him their leading questions. His work is perhaps more in the realm of suggestion than of scientific performance. Where Veblen sows, others reap. And so far is this the case that it falls little beyond the truth to say that almost all the new leads in economic thinking which have been fruitfully followed out during the past twenty years are in some degree directly traceable to him. W. C. Mitchell's *Business Cycles* is perhaps the most outstanding example of economic research built directly around the ideas of process and of the distinction between business and industry. But over the whole field of economic investigation; whether in the field of labor, or banking, or business combination, or taxation, or the relation of government to business, or what not, there are men engaged in careful scientific work, who were emancipated from bondage to the orthodox categories and who were inspired to the investigation of the institutional framework of modern economic society through Veblen's influence, direct or indirect.

The result is that there exists to-day a group of economists, engaged in the most various tasks, who may be grouped roughly as " institutional economists," and, whatever specific reservations they may individually make against the tenets of a Veblenian faith, they are collectively a tribute to the influence of his work. Even where they do not proceed in terms of his scheme of thought, the very independence of thought with which they approach their problems is in large degree due to the emancipating effect of his critical attack upon older types of theory.

The superb effrontery of his criticism and the startling heterodoxy of his analysis of current economic life have served to jar the younger generation of economists out of the rut of traditional habits of thought before they were deeply settled in them. He has made economic heterodoxy more prevalent, and at the same time less culpable. For lesser heterodoxies fade into insignificance beside his monstrous heterodoxy, and almost cease to cause comment. So far has this situation developed in the United States, indeed, that it is almost orthodox to be heterodox, and to be orthodox in the older sense is almost to be queer. In other words, economic thought is running strongly down other channels than those set by the classical tradition.

One may read into Veblen a complete determinism. Or one may find in him the lesson that our social institutions and our human behavior must be thoroughly understood, the more intelligently to control them for the common good. The former is probably the more accurate interpretation. But, since America is not temperamentally given to fatalism, it is in the latter sense that he is most commonly understood. His vogue is greatest among groups whose aim is in one way or another to reform the social order and whose watchword is "social control." The Veblenian influence, at the same time that it sets them their problems, conveys a sense of the intricacy of their task. It makes them wary of doctrinaires, avid in the pursuit of scientific knowledge, and timid in the suggestion of radical innovations. For all his condemnation of modern society, Veblen may therefore be considered something of a conservative force in modern life, somewhat the godfather of all scientifically-minded reformers.

Veblen must not, of course, be credited with too much. It lies beyond the present purpose to deal with the varied forces that have given new turns to economic theory in the twentieth century. Many of them are, as Veblen would say, contained in the material environment. The only point that need be insisted upon is that he, more than any other individual in recent years, has given a new orientation to economic thought in the United States. Gathering his ideas from the most varied sources, he has passed them through the blending processes of his mind, barbed them with the sting of his wit, and exploded them like shrapnel over the unhelmeted heads of economists. There are but few who have not been made acutely aware of their existence and their portent.

The attitude of economists toward Veblen's work is marked by the greatest diversity of opinion. In the opinion of some, he has merely stripped away a few of the less essential parts of the older types of theory, and most of his work is not conceded to be economic theory, whatever else it may be. Others feel that, without entirely discrediting the neo-classical methods, he has displayed their limitations and opened up new domains in which economists can fruitfully employ their energy. A third group would have it that he has thoroughly demolished the validity of older types of theory and has cleared the way for a new and truly scientific economics. But they are not a little vague concerning what shall be the content of this new economics. They do not know what crop they will reap from Veblen's sowing.

On the whole Veblen's followers are not greatly concerned over the future of economic theory. Anxiety on that score is more particularly reserved for the contemporary representatives of the classical tradition, who wish to see economic truth reduced to a logically articulated system of laws and principles. To those who work under the influence of Veblenian ideas, it appears not to be a defect that their tasks are of a varied and fragmentary character. Their aim is not a logical system, but a knowledge of the facts of economic life. And this they conceive themselves to be achieving by a gradual process of patient scientific investigation. It is a kind of work that can be done quite divorced from any scheme of systematic theory. It is somewhat a process of reducing Veblen's grandiose cosmic ideas to a bill of particulars. In short, Veblen's organon of thought is being applied to the study of the economic order in a wide range of ways which he did not himself envisage.

Even among those who read Veblen sympathetically there will be found little agreement concerning the relative importance of his various contributions to economic thought. Some will give precedence to his critical accomplishments; others to the evolutionary point of view; others to his genetic-historical treatment of institutions; others to his analysis of present-day economic institutions; and others, finally, to his introduction of a realistic psychology into economics. One is not called upon to choose between them here. In point of influence, the idea that economic life must be studied from the point of view of process, not of normality, would seem to have gained the widest currency, together with the related idea that a knowledge of the process is to be gained only through a realistic study of institutions and a realistic view of human nature.

Whatever may be the deficiencies of Veblen in the scientific rôle which he assumed, the effect of his work has been to stimulate some of the best scientific work of the present century in the field of the social sciences. Economists are engaged more exclusively in describing and interpreting the run of the facts. The " economic man " and competitive normality are in danger of obsolescence through disuse. Economic science is less committed to the discovery of hypothetical economic laws, and more committed to a realistic explanation of economic behavior and the functioning of the economic order. The most various factors have led to this change of direction. But no single individual has had a larger hand in it than Veblen.

We may now leave him in peace, remote and aloof in his Olympian privacy; whence may his stinging phrases continue to puncture our cherished illusions or to goad our lethargic minds.

CHAPTER IX
FREDERICK JACKSON TURNER

By
CARL BECKER
John Stambaugh Professor of History in Cornell University

FREDERICK JACKSON TURNER

CHAPTER IX

FREDERICK JACKSON TURNER

I WENT to the University of Wisconsin (in 1893 it was) for the same reason that many boys go to one college rather than another — because a high school friend of mine, whose cousin or something had "been at Madison," was going there. As youth will, I at once endowed the place, which I had never seen and had only recently heard of, with a romantic glamor. Was not Madison a distant and large city? (I am speaking now of a prairie country boy who had never ventured from his small town into the world so wide). And was it not located on a great body of water, a lake eight miles in diameter, no less? One other bit of knowledge contributed to the splendor that was Wisconsin. On the faculty of that University there was a man whom a young lawyer in my town had belauded and bragged about, and familiarly referred to as "old Freddie Turner."

"Is he old?" I asked, picturing the long gray locks of a Faust before the devil comes in the spotlight.

"Oh no, not *old*. We just called him that, I don't know why — just a rough way of showing boyish admiration without being sentimental about it, I suppose."

"What does he teach?"

"Well, he teaches American history. But it's not what he teaches, the subject I mean. The subject doesn't matter. It's what he is, the personality and all that sort of

273

thing. It's something he gives you, inspiration, new ideas, a fresh light on things in general. It's something he makes you want to do or be. I don't remember much American history, but I'll never forget that man Turner, old Freddie Turner."

So I went to the University of Wisconsin clear about one thing — I would take a course with old Freddie Turner. Unfortunately he taught history. The word held no blandishments for me. In high school I had studied (that isn't the word, but what word is there for it?) history, general history, Barnes' *General History,* or some such misdemeanor against youth; of which I remembered only one sentence: "*Egypt has been called the gift of the Nile.*" That alone of all the history of the world I remembered; and even that I hadn't learned the meaning of, hadn't indeed supposed or ever been told that it was expected to have a meaning. A dull subject, history. And yet there I was at the University of Wisconsin determined to take a course in history because, unfortunately, that was the only " subject offered " by old Freddie Turner.

I

I was not many days in Madison before the man was pointed out to me, on the campus, going somewhere in a hurry, loaded down with an immense leather portfolio bulging with books and notes; belatedly hurrying up the hill to class I dare say, probably perspiring but certainly unbowed. Of course he wasn't old — thirty-three or thereabouts at that time. To a youth of eighteen, men of thirty-three, professors at all events, might more often than not *seem* old; were at least likely to convey the im-. pression of having settled all disturbing questions, of hav-

ing as it were astutely encased themselves in a neat armor
of fixed defensive habit warranted proof against the slings
and arrows of whatever unusual experience or risky adventure the mischances of life, within cloistered academic
walls, were likely to threaten them with. No such impression was conveyed by " that man Turner " beating it
up the hill at 10:02 A.M. Even to a boy of eighteen there
was something essentially youthful in the rounded lines of
the short compact figure, in the free and unstudied swing
of arms and legs; something gay and larky about the head
ever so gallantly held, with ever so slight and so engaging
a lifted backward tilt of valiant defiance to all the associated fates; something mischievously boyish even about
the ruddy complexion, above all about the eyes and lips —
eyes and lips that seemed always smiling even in repose, or
always ready to smile, as if the world were so full of a
number of things that odd chances and interesting episodes were to be momentarily expected. Expected and
welcomed. Such was the impression. Serious indeed the
man was, you never doubted that, but not solemn, above
all not old, not professionally finished; just beginning
rather, zestfully and buoyantly beginning, out for adventure, up to something, in the most casual friendly way
inviting you to join in.

Inviting you to join in, yes. I don't mean (God for-
bid!) soliciting students to take his courses. Heaven
knows he didn't need to make sly manœuvers to get you.
Well I remember the opening day of the second year when
I stood in line by his desk, waiting to ask him a question
(totally unnecessary question, invented for the percise purpose of standing there and being spoken to). There I
stood, and presently he turned to me with the quick up-

ward flash of blue eyes that seemed to lift and throw over
and through me a shaft of live light. I seemed, dumb shy
youth that I was, to stand fully revealed in the light of
those extraordinary eyes — cool, steady, challenging, yet
friendly too, and hoping for the best. Haltingly I asked
my foolish question, and was answered. The answer was
nothing, the words were nothing, but the voice — the voice
was everything: a voice not deep but full, rich, vibrant,
and musically cadenced; such a voice as you would never
grow weary of, so warm and intimate and human it was. I
cannot describe the voice. I know only that it laid on me a
kind of magic spell which I could never break, and have
never wanted to. Well, there it was, the indefinable *charm*.
An upward lift of the eyes, a few friendly words, and I, like
I know not how many other lads of nineteen, was straightway a devoted disciple and questionless admirer of " old
Freddie Turner." I didn't care *what* he offered. For him
I would even study history.

Even then I didn't study history. I took courses in history, and in due time I took Turner's " junior course " in
American history. But I didn't study history, not really;
because I didn't know how to study it. Remembering
what things happened at what times — that was what
studying history meant to me then. Learning these things
out of a book. Well, we had a book. To begin with Turner asked us to buy Thwaites' *Colonies,* and I bought it.
I have it yet, with certain dates set down opposite the successive chapters in the table of contents; all these " assign-
ments " having been given us once for all at the beginning
of the term. Simple enough, I thought — each week I
will learn a chapter. But after the second week we were
behind the schedule, and after the fourth week we didn't

know where we were, and never found out. Of course I
read the book — I think I did; was expected to and, being
an obedient boy, must have done so. But the book was
like all history books, dull, filled with uninteresting facts
which I couldn't remember; and so it happened that when
Turner sometimes for ten minutes asked us questions, —
" Mr. Becker, what were the provisions of the Tariff Bill
of 1816? " — I never could answer, or almost never. During the second term I did answer one question, a question
which had just gone its weary round without eliciting any
response. I forget what the question was. The answer was
" 1811." " Precisely," said Turner, in a tone implying
that he now recognized me as of that select company of
scholars who would see at once the peculiar significance
of 1811.

But if I didn't study history that year, I was infected
with the desire to do so. This of course was Turner's
fault, not mine (Haskins' fault too, by the way; and if I
were writing chiefly about myself instead of Turner, which
it may be thought I am doing if I don't watch out, there
would be much to be said about Haskins). For it was
true, as my lawyer friend said, that Turner had a singular capacity for making you want to do and be something
— to do, in short, what he was doing, and to be, if possible,
what he was. And what was he? And what was he doing? Fascinated by the man, I attended to his every gesture and expression, listened to everything he said, less at
first for the content than for the voice, the intention, the
implication. The implication of the whole performance
was of something vital being under consideration, something that had in itself only incidentally to do with students " taking a course." The implication was that we (all

of us together, if *we* chose — that was our affair) were
searching for something, ferreting out hidden secrets.
Facts there were, plenty of them, and as a matter of course
to be known; but that wasn't the end. There was something concealed there, in and behind the facts, some problem that concerned humanity at large waiting to be solved.
The implication was that we might, on our own account,
turn over the dead facts once more, on the chance of finding something, something the others had missed.

Inconceivable that Thwaites had missed anything, I
couldn't suppose it! Yet so it appeared. For here was a
" teacher," who at one moment confessed his ignorance
and the next modestly questioned the textbook. Inviting
us one day to consider the problem of sovereignty, he
quoted Austin's definition; said he couldn't understand it;
admitted he wasn't blessed with the logical mind; and drew
two (or was it three?) overlapping circles on the blackboard illustrating the theory of " divided sovereignty,"
which he said seemed to fit the facts of American history better, but even of that he wasn't certain either.
Well, a " teacher " was supposed to know everything, yet
there was Turner not able to explain sovereignty. Supposed to know everything, a teacher was, but of course
not more than the textbook. Yet there another day stood
Turner saying, as casually as ever you please, " I do not
agree with Thwaites on this point." What to make of a
teacher who knew more than the textbook, but was still
ignorant of something? After I know not how long it
dawned on me, and with what a joyous sense of emancipa-
tion, that Turner wasn't, that no university professor need
be, merely a teacher. Turner obviously hadn't just learned
his history out of a book. The rash sceptic had gone out

of his way to get the "facts" somewhere else, had
"investigated"—that was the word—the documents
on his own account, had taken his own notes from the
"sources," was in short an "authority" in his own right,
and might if he wished write his own book of American
history.

From the moment Turner ceased to figure in my mind
as a teacher, I began to learn something from him. Not
"teacher" but "historian" he was, better still "author,"
whose main occupation it was, not to teach us, but to be
deeply engaged in researches preliminary to the writing
of notable books. Obvious enough, once you got the idea.
For surely no professor, coming somewhat distraitly into
class at the last moment, ever spread about such a cheerful happy air of having been interrupted in preparatory
studies, or ever more successfully conveyed the impression
of going cheerfully on, during the brief hour, for our benefit, with the morning's labors. Material evidence of those
labors there was a plenty in the stacks of notes deposited
on the desk, notes on slips of paper 6 x 8, or some such
size, filed in labeled manilla envelopes; more enveloped
notes every day brought to class than could by any chance
be looked into; as if the preoccupied scholar, leaving his
study on the run, had hastily gathered together whatever
he could conveniently lay his hands on, hoping to be prepared with illustrative material relevant to any one of a
number of interesting topics which might, happily, turn up
during the lecture.

The lecture itself, if that is the word for it, seemed never
"prepared," never studiously "got up" under the lamp.
It seemed rather the spontaneous result of preparations
always going on and never finished. The lecture was just

informal, intimately conversational talk, beginning as
might happen with this interesting matter, and ending as
might happen with that; always serious without ever being solemn; enlivened with humor and wholesome infec-
tious laughter, yet never falling to the level of the sad
professorial joke; running off into relevant digressions oc-
casioned by some student query; coming back again to the
main point; coming now and again to the full stop while
" notes " were eagerly searched for and found (oh, well,
usually found), if not in one manilla envelope perhaps in
another, notes containing some desired quotation from the
documents, with exact reference given, illustrating a point,
clinching an argument. No, lecture isn't the word. Nothing *ex cathedra* here, no musty air of academic infallibil-
ity clouding the room, no laying down of the law and gospel according to Turner; but all compact of inquiry and
novel ideas carelessly thrown out with more questions
asked than were answered, more problems posed than
solved. The professor seemed not at all concerned to ladle
out the minimum dose of American history suitable to our
complaint. He was just talking to us as a man might talk
to men, about the problems that interested *him,* problems
which he had apparently been thinking about after break-
fast, and might very likely, one felt, think some more
about after luncheon.

Such was the impression. But where then did we, poor
dazed novices astray in the bright intellectual world,
come in on this business? No doubt the method, or lack
of it, was not well calculated to send the shining morning-
faced student away rejoicing with neatly wrapped and
labeled packets of " knowledge," to be held until called
for, at examination time, and then duly returned, un-

opened. No doubt the student often felt like asking, as
students will, what precisely the " required work " was —
" Professor, what are we expected to know for examination? " Well, one could trust to luck, would have to apparently. I at least knew that something (something
about the bank was it?) happened in 1811. Curiously
enough I didn't worry, timid and cautious youth that I
was, I didn't worry much about the packets of useful information; for you see I was getting, as failing students
say, "a great deal out of the course." I was getting a
great deal out of Turner. I was daily enjoying the inestimable privilege of watching an original and penetrating intelligence at work, playing freely with facts and
ideas, handling with discrimination the problems of history, problems which so often turned out to be the problems of life itself. Unorganized the course was certainly;
but the resulting impression was nevertheless not one of
confusion. The impression always was that of a brilliant light being thrown on dark places. For the talk,
however desultory it may have been, was never merely
rambling, but went always winding in and through and
round about the matter in hand at the behest of some fresh
idea, suggestion, or tentative hypothesis. Something vital
and significant in the facts these flashed ideas and hypotheses seemed always revealing. An ordered body of information I could get, and did afterwards get, for myself;
but from no other man did I ever get in quite the same
measure that sense of watching a first-class mind at work
on its own account, and not merely rehearsing for the
benefit of others; the most delightful sense in the world
of sitting there waiting for ideas to be born; expectantly
waiting for secret meanings, convenient explanatory hy-

potheses to be discovered, lurking as like as not under the dullest mass of drab facts ever seen.

In this happy way I got a new idea of history. It was after all no convention agreed upon to be learned by rote, but just the infinitely varied action and thought of men who in past times had lived and struggled and died for mean or great objects. It was in short an aspect of life itself, and as such something to be probed into, thought about, written about. Who would not like to study history as Turner studied it? And write about it as he would write about it? Not possible of course to do it with his brilliant competence, not a chance; but still there was something to try for, a standard set, an ideal. And so in this eventful junior year I brought out my tiny little wagon and fumblingly hitched it to that bright particular star. Procuring quantities of paper and manilla envelopes, I began " pen in hand " to study history; with patient, plodding abandon pouring over such fascinating works as *Niles Register* and the *New York Colonial Documents*, or any other mouldy, crumbling old tome, provided only it contained those " original sources " which Turner, by some species of white magic, had invested with color and charm. What a joy it was in those days merely to turn the yellow pages of old books! With what a sense of solid work accomplished one extracted the substance of no matter what official document, always, with reverent piety, noting the " exact reference " — *Niles*, XII, 749. Still preserved they are, those stacks of notes in manilla envelopes, aging now undisturbed on upper shelves, long since covered with dust!

II

With the novitiate ended, one took the full vows. For three years I pursued my researches in Turner's seminary, a group of twelve or fifteen men, with a stray woman or two, meeting in the Law Building, or, better still, in the state Historical Society Library, then housed in the Capitol. Here we did our work, each man having a table, or part of one, in an alcove; and all of us assembling, on Mondays, Wednesdays, and Fridays, round one of the larger tables, with Turner in our midst. To be so commoded was to be in the very centre of the temple of learning; for we were here, all of us, professor and pupils, daily boxed about with walls of books, the books we needed and were currently using, those very collections of " documents " which exhaled the mothy odors of scholarship; so that just to sit motionless in the blest place breathing in the incensed atmosphere of research at its thickest enabled one to anticipate the illusions of the fully erudite.

Informal to a degree this seminary was, more informal even than the " junior course." Lectures there were none, or almost none, unless one prefers to say there were always lectures, or nearly always. For the engaging theory was that we were all scholars together, surveying broadly the field of American history, each man having his particular subject — the colonization of Virginia, Internal Improvements, or whatever — subjects large and unconfined, opening a career to talent. Each man was expected to master his subject as well as might be; to be responsible for it; to be ready like a cabinet minister to answer such questions, bearing upon it, as might be asked by the opposition; above all from time to time to make reports giv-

ing the matured results of his investigation. In this way
each of us, including the professor, would lecture in turn,
and all of the others, including the professor, would take
notes. The professor, such was the theory, was just one
of us, the principal one no doubt, organizing and directing the whole performance, but still not professing to
know too much, modestly deferring to any one of us where
our particular topics were concerned, and himself taking
notes, when we lectured, with an alert and convincing air
of being instructed, of having old matter freshly examined
and interpreted for him. I swear he did take notes, and
he has since assured me, with just a trace of asperity I
thought, that it was no frame-up, but that he did actually
obtain from us valuable ideas and information which afterwards he sometimes made good use of. Well, I believe
him. I do believe he did sometimes get from us some or
other odd fact, such was his inordinate thirst for facts
and his uncanny instinct for finding them in the most unlikely places, such his skill in disengaging what was significant from even the most confused jumble of the incom-
petent, the irrelevant, and the immaterial.

I took notes too, of course I did. It was part of the rit-
ual, and I was nothing if not strong in the faith — in those
old days. The notes I took are not such, I do confess,
that one could reconstruct from them an adequate account
of American history; but they had, and have had, for me
at least a high value nevertheless. Here before me, for
example, are the notes, easily contained on one sheet of
paper 6 x 8, of a two-days' report on the Mexican War.

Rogers' report — Mexican War. Polk. Taylor. Senate
Bill. Biglow Papers frequently referred to. Turner asks:
" By the way, Mr. Rogers, what exactly are the Biglow Pa-

pers? " Rogers says: " The Biglow Papers — " (Hesitates, seems a little dazed, has at last a happy inspiration) " Why, the Biglow Papers are — a well known work by — a famous author." Hilarious laughter, led by Turner, who then explains Biglow Papers. Don't myself know **B. P.** Remember look up and read B. P. Lowell, J. R.

Thus to my great regret I missed the significant points of the Mexican War, but at least I read the Biglow Papers, and have always remembered that the work is well known and by a famous author. Another sheet lies before me.

Turner asks, why the unusual literary activity in generation following 1815? Various suggestions. Becker says perhaps on account of feeling of relief and freedom after War of 1812 and Napoleonic wars. Turner says, perhaps. Is that a fact or only a plausible inference? What is an historical fact? Can you prove an inference? May historian be satisfied with inference? Have all great wars been followed by intellectual and literary activity? What in general is cause of changes in character of thought? Fifteen minute talk, mostly questions, a cascade of questions. No one answers these questions. Why doesn't Turner tell us the answers? Something to think about.

Something to think about, sure enough! Well, I have thought about it, off and on, for twenty-five years; but I don't now wonder why Turner didn't tell us the answers.

As time passed I was made aware indeed that Turner very often didn't answer questions. Heaven knows he asked enough, was always handing out some riddle to be solved, always giving us something to think about and then serenely leaving us to think about it. But there were questions he neglected either to ask or to answer. For example, did the colonies or the British government have the right of it in the War of Independence? Should one properly sympathize with Jefferson or Marshall? Was the tariff a wise policy? Was Jacksonian democracy a good or a bad thing? Were the slave states justified in seceding from the Union? Important questions these were surely; questions which a teacher who had given his life to the study of American history might be supposed to answer for students who came to college expecting to be furnished with right opinions and convictions. But I don't recall that Turner ever answered these questions, or the like of them; so that to this day I don't know what his convictions are on the great issues. Is he protectionist or freetrader? Democrat or republican? Baptist or infidel, or member of that great church which Lord Melbourne commended for never meddling with either politics or religion? Above all is he a conservative, satisfied with the evils we have? Or a liberal, willing to substitute for them others which formerly existed? Or a radical, eager for the shock of new ones never yet tried? I don't know. Turner never gave us answers to these questions. He never told us what to think.

I hope I am not conveying the impression that Turner appeared to his students in the somber light of a "strong silent man." Somber is the last word in the world to describe him, and silent isn't the word either. He talked freely enough, and he answered questions freely enough, questions of a certain sort. After I don't know how many months or years I learned that the answers he commonly neglected to give were answers which would have enabled me to borrow his opinions and judgments, and so save myself the trouble of thinking. He would do what he could to help me think, but he wouldn't if he knew it tell me what to think. He was not much given to handing down final judgments.

This is important, and I wish to emphasize it a little. Turner didn't pronounce final judgments. In those days it sometimes troubled me that he didn't. But I have long since forgiven him, blessed him indeed, for it, having seen quite enough of those complacent people who go about recreating the world in their own image and expecting others to see that it is good. Turner might have said, with Mr. Justice Holmes, that one important article of his creed as a scholar was that he was *not* God. Like Margaret Fuller, he " accepted the universe," although, unlike that voluble lady, he did it silently. I am speaking now of Turner the scholar, not of Turner the man and citizen. As man and citizen he had, and always has had, convictions, knows what he thinks right and wise, and never leaves you in any doubt about it. As man and citizen he doesn't, I am sure, think this the best of conceivable worlds, or always find it a comfortable place to be in, as what intelligent or sensitive person does? He has indeed always met the reverses of life with serenity and high courage, no man I think ever more so; but I know not how many times he may in his heart have refreshingly damned the universe to extinction, as, on occasion, all good men do I hope. But I am now concerned with the scholar. As scholar, so it seems to me, Turner accepts men and things as given, the business of the scholar being not to *judge* but only to *understand* them.

To me at least it is a matter of no slight importance that he accepted us, graduate students, in that spirit. We, too, were apparently parts of the universe, to be accepted as given. He never made me feel that I was before the Judgment Seat. He was never the schoolmaster, standing behind me prodding, with sharp exclamation points pitchforking me up the steep path of learning. He criticized my work to be sure, but it was the work he criticized, and in the most honest friendly way, without leaving any after-taste of personal depravity in the mouth. He appeared to take me as the associated fates had made me, more or less intelligent, and to assume that I would willingly do the best I could. Amazing, to me at least, was the casual friendly way he had of treating us as equals, as serious scholars with whom it was a pleasure to be associated in common tasks. Even our work he didn't criticize much, condemning it by silence mainly, commending it on rare occasions by a few hearty words of approval. How the rash man gambled on us to be sure, professing to see in us qualities and virtues marking us out for future *savants*. Perhaps there was some method in this madness. To get the best out of graduate students, or any students, it is perhaps just as well not to assume to begin with that there isn't any best there to be got out. Often enough there isn't, but then it doesn't greatly matter. If there was any best in me, I at least needed, in order to get it out, just the freedom and friendly confidence which Turner gave me, having until then been for the most part " criticized " and " trained " quite sufficiently; oh quite sufficiently told, by parents and uncles and aunts and teachers and pastors, what to do and what not to do; told in such an interesting variety of ways, and with such an implication of futility in the telling, as to leave me clutching the miserable little suspicion that I would probably never, all things considered, be much good at doing anything. Never having talked with my pastor, Turner didn't know this. He blandly assumed that I might amount to something, and at last one day told me that he thought I " had it in me " to become a scholar and

a writer — seemed really to believe it. To be told by this
admired master that I could probably do the very thing
I most wanted to do released what little ability I had to do
it. Released the ability, and intensified the desire to do it,
because I then, and ever after, worked all the harder in
order to justify Turner's faith in me.

This friendly method of dealing with graduate students
(the honest ones, I mean; the occasional fakir got the full
blaze of his hot scorn) might not have been the best
method for another, but I am sure it was the best method
for Turner. It was the best method precisely because
there wasn't any method in it. When Turner came into
class he didn't put on the teacher's manner because he
didn't think of himself as a teacher. He thought of himself — or no, he didn't think of himself, that's just the
point. He was just Turner, man and scholar, absorbed in
his work, who met us because we were interested in the
same thing he was; and who met us in the most casual
democratic way in the world because it was perfectly natural for him to meet us in that way. The easy aristocratic
grace and charm of this friendly democrat from Portage,
Wisconsin, had about it neither a shade more nor less of
any manner for his high placed colleagues than for the
obscurest graduate student. It didn't, this unstudied
friendly manner which at once put us at ease, seem to be
even second nature. It seemed to be the instinctive expression of a lively and supple intelligence restrained and
directed by some inexhaustible native fund of sincerity,
integrity, and good will. This is after all one of the reasons, perhaps the chief reason, for his success with graduate students.

It is also, I think, one principal secret of his success as

a scholar. For the scholar, the historian at all events, has to meet humanity in some fashion or other; and humanity will commonly reveal little to those who meet it with reticences and reservations and didactic motives. Even in those student days it seemed to me that Turner met humanity very much as he met us, graduate students; he didn't put on anything special for the occasion. Humanity, like graduate students, doubtless had virtues and qualities concealed somewhere about it, and might very well, such was the implication, stumble on, if you gave it rope enough, to some or other place worth going to. Best at all events to assume as much; for humanity is like graduate students in this too, that it will be more likely to do well if you trust it a little, if you have faith to gamble on its hidden capacities.

But who could tell us where poor old humanity is headed for, rope or no rope? I would not willingly charge a reputable historian with harboring a Philosophy of History. Yet I recall that one day Turner quoted Droysen, apparently with approval, to the effect that " history is the self-consciousness of humanity." And another day he said: " The question is not whether you have a Philosophy of History, but whether the philosophy you have is good for anything." In extenuation I feel moved to say that if Turner does indeed have a Philosophy of History, I can't imagine it taking the form of an answer. Much more likely to take the form of a question, thus: " If mankind could once really understand what it has done and thought in the past, is it not possible that it would stumble along now, and in the future, with more intelligence and a more conscious purpose? " I don't know whether this is a Philosophy of History or not. Whether, if it is, it is a good one, I know still less. But of one thing I feel quite sure: if Turner subscribes to it, whatever it is, it doesn't cost him much. It doesn't cost him anything in fact, for it doesn't burden him with any noticeable preoccupations or fixed ideas. He pursues his proper task, which is to find out what certain groups of men did and thought in past times, and to furnish the proximate explanation of their so acting and thinking; and this task he pursues as if he had no philosophy, as if it made no difference at all to him what they did and thought, or what the explanation might turn out to be. He pursues his task in short with detachment, with objectivity.

So at last we come to it, the inevitable word, objectivity. The word has many meanings. In those days I had myself got, or at least got up, chiefly out of books, a notion of objectivity scarcely distinguishable from complete indifference, a sort of stiff solemnity or *rigor mortis* of the spirit; so that I sometimes wondered if Turner really was " objective and disinterested," so lively and interested he always seemed. Certainly indifference, such as Renan's Man in the Moon might be supposed to exhibit, couldn't by any stretch of the imagination be attributed to Turner. Here then was a dilemma; and not being willing to abandon either Turner or the ideal of objectivity, I ended by seeing that Turner was objective in some other fashion than the Man in the Moon. The objectivity of Turner's mind, I found, was a quality he enjoyed in his own right, and not something acquired by training. It wasn't something he had painfully got up in college out of Bernheim — a set of artificially induced and cultivated repressions such as would enable any careful historian to write, let us say, an account of the Battle of Cold Harbor without revealing the fact that his father was an ardent admirer of Grant. That kind of objectivity is common enough, and often pernicious enough, being the best substitute for ideas yet invented. Turner at least didn't need it, having always more ideas than he could perhaps well manage. The objectivity he had seemed rather to spring from that intense and sustained interest which an abundance of ideas can alone generate. A hard truth for me to learn, this was, since I hadn't too many ideas; but I couldn't help seeing that Turner was so wholly absorbed in his work that he hadn't time to think of anything else, not even of the necessity of being objective. He was " disinterested " because he was so interested in the object before him that he forgot, for the time being, to be interested in anything else; he was " objective " because he was so genuinely curious about that object, desired with such singleness of purpose to know it for the sake of knowing it, that his mind was empty, for the time being, of all other objects. This kind of objectivity doesn't come by willing (not that any sane man, living in a world of action, would will to have it); it is a quality of mind, like the sense of absolute pitch, which one is or isn't born with. No doubt it may, if one has it, be cultivated, but at any rate it is inseparable from genuine *intellectual curiosity,* the lively and irrepressible desire to know merely for the sake of knowing. A rare quality indeed that is, but I think Turner has it.

Another thing about Turner used in those days to strike me as a little odd. I don't know just what to call it. " Independence " isn't quite the word. Of course he was an independent scholar; but then most professors were independent scholars in the ordinary sense of the term. His was a peculiar kind of independence which struck me then, and still strikes me, as relatively uncommon among professors. I might call it a certain obliviousness to professorial convention, an almost complete freedom from academic provincialism. I first noticed it indeed because it seemed to me then not quite the thing. For I was then doing what many college boys do — emancipating myself from one form of provincialism by taking on another. Coming fresh, or almost fresh, from the farm into an academic community, the professor's world seemed to me the last word in sophistication. The most obvious form which this sophistication took was a certain smart awareness on the professor's part of belonging to a larger and freer society than the one in which, geographically speaking, he perforce lived. Comfortable enough his ivory tower in Madison was no doubt; but he was likely to be often looking out of it towards the more splendid towers of the east, overanxiously concerned perhaps to know what the wise men there were thinking and doing. One gathered that there were decencies proper to the academic world, a minor one being that no professor should have too much confidence in himself until he received a call from Yale or Harvard, and even then a lively sense of the fitting, some hang over from colonial days perhaps, would keep him subtly servile and apologetic for being no more than an American scholar who must forever abandon hope of entering the sacred portals of Oxford, Paris, or Berlin. If all this was only a second provincialism worse than the first, I was not yet aware of the fact. It seemed to me then no more than the proper mark of those who had oriented themselves in the intellectual world, quite the attitude in short for a professor to have. Therefore it struck me as a little odd that my admired master Turner didn't have it.

For Turner didn't have it. There was no getting round the fact that he didn't have it at all. I got the distinct impression that he didn't mind living in Wisconsin, seemed to think Portage a jolly good place to come from, as if being born there, even if the fact became known, needn't seriously impair the quality of his scholarship. If he knew that Europe was infinitely richer than the United States in historic remains and traditions, I never heard him mention the fact, at least not with the appropriate air of regret for missed opportunities. He had, on the contrary, every appearance of being contented with his opportunities, seemed indeed to rejoice in his opportunities, quite as a man might who had just discovered a gold mine in his back yard. American history, he seemed to say, is a new lead, never yet properly uncovered, as rich and enticing a mine for the scholar as can anywhere be found, all the better for never having been worked by Waitz or von Ranke. It was as if some rank American flavor, some sturdy strain of backwoods independence, resisting every process of academic refinement, kept the man still proud to be an American citizen, contentedly dwelling in Madison, quite satisfied with the privilege of going every day to the State Historical Society Library where the Draper Manuscripts were.

Even in those days I felt, without quite understanding, this non-professorial attitude on Turner's part. The time was to come when I found the professorial attitude less engaging; and it was probably just because I saw Turner as " different " that these old student day impressions never faded, just because he was never quite the " professor " that his influence was more enduring than that of many professors. His influence was enduring I think because he himself didn't " date." Above all his ideas about American history didn't date, never struck one as being modeled upon any established authority or cribbed from any school of historians. Something personal there always was in his " point of view," in his " interpretations," as if the subject were being freshly looked at by a mind washed clean of scholastic dust. Not that there was anything aggressive about his independence. He never gave one the impression that, having made up his mind to be original, he was somewhat bellicosely making good. His independence wasn't an achievement. And yet I wonder. Was there not about him too (or did I just imagine it?) some indefinable but quite jolly air of conscious insubordination, just a quick little gesture of the mind impatiently dismissing the solemn snobbery of all that is academically canonized and sacrosanct? I can't be sure, but I like to think so.

That is as it may be. But this I know, that three qualities of the man's mind made upon me a profound and indelible impression. These qualities were: a lively and irrepressible intellectual curiosity; a refreshing freedom from personal preoccupations and didactic motives; a quite unusual ability to look out upon the wide world in a humane friendly way, in a fresh and strictly independent way, with a vision unobscured by academic inhibitions. These are also the qualities, I think, which have enabled him to make an " original contribution " (not so common a performance as is often supposed) to the study of American history. What then is this original contribution?

III

A distinct achievement, I count it, to have written twenty pages about Turner without having once mentioned the word " frontier." But of course this sort of thing can't be allowed to go on indefinitely. Impossible to tell the story of Turner without mentioning the frontier — as impossible as it would be to tell the story of Jack Horner without mentioning the plum. The " frontier " was a plum, sure enough; but still there is the pie, and the pie is important too, a fact often forgotten. Therefore I wish first of all to say something about the pie, in the hope that it will help us to understand how the plum came to be discovered and pulled out.

The pie of this sad metaphor (very sad metaphor indeed if it leads any one to picture Turner sitting in a corner bragging of his plum) is of course American history, or rather American history considered as an example of social evolution.

I have no desire to make Turner out a sociologist; but it must be said that narrating events was never his forte, finding proximate explanations always has been. In his first published work he raised straight off the question which has occupied him ever since. " The exploitation of the Indian is generally dismissed with the convenient explanatory phrase, ' The march of civilization.' But *how did it march?* " [1] Well, there it is, the central question of all Turner's work: How does civilization march? Not how did civilization march from January to November, but how did and does it march from simple to complex forms?

---

[1] " The Fur Trade in Wisconsin." *Proceedings of the State Historical Society of Wisconsin.* 1889. p. 53.

This is no doubt a question proper to the sociologist; and the pure sociologist, if there be any such, might attempt an answer based on the total experience of mankind up to date. What saves Turner for history, if he can be saved, is that he attempts no universal answer. It is not given to all, as he modestly says, to " bend the bow of Ulysses." He will attempt only a conditioned answer, since he deals only with a limited experience — the experience of the American people within definite space and time limits; and so, if he is concerned with the evolution of society, it is after all the evolution of a particular society. He studies American history as furnishing a concrete illustration, many times repeated, and on a relatively grand scale, of the social process.

If Turner still lies under suspicion, one thing I will stoutly affirm in his defence; the social process which entices him is not the Transcendent Idea, or any of its many poor relations. His social process isn't something in the void working over the heads of men, rough hewing them to its own ends. His social process is something that emerges from the thought and action of men, something incidental to what people do for their own ends. It wasn't the " march of civilization " that chased the Indian, nor did the poor fellow die of deficient " cultural capacity." The poor fellow died of bullets fired from rifles in the hands of Daniel Boone, and men of his ilk; men who fired the bullets, not on behalf of civilization or the social process, but on their own behalf, because they wanted land for hunting purposes or for planting, in order to feed themselves and their families and have as good a time generally as circumstances permitted. Turner seems to take it for granted that common place people, acting in common place ways, somehow or other, unconsciously for the most part, determine the social process and shape the course of history. First of all, therefore, the historian would learn what people did and why they did it.

What people did was an old story with historians, why they did it had doubtless never occupied their thought unduly. This is of course an endless question forever discussed by philosophers; and one might easily push the explanation of action back to ultimate causes — to God, or to the electron revolving rapidly round the nucleus, or, more simply, to a " stress in the ether." But such ultimates are of little use to the historian. They exhaust their virtue in explaining everything in general, so that none is left for explaining anything in particular. This is perhaps why Turner, being especially interested in the particular, is willing to leave final causes to serve the only uses they can serve, to be, that is to say, *final*, sign posts at the end of the road signifying " no thoroughfare." The explanations he seeks are proximate explanations, the causes he can make use of are causes operating above and immediately below the level of conscious purpose.

If, for example, the first settlers in New England established the " Town Meeting " that was doubtless because they consciously desired to establish it. But still one may reasonably ask what made them consciously desire to establish the Town Meeting? Perhaps it was an institution which they had, without knowing it, " brought over with them " from England, an institution which they had, in common with Englishmen and Teutonic folk generally, " inherited " from farther back, from the primitive Germans or elsewhere. Why didn't Turner accept this explanation? One naturally asks because the genetic ex-

planation of institutions was going strong at Johns
Hopkins when Turner studied there in the eighties; and
Herbert B. Adams, the teacher under whom Turner
studied, had himself published a monograph pointing out
that the New England Town Meeting was a survival from
early German custom. Turner must have been thoroughly
indoctrinated into the theory of the " continuity of history " and the " inheritance of institutions," must have
been given a full adult dose of that prolific institutional
germ known as the Teutonic Mark. Well, it was an over-
dose, I dare say. Turner couldn't stomach it. Still less
to his taste was Adams' dictum that American institutions
had already been " well done." This was really too much
for the doughty American whose ancestors had preached
and pioneered on every frontier from Massachusetts to
Nebraska. He therefore left Johns Hopkins in an unsanc-
tified state, and returned to Wisconsin proclaiming that
" the germ theory of politics has been sufficiently emphasized." [2]

Not that Turner would deny the influence of inheritance. The first settlers obviously brought with them their
English, or Dutch, habits of thought and action. These
would at first determine what institutions they would try
to establish in the new world; and no doubt it would be
possible to point out, in the Virginia Hundred or the New
England Town Meeting, vestiges of early custom, similarities to the ancient German Mark (or what Nineteenth
Century German historians, looking for political liberty
somewhere outside of France, imagined the German
Mark to be). But Turner would insist (and how clearly

[2] " Significance of the Frontier " ; *The Frontier in American History*, p. 2.

I recall his making the statement in class one day!) that
" the *similarities* of institutions are less important than the
differences." If the differences interested him more than
the similarities, the reason, I dare say, is to be found in the
man's deep-seated loyalty to America. If he has any
fundamental preconception or bias it is this. He is a thoroughly good American with never the slightest gesture of
apology. He has the rugged patriotism, seven times refined no doubt, of the middle west from which he comes.
It was this deep-seated loyalty to America that made him
" indignant " when Adams said that American institutions
had been " well done." On the contrary, Turner thought,
they had not been done at all, not really; for America was
important, not because it resembled Europe, but precisely
because it was different. He would approve down to the
ground Goethe's saying that " America has the best of it."
America has the best of it not only, and not chiefly, because
of her incomparable material resources, but because she
has brought into the world something new, something original — " the ideal of a democracy developing under conditions unlike those of any other age or country." [3] This
was what made American institutions really significant and
worth studying — this " difference." Well, you could
hardly inherit a difference. Where then did the difference
come from? Certainly not from the German Mark. Not
from the Black Forest but from the American wilderness.
American democracy " was not carried in the *Susan Constant* to Virginia, or in the *Mayflower* to Plymouth. It
came out of the American forest." [4] So Turner turned
away from the theory of inheritance as an adequate ex-

---

[3] *The Frontier in American History*, p. 335.
[4] *The Frontier in American History*, p. 293.

planation of American institutions, and set himself to study the influences of the environment. Here if at all would be found the "conditions" — geographic, economic, social — which enabled America to make its peculiar contribution to human civilization.

As a point of vantage from which to observe the influence of environment in a new country, the town of Portage was after all no bad place to be born in. With his father, the boy Turner had poled in dugouts, with Indians from "Grandfather Bull Falls" as guides, on Radisson's old route down the Wisconsin, through virgin forests of balsam firs, startling the deer that came to gaze at them through the foliage with curious frightened eyes, past Indian villages where the polesmen would sometimes stop to palaver with the Squaws standing sociably on the high bank. In Portage, coming home from school, he had seen a lynched man hanging from a tree. He had seen red-shirted Irish raftsmen tie up and "take the town," and blanketed Indians on their ponies file down the street to exchange furs for baubles and paint. The town itself was a rough frontier settlement — the meeting place of many nationalities. It had its Irish ward into which boys of Turner's sort ventured, with whatever tense bravado they could muster, only in gangs; its Pomeranian ward where kerchiefed women in wooden shoes still drove community cattle to common pasture; and, in the country round about, there were Scotch, Welsh and Swiss settlements. What doubtless helped to make vivid the significance of such folk was the fact that Turner's father, the editor of a local paper, was a politician of sorts, who "sheparded all these new people," lectured them in his editorials on farming and politics, and was wonderfully trusted and followed

by them. Here it was then, before his very eyes, the past
and present curiously joined together; the frontier in many
stages — virgin forest, Indian villages, lawless raftsmen,
fur trade, the rough frontier town a simmering pot skillfully stirred by the descendant of Connecticut Yankees
who, in every generation since the seventeenth century,
had got on the " wrong side of the hedge." Here it was to
be observed by one who had eyes to see, the very process
which had been making America, such as it was, so different from Europe — and, for that matter, why shouldn't
it be?

This youthful experience Turner didn't put aside in
some unused garret of the mind when, at the university, he
came to study history. The past seemed to him a dead
thing except as he could see it still living in the present.
Tenuous and vanishing vestiges of ancient custom interested him but little, so that when his teacher, William F.
Allen, suggested that he look into the faint remaining evidences of common lands in the region round about Prairie
du Chien, he soon found that he " couldn't get very far
with that." He didn't get any where with it in fact, but
presently turned up, in his rakish independent way, with
an essay on " The Fur Trade in Wisconsin." [5] This fresh
topic, redolent of Indians and balsam trees, he took with
him to Johns Hopkins, afterwards presenting it there, with
revision and enlargement, as a doctor's thesis. In due
time it was published under a new title in the Johns Hopkins Studies,[6] where it may still be seen curiously hobnobbing with sedater monographs on local government and

[5] *Proceedings of the State Historical Society of Wisconsin,* 1889.
[6] " The Character and Influence of the Indian Trade in Wisconsin " : *Johns Hopkins University Studies,* 1891.

comparative institutions. In this essay one may find, dimly suggested, the ideas, or some of them, which shortly after were presented in the now famous paper, " The Significance of the Frontier in American History." [7]

The significance of the frontier in American history was just this, that America was itself the frontier, the march lands of western civilization, the meeting place of old and new, the place in the world where one could still observe the civilized man adjusting his habits to the rude conditions of life in a primitive environment. From the civilized man the frontier " strips off the garments of civilization and arrays him in the hunting shirt and the moccasin." It drags him out of his coach-and-four and throws him into a birch-bark canoe, deprives him of his panelled halls and gives him a log cabin. A rude shock this to the civilized man, who finds that his traditional habits and ideas serve him but inadequately in the new world; and so, the environment proving at first too strong for the man, he temporarily reverts to the primitive, to something half savage. But little by little he masters his environment, by ingenious devices fashions rude comforts, falls into a rough routine of life, imposes crude laws and a ready-made justice, snatches at such amusements and amenities as are to be had for the taking — in short, painfully builds up once

[7] The essential ideas of this paper were first presented in an article ("The Problems of American History ") written for the student periodical, *The Aegis*, November 4, 1892. In its present form it was read before the American Historical Association at its meeting in Chicago, July 12, 1893. First printed in *Proceedings of the State Historical Society of Wisconsin*, December 14, 1893, and again in *Report of the American Historical Association*, 1893. Similar ideas were set forth by Woodrow Wilson in his review (*Forum*, December, 1893) of Goldwin Smith's *History of the United States*. But Turner had, in his house at Madison, read his paper to Wilson before the latter wrote his review.

more a " civilization," a civilization all compact of memories and experience. The memories are old, but the experience is new. And the experience modifies the tradition,
so that in the end the " outcome is not the old Europe, not
simply the development of Germanic germs. . . . The
fact is that here is a new product that is America." [8]

Here then was a fresh field for the historian. Not that
American history had more importance than European,
but certainly it had not less importance. The point was
that it had a *peculiar* importance, and this peculiar importance was that it presented an unrivalled opportunity
for studying the general in the particular. " Loria, the
Italian economist, has urged the study of colonial life as
an aid to understanding the stages of European development. . . . ' America,' he says, ' has the key to the historical enigma which Europe has sought for in vain, and
the land which has no history reveals luminously the
course of universal history.' There is much truth in this.
The United States lies like a huge page in the history of
society. Line by line as we read this continental page
from west to east we find the record of social evolution." [9]
Complex it was, this social evolution, because of the vast
extent of the country. " All peoples show development.
. . . In the case of most nations, however, the development has occurred in a limited area. . . . But in the case
of the United States we have a different phenomenon.
Limiting ourselves to the Atlantic coast we have the familiar phenomenon of the evolution of institutions in a
limited area, such as the rise of representative govern-

[8] " The Significance of the Frontier ": *The Frontier in American
History*, p. 4.
[9] *The Frontier in American History*, p. 11.

ment; the differentiation of simple colonial governments
into complex organs, progress from primitive conditions of
society, without division of labor, up to manufacturing
civilization. But we have in addition to this a recurrence
of the process of evolution in each western area reached
in the process of expansion. Thus American development
has exhibited not merely advance along a single line, but a
return to primitive conditions on a continually advancing
frontier line, and a new development for that area. American social development has been continually beginning
over again on the frontier. This perennial rebirth, this
fluidity of American life, this expansion westward with its
new opportunities, its continuous touch with the simplicity of primitive society, furnish the forces dominating
American character." [10]

All this might mean but little to those for whom "history is past politics." But those who wished to look behind institutions might find much in it. A quite unrivalled
opportunity they would find, in this perennial rebirth on
different frontiers, for studying the evolution of a society
from simple to complex forms under conditions generally
similar but differing in point of detail; an unparalleled
opportunity to note the interaction of all the " influences "
(geographic, economic, social, and whatever others might
be found) that shape the thought and action of men. Regarding history in this novel way, the historian would of
necessity be less concerned with the " what " than with the
" how," less with the result than with the process; less
concerned with chronicle, the narrating of events from decade to decade, than with the description and comparison
of regional and sectional societies, and with the complex

[10] *The Frontier in American History*, pp. 2, 3.

of influences creating, in each of these regional societies, certain economic interests and political activities. Chronology, being treated with scant respect, would inevitably lose something of its commanding position and high repute, since the historian would be continually throwing past and present, as warp and woof, back and forth to make the woven fabric of a living civilization. " Continuity " there would be, certainly so, but the continuity would be found, not in the sequence of little event following on little event, but in the persistence of certain general conditions, in the recurrence of certain psychological reactions determined by the conditions, above all perhaps in the emergence (the evolution if you like), out of the interaction and conflict of regional societies ranging from the relatively primitive to the relatively complex, of a distinctively American society with its peculiar traditions and ideals.

Regarded thus, not as a sequence of events, but as a social evolution, American history up to the present could be regarded as a single phase of universal history; could be regarded as the history of the frontier, which is not so much a region as a process. " The West, at bottom, is a state of society rather than an area. It is the term applied to the region whose social conditions result from the application of older institutions and ideas to the transforming influence of free land." [11] Up to the present, or the very recent past, it is above all the abundance of free land, underlying and equalizing the diverse influences of regional geography, that has made America a frontier society, that has made possible the " perennial rebirth," that has kept society always in touch with the primitive. These are the

[11] *The Frontier in American History*, p. 205.

conditions that explain the essential traits of American character — " that coarseness and strength combined with acuteness and inquisitiveness; that practical, inventive turn of mind, quick to find expedients; that masterful grasp of material things, lacking in the artistic but powerful to effect great ends; that restless, nervous energy; that dominant individualism, working for good and for evil, and withal that buoyancy and exuberance which come with freedom." [12] And these also are the conditions that explain American institutions, American " democracy " — the questionless faith in " liberty " and " equality " and the right and the capacity of the people to govern themselves; not by the " glorious constitution " are these ideals to be explained, but by the conditions peculiar to our situation — our situation on the frontier of western civilization. " The larger part of what has been distinctive and valuable in America's contribution to the history of the human spirit has been due to this nation's peculiar experience in extending its type of frontier into new regions; and in creating peaceful societies with new ideals in the successive vast and differing geographic provinces which together make up the United States." [13]

This first phase, the phase of the frontier, is obviously passing. For a quarter of a century now there has been, relatively speaking, no free land. Westward expansion has ceased, and with it the " perennial rebirth," the continual return to primitive conditions. The country becomes increasingly urban, increasingly industrial. Classes tend to become fixed. Parties show signs of dividing on economic and social issues. Accumulated capital, seeking

[12] *The Frontier in American History*, p. 37.
[13] Preface to *The Frontier in American History*.

investment throughout the world, proves more powerful than senatorial oratory, and the old isolation gives way to imperial entanglements and conflicts. The United States is ceasing to be a country on the frontier of European civilization in which the cardinal fact is the steady expansion of population into the unoccupied areas of free land. It too is now becoming " old," " eastern," a settled community, a federation of sections, varying greatly in point of geographic and economic conditions, but approaching uniformity in point of social evolution.[14]

The first phase is passing; and Turner, always occupied primarily with the present, and with the past as illuminating the present, has in recent years turned his attention to the fascinating problem of the United States as a federation of sections. In two of his most brilliant essays [15] he has developed this idea. Underlying the formal federation of states, he points out, is the real federation of great geographic and economic areas, each one comparable, in extent and variety, to the most important of the European nations; so that the problems of American political history are in a measure comparable to those of European history. There are striking differences surely. We have not the racial and religious antagonisms of Europe. We lie less uneasy under the heavy weight of tradition. Nevertheless the great sections of our country have their deep-seated

[14] In his presidential address before the Historical Association in 1910, Turner took occasion to emphasize the passing of the first phase of American history, and to suggest ways in which present problems might be illuminated by a study of the past. " Social Forces in 1911 " ; *American Historical Review*, January, 1911. Reprinted in *The Frontier in American History*, p. 311.

[15] " Sections and Nation "; *Yale Review*, Oct. 1922. " The Significance of the Section in American History " ; *Wisconsin Magazine of History*, March, 1925.

differences of interest, they have their differences of temperament and ideals. Their antagonisms are such that, if fortune had separated them into independent states, they would, like the European nations, be engaged in a new world struggle for the balance of power. Happily we have a federal government which holds us together in a league of sections; so that while the European nations employ diplomatic negotiations, conference, and war for the settlement of their conflicts, the American sections manage to get on amicably by peaceful bargains and compromises legally negotiated through the national party system and the Federal government.

And what of the future, since the first phase is passing? Since the peculiar conditions under which American institutions have hitherto developed no longer exist, what is to be the fate of American " democracy," of American " ideals," such as we have known them? " Can these ideals of democracy and individualism be applied and reconciled to the twentieth century type of civilization? " [16] It is Turner himself who asks this question, and it is perhaps with a certain note of apprehension that he asks it. In recent addresses he has asked it repeatedly, and, one feels, with a somewhat diminished zest and optimism. The answer would seem to be obvious. If American institutions and ideals, such as we have known them, have been the result of primitive frontier conditions, it would seem that they must, with the passing of those conditions, be transformed into something different — perhaps into something altogether different. At least this is so unless there is more efficacy in the " inheritance " of institutions and ideals than Turner has led us to suppose.

[16] *The Frontier in American History*, p. 203.

Turner the scholar sees that this is so; but Turner the frontier democrat from Portage, Wisconsin, addressing students at commencement time, and wishing (rightly enough!) to say something appropriately hopeful for the occasion, regrets it — I was about to say, for the moment seems almost to forget it. But no, that cannot be, since it is precisely Turner's contribution to the study of American history that makes it impossible to forget it. For his contribution, from the point of view of a general interpretation, is just this, that American institutions and ideals are the result of a primitive, and therefore surely a passing stage of social evolution.

IV

Turner's contribution to history and the social sciences has been set forth in monographic studies, essays, occasional addresses, and the volume which he contributed to the American Nation Series.[17] In addition, so he as-

[17] The following list is, aside from book reviews and newspaper articles, all of Turner's writings, unless I have missed something. Those who have thought of Turner as exclusively occupied with the "frontier" or the "West," should note the important contributions he has made to diplomatic history.

(1) "The Character and Influence of the Fur Trade in Wisconsin"; *Proceedings of the State Historical Society of Wisconsin*, 1889. (2) "The Problems of American History"; *The Aegis*, 1892. (3) "The Character and Influence of the Indian Trade in Wisconsin"; *John Hopkins University Studies*, 1891. (A revision of No. 1). (4) "The Rise and Fall of New France"; *Chautauquan*, XXIV, 31, 295. (5) "The Significance of the Frontier in American History"; *Proc. State Hist. Soc. Wisc.*, 1893. (A revision and enlargement of No. 2.). (6) "Western State Making in the Revolutionary Era"; *American Historical Review*, Oct.-Jan., 1895–1896. (7) "The Problem of the West"; *Atlantic Monthly*, 1896. (8) "The West as a Field for Historical Study"; *American Historical Association Reports*, 1896. (9) "Correspondence of Clark and

sures me, he is now " finishing up a book on the period
1830–1850," a book in which he endeavors " to sketch
the characteristics and development of the leading sections during those decades, and briefly to indicate . . .
the intersectional aspect of political history." Even
with this book completed, Turner's collected works will
not fill much space, would doubtless leave much of a
five-foot shelf open to the collection of dust; and many
devoted, if not always discriminating, disciples and publishers have grown gray expectantly waiting for the " great
work " which does not appear. Seven volumes at the very
least they seem to demand, stately leather-backed tomes

Genet "; *Ibid.*, 1896. (10) " Dominant Forces in American Life ";
Atlantic Monthly, 1897. (11) " Margourit Correspondence in Re-
spect to Genet's Projected Attack "; *Am. Hist. Assoc. Rep.*, 1897.
(12) " Diplomatic Contest for the Mississippi Valley "; *Atlantic
Monthly*, 1898. (13) " Documents on the Relation of France to
Louisiana "; *Am. Hist. Rev.*, April, 1898. (14) " Origin of Genet's
Projected Attack on Louisiana and the Floridas "; *Ibid.*, July, 1898.
(15) " The Middle West "; *International Monthly*, Dec., 1901. (16)
" English Policy towards America in 1790–1791 "; *Am. Hist. Rev.*,
July-Oct., 1902. (17) " Contributions of the West to American
Democracy "; *Atlantic Monthly*, 1903. (18) " Significance of the
Louisiana Purchase "; *Review of Reviews*, May, 1903. (19)
" Correspondence of the French Ministers to the United States,
1789–1797 "; *Am. Hist. Assoc. Rep.*, 1903. (20) " Democratic
Education of the Middle West "; *Worlds Work*, Aug., 1903. (21)
" Problems in American History "; *Congress of Arts and Sciences:
The Universal Exposition, St. Louis*, II. 1904. (22) " Documents on
the Blount Conspiracy, 1795–1797 "; *Am. Hist. Rev.*, April, 1905.
(23) " Policy of France toward the Mississippi Valley in the Period
of Washington and Adams Administrations "; *ibid.*, 1905. (24)
" The Historical Library in the University "; *John Carter Brown
Library*, 1905. (25) *Rise of the New West*, (Vol. XIV of the American Nation Series), Harpers, 1906. (26) " The South, 1820–1830 ";
Am. Hist. Rev., 1906. (Incorporated in substance as Ch. 4 of No.
25). (27) " The Colonization of the West, 1820–1830 "; *Ibid.*,
1906 (Incorporated in substance as Ch. 5 of No. 25). (28) " Is

for preference, something they may point to with pride as an achievement, a life work, one of those " comprehensive " and " definitive " histories no doubt which posterity may be expected to label " standard," and straightway shelve with Gibbon and Grote behind glass doors, rarely opened.

Such expectations, I think, will not be fulfilled, for many reasons no doubt, but at least for one very good one, which is that history, as Turner conceives it, is not well adapted to quantity production.   The easiest kind of history to write is the kind that lends itself to narrative — history

Sectionalism in America Dying Away? "; *American Journal of Sociology*, 1908.   (29) "The Old West "; *Proc. State Hist. Soc. Wisc.*, 1908.   (30) "The Ohio Valley in American History "; *Ohio Valley Historical Association*, 1909.   (31) "Significance of the Mississippi Valley in American History "; *Proc. Miss. Valley Hist. Assoc.*, 1909–1910.   (32) *Pioneer Ideals and the State University;* University of Indiana, 1910.   (33) "Social Forces in American History "; *Am. Hist. Rev.*, Jan., 1911.   (34) "History of the United States, 1865–1910 "; *Ency. Brit.*, 1911.   (35) *Guide to the Study of American History*, 1912 (Joint author with Channing and Hart; author of part from 1865 on).   (36) *List of References on the History of the West*, 1912.   (37) Hart and McLaughlin's *Cyclopedia of American Government*, 1914.   (Author of articles: "The Frontier in American Development "; "Sectionalism in the United States "; "The West as a Factor in American Politics ").   (38) Reuben Gold Thwaites; "A Memorial Address "; *Hist. Soc. Wisc.*, 1914.   (39) "The First Official Frontier of the Massachusetts Bay "; *Publications of the Colonial Society of Massachusetts*, 1914.   (40) *The West and American Ideals;* University of Washington, 1914.   (41) *Middle Western Pioneer Democracy;* State Historical Society of Minnesota, 1918.   (42) "Greater New England "; *American Antiquarian Society Proceedings*, 1919.   (43) *The Frontier in American History.* Holt, 1920.   (Reprinting studies noted above, viz: Nos. 5, 7, 10, 15, 17, 29, 30, 31, 32, 33, 39, 40, 41.).   (44) "Sections and Nation "; *Yale Review*, Oct., 1922.   (45) "Since the Foundation "; *Historical Outlook*, XV, 335 (Address at Clark University).   (46) "The Significance of the Section in American History "; *Wisconsin Magazine of History*, 1925.   (47) Children of the Pioneers; *Yale Review*, July, 1926.

conceived as a succession of events in a time series. The factual substance is there, inexhaustible, lying conveniently under the hand, needing not to be invented or imagined, needing only to be carefully searched out and verified. The problem of the correlation of ideas scarcely presents itself, since, strictly speaking, none but rudimentary ideas are essential. Even the problem of arrangement lays no great strain on the intelligence, being already half solved by the accidents of time and space. With industry and patience, therefore, the manuscript runs to seven volumes (or even, unless cruel and unusual precautions are taken, to ten) by the simple process of narration, the process of telling concretely what happened in such abundance of circumstantial detail that, as Leslie Stephen says, " an event takes longer to describe than to occur."

In this sort of history, history conceived as a succession of events in a time series, Turner is but little interested. If in all his published work there are five pages of straight narrative I do not know where to find them. His writing is all essentially descriptive, explicative, expository. Heaven knows he doesn't lack " material." Always on the still hunt for " data," he has facts enough; quantities of facts and events, but all wrenched loose from their natural setting in time and place by his curious inquiring mind in order to be assembled again in support of some idea that has occurred to him, or for the illumination of some problem that he has found interesting. This is the chief reason why he goes his own way, heedless of voices in the wilderness calling for the " comprehensive history." Left to his own devices, he gives us work suited to his objectives and his methods of approach — he gives us monographs and essays; and even when, on one happy occasion, he was caught by his friends and set the task of writing ten years of history for the American Nation Series, he produced a book that fits but oddly into the scheduled plan. In place of telling us what happened by narrating the succession of events, he endeavored to make intelligible what happened by describing the economic, social, and cultural conditions which, in each of the great geographic sections of the country, determined the political interests and conflicts of the time.

Well, one point is that in this kind of history many volumes are not required for presenting the results of wide researches and much reflection. The detailed and orderly narrative gives place to the static description of environment; and for such description a hundred details (details relating to climate, geography, psychology, economic technique, social custom), which would fill ten pages if narrated for their own sakes, are enclosed in a few compact generalizations which may be set forth in a brief paragraph or two. The point is that the generalized description, by virtue of condensing and symbolizing the bulky concrete, does not easily run to many volumes. Consider the extended researches concealed beneath the modest surface of those admirable opening chapters in Turner's *Rise of the New West*. To raise the completed structure of American history on such solid foundations throughout would be a herculean task indeed. Men there have been no doubt who might have done it — a Gibbon, a Mommsen, a Sorel. But Turner at least has not the encyclopaedic or the systematizing mind for it.

The "comprehensive history" presents another difficulty to those who, like Turner, are primarily interested in the complex of influences that determine political events.

This is a difficulty in what is called synthesis. It is true that historians, the " Newer Historians " at all events (and who would wish to be excluded from that ancient and honorable company!), have long since agreed that the business of the historian is to make a " synthesis of social forces," and at the same time to " trace the evolution of society " (or whatever you wish to call it). We even boast of it in a casual, off-hand way, as of a thing often done. But I suspect that all we have as yet done is to invent various methods of avoiding the difficulty. One method of avoiding the difficulty is triumphantly illustrated in the *Cambridge Modern History*. The difficulty is more resolutely faced, but not by any means overcome, in Lavisse's admirable *Histoire de France*. Lamprecht may really have solved the problem for all I know; but if so, then he has solved it, so far as I am concerned, at the heavy expense of rendering the experience of mankind thoroughly incomprehensible. The difficulty (well enough illustrated in Turner's *Rise of the New West*) is fundamental, and, I think, radically unsolvable. The point is that for the " synthesis of social forces " one must employ the method of generalized description; while for the " evolution of society " (in the chronological sense that is) one must narrate the forward march of events. Well, the generalization spreads out in space, but how to get the wretched thing to move forward in time! The generalization, being timeless, will not move forward; and so the harrassed historian, compelled to get on with the story, must return in some fashion to the individual, the concrete event, the " thin red line of heroes." Employing these two methods, the humane historian will do his best to prevent them from beating each other to death within the covers of his book. But the strain is great. And while any courageous historian may endure it for one volume, or even for two, few there are who can survive ten.

If these pages are expected to label Turner — to say whether he is historian, or sociologist, or historical sociologist, or sociological historian — there must inevitably be disappointment. For labels do not rightly describe any one. Certainly no label rightly describes Turner. He is, strictly speaking, neither historian nor sociologist. He is at all events not the academician, systematically preparing standard works according to scheduled plan. In his writings, as in his teaching, he is not quite the " professor," not quite what you look for in the " historian." He is just himself, a fresh and original mind that goes its own way, careless of the proprieties, inquiring into everybody's business, hobnobbing with cartographers, economists, sociologists, geographers, census compilers, editors of *Who's Who*. In his writings, as in his teaching, he is forever the inquirer, the questioner, the explorer; a kind of intellectual Gentleman Adventurer, fascinated by " this new world called America," fascinated above all by the American people and by their habits of thought and action, avid for " data " about them, wishing for his own peace of mind to understand them, to know what their " significance " may be. With this end in view he ranges far and wide through their history, past and present, in the ceaseless search for facts and for explanatory ideas; ranges far and wide on his own hook, poking into every sort of unlikely place, getting lost it may be, yet always finding himself again, and always buoyantly turning up at last with a rich freightage of information and notions; a rich freightage which he lays before us as best he can, in collections of documents, heavily weighted monographs, illuminating charts and graphs, dreadfully informing statistical tables, or brilliant essays in which happy ideas and analogies elbow one another for standing room. He lays it before us, this rich freightage of information and ideas, and asks us to take it, not as an exhaustive and definitive contribution, but only as an accumulated capital for new and larger ventures. And how many men, rummaging in this rich store, have carried away something useful for their purpose? How many graduate students, colleagues, scholars at home and abroad? And not historians only, but geographers, sociologists, economists, lawyers and political scientists.

Yes, quite beside the mark to expect, or ever to have expected, the ordered history in ten volumes from this lively intelligence! We must take Turner as he is, must be content with the qualities he has, with what he has given us, and will give. Content? But content is not the word. We must be grateful for these qualities, so rare they are, and for this work which has proved so fruitful. Turner's fame must rest, not upon the massed bulk of books published, but upon the virtue and vitality of the ideas he has freely scattered about. For my part I do not ask of any historian more than this, that he should have exerted in his generation a notable influence upon many scholars in many branches of humanistic study. This is enough; and this, I think, must be accorded to Turner.

Not everyone, I find, can quite understand the influence of Turner upon this generation of scholars. It is indeed not easily understood by those who know only his published work, by those who have not well known the man. But his friends and colleagues understand it. And his pupils understand it better than any others, because his pupils know, better than any others, that the man is more than his work. And so I end as I began — with " that man Turner," who laid and still lays upon us all the spell of his personality. Some indelible impression of him, some virtue communicated to us from the alert intelligence and the fine integrity of a high-minded gentleman, still shapes our lives and gives added substance to our work. I have said this before, and now I say it again. And yet, when all is said, something still escapes the crude phrase — some rare and moving quality in the man, some lifted light of the human spirit which no words of mine can adequately convey.

CHAPTER X
JAMES HARVEY ROBINSON

By

HARRY ELMER BARNES
Professor of Historical Sociology in Smith College

JAMES HARVEY ROBINSON

CHAPTER X

JAMES HARVEY ROBINSON

In an earlier chapter Professor Vincent has described the work of Herbert Baxter Adams in establishing the cultivation of history in the United States as a science of accurate documentation in the study of the political evolution of the past. We shall here indicate how James Harvey Robinson, in the next generation, carried the development of history one step further and made it a genetic social science concerned with tracing the development of civilization as a totality.

James Harvey Robinson was born in Bloomington, Illinois, June 29, 1863. From the same state came various others, as William Jennings Bryan, three years older, Elbert Hubbard, E. J. James, Simon Patten, E. B. Wilson and H. S. Jennings, who were, in quite different ways, destined to exercise a somewhat wide-spread influence upon their generation.

The subject of this biography was born into a well-to-do family where books and intelligent conversation were available. His eldest brother took the trouble to learn German and collect a library of old volumes selected from second-hand catalogues. His younger brother was to become the head of the Harvard Herbarium. One of his sisters interested herself in reproducing illuminated manuscripts. His father, born near Saratoga, N. Y., had advanced from the keeper of a general store to the presidency of the leading bank; and his mother — the daughter of a highly Calvinistic clergyman, who had been earlier a printer and the publisher of a little newspaper in the Mohawk valley — was fond of etymologies and possessed a more ambitious and skeptical mind than circumstances encouraged her to develop. When Robinson was eleven years old his father died and before many years he was in entire control of a moderate income, which serves somewhat to explain the independence of his thought, since he could, so far as his natural timidity, innate frugality and respect for his mother's opinions permitted, fare his own way. He never had to earn his living, and that, in his case, was a great advantage.

Robinson was rather over-prepared for the common schools and remembers little advantage from attending them, except in the way of enlarging the less respectable aspects of his vocabulary. He was a good boy, and liked to fuss with carpenter tools and a make-shift printing-press. His grandfather set up for him, in diamond type, the passage, from the Gospel according to John, " God so loved the world. . . ." He also bought some chemicals from the local druggist, and sulphuric acid had a fatal effect on his coat-sleeve, but he learned of the strange conduct of metallic potassium. He perused Appleton's *Encyclopedia* and Kames' *Elements of Criticism*. " From the former," says Robinson, " I learned about the strange crystals to be found in the urine, from the latter something of ' The Mourning Bride.' " Then there was Chambers' *Book of Days,* and a four-volume theology by a certain Spencer, as he recollects, which had the most terrifying statistics in regard to the prospect of eternal damnation for those who were not converted by the time they were eighteen.

The graph of salvation fell off shockingly, however, after twenty. He wondered what it was to "come to Jesus," as he was exhorted to do when an evangelist, or "ambassador of God," as he modestly called himself, appeared in the First Presbyterian Church. He was connected with this edifice on his mother's side, and can still scent its musty atmosphere. Later Dr. Frank Crane was to preside over the First M. E. Church across the street. Robinson marvelled at the sayings of the Seventh Day Adventists who used to camp in a grove just to the west of his home. He wondered if they were right about the approaching judgment day as indicated by the increase of earthquakes and meteorites. His mother had taught him that the decline of the Turkish Empire had a prophetic significance. Then all the evangelical preachers would get busy to refute the idea of obeying the Decalogue in regard to the observation of the Sabbath on Saturday. Only much later did he see how troublesome it was for them to explain the substitution of Constantine's "great day of the sun" for the Jewish sabbath. Meanwhile he suffered much from his respectful observation of the taboos associated with this great day of the sun; and the boredom of the first day lingered long after he had learned about the notions of the Brownists, from whom he was descended both spiritually and "genealogically" (which he long after learned had little to do with "biologically").

Robinson was afflicted with what Job calls a "wandering desire." He wandered from the Bloomington high school, after half pursuing the course, to Normal, just north of Bloomington, where there is an institution that has sent forth a number of men of importance. Here Edmund J. James was teaching Latin and Greek, and writing on the tariff and banking. Later he was to be the head of the Wharton School in the University of Pennsylvania, a professor in the University of Chicago, President of Northwestern University and finally of the University of Illinois. In due time, James's career was significant in Robinson's, but the latter soon fell away from Latin and began to fool about in the natural history museum, which was under the charge of a man of genius, Stephen A. Forbes, now a veteran in the University of Illinois. Here Robinson learned in boyish earnestness to manage a microscope and prepare slides, and soon came to apprehend something of nature's wonders. He procured a stately binocular microscope from an ingenious manufacturer in Chicago, and still has the Zeiss objectives which went with it. His brother, later to become a distinguished botanist, had an Alvin Clark four-inch refractor telescope, so that the stars were also a matter of family discussion.

These early observations and musings before the various biological exhibits " enabled me," writes Professor Robinson,[1] " to consort without embarrassment with embryologists and biologists." By thus acquiring the fundamentals of biology and sex through the natural history museum and the ministrations of a discerning biologist, instead of by the usual avenue of the Methodist or Baptist Sunday School, Robinson was from the first free from that impurity-complex which has oppressed and stultified the thought of so many of our eminent and respectable historians. He never felt it necessary, as does one of our pompous contemporary historians, to offer his women students the option of leaving the lecture room prior to his discussion of the " Rump Parliament." This early bio-

[1] Letter to the writer, March 10, 1926.

logical knowledge not only freed Robinson to study history without any compulsive necessity of passing austere moral judgments on the matter of the conventional morality of the leading characters and epochs of history, but it also impressed upon him at an early age the all-important fact of the genetic principle in nature. Though still theoretically orthodox when he entered Harvard, Robinson was from his youth onward an evolutionist in his scientific thinking, and it was but a step from bio-genesis to a proper appreciation of the genetic nature of civilization-building. In fact, Robinson has himself stated that the genetic principle was not originated by the historians but gradually taken over by them from the biologists and geologists.

" It would seem as if the discovery of the incalculable value of genetic reasoning should have come from the historians, but, curiously enough, instead of being the first to appreciate the full significance of historical-mindedness, they left it to be brought forward by the zoölogists, botanists and geologists. Worse yet, it is safe to say that, although the natural scientists have fully developed it, the historian has hitherto made only occasional use of the discovery, and history is still less rigidly historical than comparative anatomy or social psychology." [2]

This early interest in biology was kept alive by subsequent reading, by visits to his brother, Benjamin Lincoln Robinson, the distinguished Harvard botanist, and by association at Columbia University with the large and active group of students of genetics in that institution. Robinson took a personal part in the campaign to repel the imbecilities of " Bryanism," contributing a notable defense of evolution to *Harpers Magazine* for June, 1922, entitled " Is Darwinism Dead? "

[2] *The New History*, p. 77.

In 1882 Robinson wandered to Europe and spent over a year in rather unintelligent efforts to improve his French and his flute-playing. He recognizes that he might have been a biologist but never a musician. On his return to Bloomington he was urged to go into business. He had three months of experience in a local " notion " store and learned to dust off boxes of suspenders and pipes, on nothing a month. He was then offered thirty dollars a month to remain after his novitiate, but accepted instead a position in the paternal bank with a salary of twenty-five dollars a month as " collector " and writer-up of pass books. Then he seemed to need a rest and went to the Maine coast. On his way home in the summer of 1884 he decided, while sitting on a trunk in the baggage-car and viewing Lake Memphremagog, to go to Harvard, where his well-prepared younger brother was going. He resolved, too, to get through Harvard in three years, since his younger brother was entering as a sophomore. And this he did, at no sacrifice of education but, incidentally, with somewhat indifferent academic ranking. He remained a fourth year, worked on the topic that was later to be his doctoral thesis in Freiburg, and suffered from that psychic depression that has been his special " cross." He married Grace Read of Bloomington in September, 1887, just before starting his graduate work at Harvard.

Though Robinson spent four years at Harvard, taking his master's degree in 1888, he assures the writer that William James was the only teacher that left any significant or permanent impression upon him, or in any way influenced his subsequent thinking. James not only encouraged a pluralistic and pragmatic philosophy and a critical view of knowledge, but also first aroused in him that vital interest in psychology which has continued throughout his life and undoubtedly contributed much to his subsequent excursions into the psychological interpretation of history. In 1888 he went to Strassburg where his brother was studying botany with Count Solmes, and, after a semester of learning German, he moved on to the University of Freiburg where von Holz received him with friendliness and encouraged him to elaborate his work at Harvard on *The Original and Derived Features of the Constitution of the United States* as his dissertation. He received his doctor's degree at Freiburg in 1890.

At Freiburg Robinson began to acquaint himself with the technique and methodology of historical research, particularly in the study of original sources, which involved easy familiarity with the great collections of source-material, the guides which facilitate their exploitation, and the auxiliary sciences such as paleography, medieval lexicography and *diplomatique*. It was here that Robinson began to develop that facility for minute and painstaking historical research which was soon to impress his colleagues, Munro and Cheyney, at the University of Pennsylvania. It has been supposed by many that Robinson's chief historical interests in Germany were in medieval history, and that his work on the Bundesrath was wholly incidental to these medieval studies. This is not the truth, however, for, strange as it may seem for the author of *The New History* and *Mind in the Making*, his dissertation subject represented the core of his university work at Freiburg. For some unexplained reason Robinson had become, for the time being, vastly interested in German constitutional law and read avidly all the literature relating to the federal constitution. This led him to write his

German Bundesrath, an institution which he felt was fundamental and very ill-understood in foreign parts. At one period, therefore, he probably knew as much about German public law as any outsider was likely to know. Later he coöperated with E. J. James in translating and editing the Prussian Constitution.

After finishing his work at Freiburg, Robinson remained for a time in Germany, visiting Halle and Berlin. At Halle he met Simon Patten and made such an impression on him that he was invited to accept a modest position in the University of Pennsylvania. He entered upon his work in Philadelphia in the fall of 1891. At the University of Pennsylvania his immediate associates in the field of history were Dana C. Munro and Edward P. Cheyney. The mutually stimulated enthusiasm of these young men led to the initiation of the famous series of *Translations and Reprints from the Original Sources of European History,* which represented the first serious and important effort in the United States to introduce source material into the college teaching of European history.

Robinson's Pennsylvania experience doubtless helped along notably that thoughtful attitude towards history and social science which has distinguished all his writings. Munro and Cheyney were capable and enthusiastic students of history and there was much exchange of opinion between these three original young scholars. Moreover, Cheyney has ever been one of our most open-minded and analytical historians, distinctly a member of the more progressive group in the American Historical Association. While he modestly states that the stimulus to original thought came chiefly from Robinson, there can be no doubt that Cheyney contributed much to their joint interests and their discussions of historical topics. McMaster was working on the first important historical product in this country which definitely repudiated the political narrative as the backbone of respectable historical writing. There can be no doubt that Simon N. Patten exerted a considerable influence on Robinson at Pennsylvania. Patten possessed the most original and suggestive mind which permanently graced the University of Pennsylvania, and he and Robinson were close friends from European days. While professionally an economist, Patten was always much interested in the history of thought and institutions. It was also at Pennsylvania that Robinson first became acquainted with E. G. Conklin, who has been one of the leaders in the effort to indicate the historical and cultural implications of modern biology and genetics. Likewise, Robinson began early that extremely valuable and illuminating practice of discussing topics of historical interest and current importance with people outside of his department, and, indeed, outside of the university itself. This habit has doubtless done much to prevent Robinson from being an esoteric and monastic scholar, has stimulated his humanistic tendencies, has broadened his vision, and has added much to his concrete knowledge. Cheyney remarks of the existence of this extramural association at Philadelphia:

"I might add, if you can make any use of the fact, that promptly after he came to Philadelphia Robinson obtained recognition and received much appreciation from many of the more intellectual and 'select' people of Philadelphia, both within and outside of the University. He was also given cordial entrée into their homes and social circles, something not always or easily obtained. This testifies to his personal charm and easy poise. There was no society, apparently, in which he did not feel at home and to which he was not welcomed." [3]

In 1895 Robinson was called to Columbia University as Professor of European History. Here, he states, the process of education, begun under Forbes and William James, was renewed and has never ceased. Later, in association with Dewey, he found a mutual interest in the history of ideas which was subsequently to absorb most of his professional interest and enthusiasm. E. L. Thorndike suggested a more exact and modernized knowledge of psychology. From E. B. Wilson and from the geneticists at Columbia his early interest in biology and evolution was revived and stimulated. From the scientists and technologists at Columbia, Robinson obtained a reinforcement of his observations with respect to the stupendous changes which pure and applied science had brought into existence in transforming the material culture of the modern world. Boas and the anthropologists served to connect up biological and human evolution, and to impress upon him the enormous period of time which had elapsed between the appearance of man upon the planet and the origins of written history. Toward the close of his career at Columbia the psychoanalysts began to influence Robinson though he had long suspected the small amount which man really knows about the fundamental reasons for his conduct, and the slight reliability of his rationalized explanations of his motives and purposes in life.

Following 1910 Robinson made the acquaintance of the works of Thorstein Veblen, which impressed upon him the importance of the interrelation between the history of technology and economics, on the one hand, and the his-

[3] Letter to the writer, March 3, 1926.

tory of ideas and institutions, on the other. Veblen's works also emphasized the weaknesses, wastes and dubious rationalized apologetics of contemporary capitalism and the theory of business enterprise. Veblen's influence through his writings was extended by personal association when Robinson and Veblen were colleagues at the New School for Social Research from 1919 to 1921.

Robinson's intellectual development was also, quite naturally and inevitably, conditioned by his own studies in the field of history and the social sciences during his long teaching career. Few men have interested themselves in more fields of history than Robinson, and no one has studied any field of history more thoughtfully than he. Hence, his thinking has been profoundly affected, not only by the facts and events dealt with, but also through the theories and doctrines of the leading figures in the various periods of history with which he has been concerned. The latter influence was particularly potent during his study of the history of the intellectual class in Europe, the subject to which he devoted his best thought during the last ten years of his career at Columbia. He was particularly influenced by the views of the French and English Rationalists from Montaigne to Condoret.

Then, Robinson has always been intensely alert to what is actually going on in the world about us. In many ways the changes in the culture, knowledge and outlook of man from 1885 to 1925 have been more striking than those which have occurred in the whole previous history of humanity upon the earth. These changes have been particularly evident and impressive in New York City. To a man as alive to these facts as Robinson, the impress left upon his psyche by these contemporary developments was truly

stupendous.   Some slight conception of Robinson's appreciation of the momentous nature of the transformations
through which he has himself lived appears in the stirring
concluding chapter which he contributed to the original
edition of the *Development of Modern Europe*, in the
last three chapters of the new edition of his *History of
Western Europe,* and in the *Survey* for October 1, 1924.

Finally, as is the case with all stimulating teachers, Robinson learned much from his former students who later became his colleagues in the Columbia department.   His
broad outlook was further expanded through association
with Professor Shotwell.   As far as is known to the writer,
no other historian has even faintly approximated Shotwell's gift for linking up the cosmic and historic, which
is well illustrated by the following brief quotation from his
stimulating address on " Mechanism and Culture ":

" Go down to the great power-house where the force is generated to drive these subway trains and see what degree of control
over nature has been reached with reference to the needs of civilization.   There the power is generated from the coals of Pennsylvania.   The heat stored up from suns of geologic ages is released once more under the exacting control of an engineer and
adjusted by automatic devices to correspond with the weight
upon the floors of the cars, so that it is hardly a figure of speech
to say that as you step upon the train a few more leaves of prehistoric forests crackle away in the energy of heat, and that
energy becomes a substitute for the human energy of the
traveller."[4]

Through the influence of Shotwell and Charles Austin
Beard, Robinson received encouragement in the study of
material culture, economic institutions and the common-

[4] J. T. Shotwell, " Mechanism and Culture," in *Historical Outlook*, January, 1925.

place needs and activities of everyday life. The effect of this influence appears, among other places, in his striking address on " History for the Common Man " reprinted in *The New History*. From Professor William R. Shepherd he received suggestions as to the interaction of cultures upon one another, particularly the influence of the reaction of European expansion upon European thought and culture from the time of the Crusades to the French Revolution.

The above appear to the writer to have been the chief personalities, influences and factors involved in the psychogenesis of James Harvey Robinson, in so far as these were derived from academic associations and external surroundings.

Robinson's career as a teacher of history began at the University of Pennsylvania, where he went as a Lecturer in European history in 1891. He was promoted to an associate professorship the next year, and held this title until he resigned in 1895 to accept a professorship in European history at Columbia University. The Wharton School of Finance was then being established at the University of Pennsylvania, and undergraduate work in history and the social sciences was being greatly extended in the new Wharton School and in the college. Edmund Janes James, Simon N. Patten and Joseph French Johnson were the leading figures at that time in the Wharton School. At Pennsylvania, Robinson exhibited those interests and characteristics which were ascendant in the first two decades of his teaching and study of history. Here, he was the careful, painstaking student of historical sources and textual material, the exacting editor and the intensive teacher who illuminated his serious interpretation of textual material with flashes of wit and penetrating reconstruction of historical situations. His colleagues of those days, Professors Cheyney and Munro, have furnished the writer with their impressions of Robinson in his Pennsylvania period. Professor Cheyney says, among other things:

" I remember very well the first time I met Mr. Robinson, in 1891, I think. He was brought to the University as the " new man in History " when the Wharton School was being established and college work extended. It was almost a matter of chance that he took the European and I the English field for teaching; we were then both equally interested in both fields.

I was much impressed then with his delicate, intellectual face and manner, and with the fact (as I was home-bred) that he had his undergraduate degree from Harvard and his Ph.D. from Germany. This last fact I think is significant in his whole career, that is to say that Robinson is fundamentally a well-trained, solid historical student with all the rigorous conceptions of historical research and statement that even the most pharisaical of the profession can lay claim to. However much he may have devoted himself through later life to criticism and speculation, and however much he may have wandered in other regions, he is fundamentally a historian. He has done a great deal of genuine, minute research. I have never felt at all reconciled to his failure to complete the large work on the History of the Intellectual Classes in Europe that he had projected and which he had in fact largely put into written form. It would last longer than his critical work."

Professor Munro agrees with Cheyney in all essential matters:

" Robinson was noted at Pennsylvania and later for his independence of thought, keen critical ability, and for the interest which he imparted to all his teaching. He was acting as one of

[5] Letter to the writer, March 3, 1926.

the assistant editors of the *Annals of the American Academy,* in addition to doing his regular teaching.

I think the most interesting feature of the beginning days of his teaching was the ignorance in which we all were of the fundamental tools of the trade, which every graduate student is now expected to know. We were constantly making discoveries of essential books, and Robinson was keen to master every one. He was quick to appreciate the fact that a reading of the sources is the real short cut to a knowledge of history and also to independent judgment.

He contributed, as you know, several numbers to the series of *Translations and Reprints,* and he did the work so thoroughly and conscientiously that, as he said, it would have been easier to write a volume on the subject than to prepare one of these numbers." [6]

While at Pennsylvania Robinson revised his work on the *Bundesrath* and published it in an English edition, edited five numbers of the *Translations and Reprints,* and initiated that friendship with Professor Henry W. Rolfe of Swarthmore College, which led to the publication of their joint work on Petrarch in 1899.

In 1895 Robinson accepted a professorship in European History at Columbia University. Technically his appointment was to Barnard College, and, though few of his colleagues or students have been aware of the fact, his salary and professorship, until his retirement in 1919, were based on the Barnard Foundation. Indeed, in 1900–1 Robinson was acting dean of Barnard College. From the beginning, however, it was arranged that his work should be divided between Barnard and the Columbia Graduate School, and all of his more notable teaching activities were carried on with his graduate students in the University. Barnard

[6] Letter to the writer, February 25, 1926.

seniors, however, had the inestimable advantage of attending his famous course on the " History of the Intellectual
Class in Western Europe," to which the graduate students
on the other side of Broadway flocked in such great numbers. This was easily the most popular course in the college, and something which was anticipated by Barnard
students with even greater ardor than the approach of
Commencement Day.

Robinson's call to Columbia came as an important incident in a general effort to strengthen the new Faculty of
Political Science. There was a movement on foot to bring
to Columbia from Pennsylvania not only Robinson but
also the economists, Edmund Janes James and Simon N.
Patten. Robinson was, however, the only one of the three
who was actually translated to Morningside Heights.
Robinson's invitation to join the Columbia faculty was
based upon both professional and personal grounds. Up
to 1895 there had been no one at Columbia who was a
specialist in European history, a subject in which President Seth Low was much interested. The only courses in
this field were a general course on the political history of
Europe from the " fall of Rome " to the Revolutions of
1848, offered by Professor Herbert L. Osgood, and another
on the history of European political theories taught by
Professor William A. Dunning.

Dean John William Burgess and Professor Dunning
agreed in 1894 that the time had come when a specialist
should be added in the general field of medieval and modern European history. Dean Burgess has recently informed the writer that the responsibility for the choice of
Robinson for this post rested with the late Professor Dunning. He states that Dunning was impressed by Robinson's

capacities as a close student of original source material, and as a skillful editor. When Robinson was at Pennsylvania he had not only edited certain numbers of the *Translations and Reprints,* but was also an associate editor of the *Annals of the American Academy of Political and Social Science.* Dunning was at this time editor of the *Political Science Quarterly* and he wished to have the aid and counsel of so promising a man as Robinson in his editorial duties. [7]

At Columbia, Robinson worked out the full sweep of his career from the editor of *Translations and Reprints* to the author of *Mind in the Making,* which was actually first delivered as the Kennedy Lectures before the New York School of Social Work during the last semester of Robinson's connection with Columbia. In a later section of this chapter, treating of Robinson as an historian, we shall deal with greater thoroughness with the evolution of Robinson's historical interests and concepts. It will suffice to point out here that during the first third of his quarter of a century of teaching at Columbia he manifested, for the most part, the characteristics he had exemplified at Pennsylvania, namely, an unusually intelligent, discriminating and interesting interpretation of the history of restricted periods directly from the available original sources. In other words, he was then an "objective historian"— whom Robinson has himself so well described as " an historian without an objective." Approximately the next third of his Columbia term was transitional. He developed that genetic interest which took him from the *Cahiers* of 1789 back to the origins of the cosmos, as set forth in modern astro-physical theories, and forward to

[7] Letter of J. W. Burgess to the writer, March 8, 1926.

Dewey, Edison, Marconi and Mencken. By 1910 Robinson had become primarily an interpreter of history, centering his efforts around his popular and ever growing course on " The History of the Intellectual Class in Western Europe." His success as an individual and a teacher was distinct and notable from the outset, but the change in the nature of his historical interests and in the type of course offered by him during his Columbia professorship inevitably resulted in an ever increasing popularity of his courses. It also produced a much greater interest in the man and his work on the part of a progressively expanding group of admiring students.

His influence as a teacher while at Columbia was enormously extended in an indirect fashion through the impression left by his personality and teachings upon his more conspicuous students. A list of a few of these, which would include such names as James Thomson Shotwell, Charles Austin Beard, Carl Becker, William R. Shepherd, Preserved Smith, J. Salwyn Schapiro, Carlton J. H. Hayes, Lynn Thorndike, Alexander C. Flick, Howard Robinson, Arthur M. Schlesinger, Harold U. Faulkner, Benjamin B. Kendrick, Dixon Ryan Fox, Louise R. Loomis, James E. Gillespie, G. G. Benjamin, J. Montgomery Gambrill, Edwin P. Tanner, Henry Johnson, Emma Peters Smith, Joseph Ward Swain, Parker T. Moon, Leland Jenks, Martha Ornstein, Harry J. Carman, Ann Elizabeth Burlingame, Edward M. Earle, Max Cushing, John Herman Randall, Jr., Wallace E. Caldwell, C. P. Higby, and many others, will suffice to indicate to what an amazing degree the development of the newer and broader tendencies in historical interpretation has been associated with the Robinsonian ancestral tree. Then, we should not over-

look Robinson's influence upon other important centers
of the development and dissemination of the "new
history," the department of history at the University of
Pennsylvania under the aegis of E. P. Cheyney, and the
later work of James Henry Breasted of the University of
Chicago.

The last four or five years of Robinson's connection with
Columbia were not particularly happy as far as the institutional aspects of the situation were involved, though his
popularity as a teacher continued to increase to the last,
and it was necessary to resort to the chemistry amphithe-
ater in Havemeyer Hall in order to find a room large
enough to seat his class in intellectual history when the
course was offered for the last time at Columbia during
1918–19. The increased regimentation and the dogmatism, intolerance and super-Rotarian enthusiasm engendered by the World War were extremely distasteful to
Robinson's refined and discriminating intellect, and he
wrote a vigorous protest in the *Atlantic Monthly* on " The
Threatened Eclipse of Free Speech." He particularly re-
sented that intrusion of these influences and traits into the
Columbia academic atmosphere which was notoriously exemplified in the persecution of Professor Beard for his
work, *An Economic Interpretation of the Constitution,* in
the rebuke of Professor Kendrick for some well-chosen remarks on Henry A. Wise Woods' eulogy of military training as the highest ideal of college education, and in the
dismissal of Professors Cattell and Dana for appealing to
Congress to withstand the pressure of the war-makers. Beyond this, Robinson had become more and more interested
in the world outside college walls. He also became ever
more impatient with the punitive and penitential theories

of education and with the growing secondary school type of regimentation and procedure in colleges and universities. He was equally out of sympathy with their archaic, stereotyped and rigid curricula, stated examinations, and solemn degree-granting convocations.

In short, the World War made university teaching particularly distasteful to Robinson just at the time when his intellectual interests and convictions were already leading him toward an ever increasing belief in the fundamental futility and sterility of academic routine and procedure. Hence, it was but natural that he should have been attracted by the proposition to establish a novel institution for study and research in the field of history and the social sciences entirely free from entrance requirements, examinations and degrees. This brings us to the last phase of his academic career, if it may be called academic, namely, his part in launching the New School for Social Research.

While the " New School " was first opened in a formal fashion with a partial program in the spring of 1919, and with a full offering in the fall of the same year, its initiation was not a sudden or dramatic matter. It had grown up as an idea embodying the general spirit of revolt against conventional higher education which was evident in Robinson and many of his intimate friends, such as Beard, Dewey, Hayes, Emily James Putnam, Alvin Johnson, Wesley Clair Mitchell, Thorstein Veblen and others. These liberal spirits had often depicted in their conversation an ideal institution where teacher and student might meet for mutual edification and enlightenment free from the paralyzing and dementing influence of the fear of examinations and the protective psychosis of academic dignity. Effective publicity for such an organization was assured by the conversion of Herbert Croly of the *New Republic* to the " idea," and financial support for the enterprise was found through the donations of Mrs. Charlotte Sorchan, Mrs. Willard Straight and many others. In this way the dream of conversational ecstacy was transformed into an experimental actuality. The ideals underlying the New School for Social Research were stated in the most comprehensive and effective fashion by Robinson himself in an article published in *School and Society* for January 31, 1920:

Teaching and learning are assumed to go hand in hand. But no one who is not professionally pledged to this assumption can fail to see that teaching commonly fails to produce learning, and that most we have learned has come without teaching, or in spite of it. The gestures and routine that make up teaching are familiar enough and can easily be acquired. Recitations, lectures, quizzes, periodical examinations, oral and written, textbooks, readings, themes, problems, laboratory work, culminating in diplomas and degrees *cum priviligiis ad eos pertinentibus,* form the daily business of tens of thousands of teachers and hundreds of thousands of boys and girls in thousands of smoothly working institutions dedicated to the instruction of the young. Teaching in all its various manifestations can readily be organized and administered.

As for learning, that is quite another matter. It is highly elusive and no one has yet discovered any very secure ways of producing it. Being taught and learning are obviously on different psychological planes; they involve different processes and emotions; are subject to different stimuli and spring from different impulses. Our " institutions of learning " are essentially institutions for teaching. Teaching is easy but learning is hard and mysterious, and few there be that attain to it. It seldom forms the subject of discussion in faculty meetings where it is tacitly assumed that pupils and students rarely wish to learn, and that the main business in hand is to see that those obviously indifferent to being taught are suitably classified and promoted or degraded according to the prevailing rules of accountancy. . . .

However this may be, one can conceive of a school which would be frequented solely by those who thought that they wished to learn and where there would be no other inducement than the proffered opportunities to learn.

Such is the *New School for Social Research*. It appeals to adults who, after some experience in life, are eager to extend, elaborate and elucidate their personal experience by studying matters which have aroused their curiosity, shown up their ignorance or puzzled them. No one comes to the New School because he is sent; or hopes for a degree or diploma, or even for the momentary relief that comes from pleasing teacher by matching a series of questions with acceptable answers. This greatly simplifies the problem of encouraging learning. We do not have to generate the preliminary sense of need which forms the heaviest responsibility in school and collegiate education.

A second simplification consists in confining our studies to mankind and his present predicaments — to public affairs and human organizations; — all, of course, in the light of man's history and nature as now understood. History, anthropology, psychology, biology, economics, sociology, public law and the rest of the disciplines which have man, his nature and social organization for their theme are not set off in departments but are concentrated into a common effort to state and explain so far as may be human conduct, aspirations and organization. . . .

We in the New School can venture to be shamelessly interested in current conditions just because we can treat them without the reservations imposed by the educational *mores*. We can think as freely as we are capable of thinking just because we are not afraid that too much thinking is likely to be done either by ourselves or by our students. The excessively retrospective tendency of much of the teaching in the social sciences is merely an attempt to escape from the hazards of talking honestly about prevailing conditions. The policy of the Hanseatic League can be treated with a freedom impossible in the case of the United States Steel Corporation. One may venture to say all he knows of such long-dead pacifists and radical reformers as Pierre Dubois and Marsiglio of Padua; an equally fair statement of the contentions of Lenin or Victor Berger would obviously be offensive and tend to create intellectual " unrest." But our object is not to allay doubts and rationalize what exists, but frankly to stimulate questioning and investigation among the men and women that come to us. Our only fear is that the questioning and investigation will not be thorough-going enough, not that it will be dangerously free. The New School is no guardian of the morals of the young; it does not function *in loco parentis*, or even *in loco almae matris*. Its instructors are scientifically interested in the subjects they deal with; they all believe that fundamental social readjustments are inevitable, but they are pledged to no program of social reform, old or new; they are simply looking for light, and encouraging others to do so. Facts are not classified in their minds as safe or dangerous; radical or conservative; suitable for the young or adapted only for the old and settled.

Unfortunately, from the point of view of Robinson's interests and associations the New School proved a personal disappointment which was mitigated only by the astonishing success of *Mind in the Making*. The reasons for the failure of the New School to measure up to Robinson's expectations were numerous and vital. First and foremost, the institution was launched at least a year, if not two years, earlier than it should have been. It opened its doors before it had money enough to insure its existence and perpetuity independent of students' fees. It had no permanent endowment and, hence, it was dependent to a large extent upon tuition paid by those enrolled in classes. The pledges made by wealthy supporters of the school were to run for only a limited period of years and, for the most part, have not been renewed. The institution then, was forced to make an appeal for large attendance without being able to lure serious students by means of the only seductive bait known to modern higher education, namely, academic degrees. While a lecturer at the New School during its first year, the writer was on numerous occasions assured by graduate students from Columbia that the New School offerings were much more attractive than most of the courses then offered by the Faculty of Political Science at Columbia, but that they simply could not attend the New School regularly because they had neither time nor money to invest in an educational enterprise which would produce nothing more than increased erudition, intellectual development and improved cerebration. Professional ambitions and conjugal responsibilities or aspirations forced upon these students diligent and solemn devotion to those courses which would ultimately secure for them the magic doctor's degree that would open the way to an instructorship in a state university and then, if married, to the office of the obstetrician or, if unmarried, to that of the marriage-license clerk in the county administration building. It seems to the writer that this lack of adequate initial endowment was the crucial and all-important factor in producing the early trials and difficulties of the new institution.

Again, some originally interested when the institution was still in the stage of discussion, took no active part in launching the enterprise. The premature death of Carlton H. Parker was a heavy blow to the prospects of the school. His great personal force and inordinate enthusiasm for the enterprise might have carried it successfully through the initial handicap of inadequate endowment. Then, popular teachers, such as Hayes and Dewey, who were expected to accompany Robinson and Beard in the secession from Columbia, were made such attractive offers to remain at Columbia that they felt it to their best interests to do so. Many sympathetic spirits at Harvard, Yale and other university centers in the East, who had been originally interested in the project and had promised active aid, proved too busy or timid to participate when the test came with the opening of the institution, though Harold J. Laski and Thomas S. Adams actually offered courses during the first year of the school.

Further, there were wide differences of opinion among the real founders of the school as to its fundamental purposes and objectives. Beard, with memories of his part in founding Ruskin College at Oxford, and disgusted with conventional academic methods, desired to house the New School in humble quarters located over a livery stable, garage or brewery where even the olfactory stigmata of conventional education would be effectively obscured. He desired to have the institution strictly a research organization, with the students exploiting the remarkable library facilities of New York City and with lectures reduced to a minimum. In this general attitude he was supported by Mr. Croly. Robinson, on the other hand, with his primary interest in potently and directly influencing public opinion and educational procedure, was mainly desirous of attracting large groups of students and effecting their intellectual seduction.

Finally, the very nature of the institution and its administration made its successful conduct difficult. The advanced, daring and original nature of the institution naturally and inevitably attracted to it independent and somewhat uncompromising intellects. At the same time, faculty policies were decided in an absolutely democratic manner which, given the nature of the faculty, invited immediate and serious dissent and discontent. Such a faculty as that originally assembled at the New School could probably have been maintained in peace and efficiency only in connection with direction by a benevolent bureaucracy which decided upon the nature of the courses desired and the appropriate instructors to be engaged, and then granted to these instructors absolute freedom in the conduct of their courses but no participation in determining the policies of the institution. The above factors led to Professor Robinson's resignation from the New School in 1921 and to his expression of no little understanding of, and personal sympathy with, the administrative problems and trials of university executives. Beard had a great influence in inducing Robinson reluctantly to sever his connection with the New School. He urged that the pen was far wider in its influence than talk.

After a number of subsequent experiments, the administration of the New School was taken over by Dr. Alvin Johnson of the *New Republic*. By skillful concentration upon specialized phases of adult education, and by encouraging student participation in administration and endowment, the institution has now become almost self-supporting and an extremely vital and progressive element in Metropolitan education. It is now beginning actually to realize the ideals and influence Robinson had in mind in 1918.

While Robinson formally withdrew from the New School he has retained his interest in adult education, which represents his closest approximation to a program of social reform. His general answer as to what he really meant by adult education — a question often put to him at the New School — was embodied in belated form in his *Humanizing of Knowledge*. Robinson contends that the first step to be taken in adult education is to provide the right sort of books for the intelligent reader which will present a clear summary of the progress being made in the various fields of human knowledge. Hence, he has refused to associate himself with any schools or organizations for the purpose of forwarding adult education, but has preferred to give such time as he can find to the program of planning out and editing such a list of books as he has in mind.[8]

We may now consider briefly the evolution of James Harvey Robinson as an historian, leaving an analysis of his qualities as a teacher of history for more thorough consideration later in the chapter. As we pointed out above in connection with the work of Professor Robinson at the University of Pennsylvania, he started on his historical career as a rigorous and exacting student of texts and documents. His interests were in the Middle Ages, the Reformation and the French Revolution. His early career as an historian, then, exhibited an alert mind illuminating obscure sources which dealt with a restricted range of subjects. He was always original in his outlook, but did not at this time reveal the cosmic and genetic point of view or that interest in contemporary problems and social reform which came to characterize his later teaching and writing. One of his most distinguished former students thus describes his interests and methods at the opening of the present century:

[8] These books will appear as *The Modern Readers' Bookshelf*, published by the George H. Doran Company.

" When I first knew him back about 1903, he was not visibly disturbed by the forces of modernism. He was teaching the Protestant Revolt, medieval institutions, and the French Revolution in a fashion never heard of before in all the land. He was always shooting out such things as: Erasmus was like Mathew Arnold, Luther like Charles Spurgeon — delicious and illuminating bits — but he was not running a rapier through the substance of things. It was long afterwards that he turned modernist with a vengeance. Still his interest in the intellectual life was even then predominant with him. Of course there was nothing pontifical about him even in the old days. He saw through the clap-trap of most of the so-called research which is merely adding machine business. No student would ever die for a document after hearing him, but he might get into jail for having an idea." [9]

Robinson's great effort during this period was to fulfill completely Leopold von Ranke's conception of the function of the historian to reproduce exactly from the sources an historical situation as it actually existed at the time of the event, without reference to the causes or the results of the situation thus being reconstructed. Professor Shotwell, who enjoyed special advantages in the way of studying historical documentation with the leading medievalists of England and France, has assured the writer that he never studied with another man who possessed even a reasonable approximation to Robinson's almost uncanny ability to make a situation live again from an interpretation of the sources. Professor Shotwell's verdict has been confirmed by other highly reliable testimony from Robinson's colleagues and students throughout the first fifteen years of his teaching experience. In a letter to the writer, Professor Shotwell thus describes Robinson's thorough

[9] Letter to the writer, March 13, 1926.

mastery of source-material and his insistence upon its exploitation:

" The great influence which Professor Robinson has exerted
upon the study and teaching of history in this country cannot
be explained in any single formula. But the aspect of his work
upon which I have been asked to comment is the one which will,
I think, appeal most strongly to those who had the good fortune
to be his students in the years gone by. Historical scholarship
controlled with relentless precision his reconstruction of the
past. Textual criticism was the foundation of everything. No
careless reference to secondary material was ever allowed to
pass muster; the original sources were interpreted strictly in
the setting of their own time. The contributions to historical
synthesis which Professor Robinson has made in these later
years have been based upon long and close analysis of first-hand
material. If in the criticism of recent historiography he has
from time to time emphasized the limits of our knowledge of
historical phenomena, it should not be forgotten that few among
living historians know more about the textual basis of our historical knowledge in the field of European history than he.

" I recall the classroom of more than thirty years ago when
the Seminar of Mediaeval History met under his direction.
Whether it was the structure of the Mediaeval Church or the
growth of the monarchy in France in the Thirteenth Century,
the subject was always approached from the original material
first, and the student was never permitted the easy path of a
mere restatement of the narrative of manuals or non-contem-
porary documents. One had always the sense of working directly with the sources themselves. The closest application of
the historical disciplines controlled the imagination, while stimulating it by this contact with the genuine records of events or
institutions." [10]

Robinson has himself stated the basis for his original
enthusiasm in that cultivation of the original sources of

[10] Letter to the writer, April 15, 1926.

European history which led him from the initial labors on the *Translations and Reprints* to the much more extensive and laborious enterprise of preparing his four volumes of *Readings* on European history:

" No improvement in the methods of historical instruction in our high schools and colleges bids fair to produce better results than the plan of bringing the student into contact with the first-hand accounts of events, or, as they are technically termed, the *primary sources.*

" This term may perhaps call up in the minds of some the vision of a solitary stoop-shouldered, spectacled enthusiast, engaged in painfully deciphering obscure Latin abbreviations on yellow parchment. But it is a mistake to conclude that the primary sources are always difficult to get at, dull, and hard to read. On the contrary, they are sometimes ready to hand, and are often more vivid and entertaining than even the most striking descriptions by the pen of gifted writers like Gibbon or Macaulay. . . .

" It may, of course, be urged that the trained historian, after acquainting himself with the men and the circumstances of a particular period, can make better use of the sources than any relatively unskilled student. But, admitting the force of this argument, there is, nevertheless, so much to be learned from a study of the original accounts that cannot be reproduced by the most skilled hand, that no earnest student or reader should content himself with second-hand descriptions when primary sources are available.

" The sources are unconsciously molded by the spirit of the time in which they were written. Every line gives some hint of the period in which the author lived and makes an impression upon us which volumes of second-hand accounts can never produce. The mere information, too, comes to us in a form which we do not easily forget. The facts sink into our memory. . . .

" Moreover, the study of the sources enables us to some extent to form our own opinions of the past, so that we need not rely entirely upon mere manuals, which are always one, and generally two or three, removes from the sources themselves. When we get at the sources themselves we no longer merely read and memorize; we begin to consider what may be safely inferred from the statements before us and so develop the all-important faculty of criticism. We are not simply accumulating facts but are attempting to determine their true nature and meaning." [11]

This occupation with the sources necessarily involved a thorough mastery of the guides to the sources, as well as of the leading works on the methodology of historical research and the diverse auxiliary sciences essential to a successful study of source-material. Consequently, as Professor Cheyney points out, Robinson was able to hold his own with any esoteric medievalist in facing unabashed the *Monumenta*, the *Documents inédits*, the *Rolls Series* and Migne's *Patrologia*. Likewise, he could vie successfully with the best of them in wielding his Du Cange, Potthast, Molinier, Giry and Wattenbach, as well as in expounding the subtle secrets of Bernheim. Those critics of Robinson among the less imaginative and more arid of American historical students — who agree with Gibbon that " diligence and accuracy are the only merits which an historical writer may ascribe to himself " — might fruitfully accept the invitation to examine the list of historical sources from which Robinson selected his four volumes of *Readings* in European history. They might be astonished to learn that even Lamprecht regarded these bibliographies of sources as an excellent guide for students in his German university seminars. These facts will serve to put at rest for all time the absurd allegations of cub reviewers or of offended Catholic Clergy who believed that they discerned

---

[11] *Readings in European History*, Vol. I, pp. 4–6.

in Robinson's popular and light-hearted treatment of the Middle Ages in *Mind in the Making* evidence of loose scholarship and unfamiliarity with the original sources for this period. Some even went so far as to liken him to H. G. Wells as an historical scholar.

If Robinson has in subsequent years become more generalized and popular in his historical teaching and writing it is simply because one of the most competent textual scholars this country has produced gradually came to the conclusion that he had a field of greater personal usefulness as an interpreter of the vast accumulation of the hitherto largely inert and irrelevant mass of historical materials which had been brought together by earlier researchers. He has himself explained and justified this transformation in his notable article " After Twenty Years," in the *Survey* for October 1, 1924. But, with all of his insistence upon a first-hand study of original sources, he was not foolish enough to carry on such studies independent of the best judgment of others who had made a similar excursion into the source-material. He was always as familiar with the chief monographs on any period as he was with the great collections of documents. This fact is well brought out in his famous article on " The Study of the Lutheran Revolt " in the *American Historical Review* for January, 1903.

In effecting this transition from an intensive student of historical texts and methodology to a cosmic interpreter of historical materials, Robinson's studies of the French Revolution proved the pivotal and decisive factor. As we shall point out more thoroughly below, his concern with the French Revolution was almost exclusively with its causes. From this type of approach he developed an interest in the general problem of the genesis of institutions and of civilization as a whole. In addition to the inevitable effect of a genetic approach to the French Revolution, the study of French history in the eighteenth century furthered the gradual development of the genetic point of view on the part of Robinson through his interest in the great leaders of rationalist thought during this period. The Rationalists were much interested in the origins of civilization and the philosophy of history. Voltaire was ever his chief hero in this age, and, as we know, Voltaire wrote the first history of civilization worthy of the name. It was the interest in, and mode of approach to, the French Revolution which led Robinson back, first to the Reformation and the Middle Ages, and ultimately to *Pithecanthropus Erectus*. Professor Robinson has himself well stated this fact in an answer to a query by the writer, who assumed that his interest in medieval history had come from his original studies in Germany:

" In regard to my interest in medieval history it did not come in Germany but rather as a tendency to move back slowly from the guillotine to the first hatchet. I found my interests naturally aroused in what went before, which is only too often what now is. I could not understand the indifference of most historical men to the antecedents of their heroes and institutions." [12]

The manner in which he was led from the Middle Ages back to the eoliths is described by Robinson in his article in the *Survey* for October 1, 1924:

" In writing history it is also becoming harder and harder to justify any particular point of departure. It is as difficult to tell where to start as where to stop. One has somehow to scotch the eternal snake without killing it. The Middle Ages, after

[12] Letter to the writer, March 27, 1926.

the works of Harnack, Dill, Taylor, Glover, Cumont and many others, appear, from a cultural standpoint, to be a sort of attenuated later Roman Empire. And the later Roman Empire witnessed the lapsing of borrowed Greek culture; and the Greeks, we now know, were pretty dependent on all the wonders that were achieved by Egyptians and Western Asiatics, who built on the fundamental discoveries of neolithic mankind, whom we must recognize as incredible progressives compared with their predecessors. It took the race, with its humble origins, so long to make a hatchet to be held in the hand, then so long to set it in the handle, then so long and so recently to set the handle in the hatchet! " [18]

Of course one must not overlook Robinson's early interest in evolution, as well as in natural history, in explaining the origins of his genetic view of human development. Indeed, in the above quoted *Survey* article, he explicitly says: " This so-called genetic or historical approach is the discovery, I conjecture, not of the historians but rather of the natural history people, who taught the historian this most important of lessons." [14] Likewise, his growing interest in anthropology served to emphasize the relative chronological insignificance of the period which has elapsed since the dawn of history, as compared with the vast expanse of time between the Egyptians and the eolithic age. Perhaps the best statement of his appreciation of both the genetic point of view and the new time perspective is to be found in the following quotation from *The New History:*

" In order to understand the light which the discovery of the vast age of mankind casts on our present position, our relation to the past and our hopes for the future, let us borrow, with some modifications, an ingenious device for illustrating modern

[18] *Loc. cit.*, p. 19.   [14] *Ibid.*, p. 20.

historical perspective. Let us imagine the whole history of mankind crowded into twelve hours, and that we are living at noon of the long human day. Let us, in the interest of moderation and convenient reckoning, assume that man has been upright and engaged in seeking out inventions for only two hundred and forty thousand years. Each hour on our clock will then represent twenty thousand years, each minute three hundred and thirty-three and a third years. For over eleven and a half hours nothing was recorded. We know of no persons or events; we only infer that man was living on the earth, for we find his stone tools, bits of his pottery, and some of his pictures of mammoths and bison. Not until twenty minutes before twelve do the earliest vestiges of Egyptian and Babylonian civilization begin to appear. The Greek literature, philosophy, and science of which we have been accustomed to speak as " ancient," are not seven minutes old. At one minute before twelve Lord Bacon wrote his *Advancement of Learning*, to which we shall recur presently, and not a half minute has elapsed since man first began to make the steam-engine do his work for him. There is, I think, nothing delusive about this reduced scale of things. It is much easier for us to handle and speculate upon than the life-sized picture, which so transcends our experience that we cannot grasp it.

" Two reflections are obvious: In the first place, those whom we call the ancients — Thales, Pythagoras, Socrates, Plato, Aristotle, Hipparchus, Lucretius — are really our contemporaries. However remote they may have seemed on Archbishop Usher's plan of the past, they now belong to our own age. We have no reason whatever to suppose that their minds were better or worse than ours, except in point of knowledge, which has been accumulating since their day. In the second place, we are struck by the fact that man's progress was at first shockingly slow, well-nigh imperceptible for tens of thousands of years, but that it tends to increase in rapidity with an ever accelerating tempo. Our forefathers, the drift men, may have satisfied themselves for a hundred thousand years with a single stone implement, the so-called *coup de poing* or fist hatchet, used, as Sir John Lubbock surmises, for as many purposes as a boy's jackknife. In time they learned to make scrapers, borers, arrowheads, harpoon points, and rude needles of flint and bone. But it was scarcely more than half an hour before twelve by our clock that they can be shown to have invented pottery and become the possessors of herds. The use of bronze and iron is much more recent, and the men of the bronze age still retained a pious devotion to the venerable stone hatchet, which the priests appear to have continued to use to slay their victims, long after the metals began to be used." [15]

Robinson was always careful to make it clear that, as far as he dealt with " causes " in history, he was concerned only with genetic antecedents and not with metaphysical obfuscation. In a recent letter to the writer he says:

" I have little use for the word " cause " which appears to me to imply a misapprehension of the infinite interworking of things. We are up against situations and always have been. William James has stressed this and Shotwell in his *Interpretation of History* shows that interpretation consists in pointing out neglected concomitants and antecedents. Mark Twain's *Mysterious Stranger* puts the interlocking of all things in an impressive allegory."

In the same way that Robinson's genetic view of things led him back to the origins of man, so his interest in science, technology and everyday matters directed his attention to contemporary developments and problems. He was also helped towards this conception of the supreme importance of the present day through the influence of Shotwell, Beard and Veblen, as well as through his readings of Marx and the economic historians. His first confession of a capitulation to the modern field is to be found

[15] *Op. cit.*, pp. 239–41.

in the preface which he wrote for the *Development of Modern Europe* in 1907:

" It has been a common defect of our historical manuals that, however satisfactorily they have dealt with more or less remote periods, they have ordinarily failed to connect the past with the present. And teachers still pay a mysterious respect to the memory of Datis and Artaphernes which they deny to gentlemen in frock coats, like Gladstone and Gambetta. The gloomy incidents of the capture of Numantia are scrupulously impressed upon the minds of children who have little chance of ever hearing of the siege of Metz. The organization of the Achaean League is given preference to that of the present German Empire." [16]

Even more striking are the following excerpts from the *Survey* article cited above:

" It happened that some twenty years ago I completed a brief review of the History of Western Europe, from the break-up of the Roman Empire onwards. Today I am called upon to revise it. The editor of the *Survey* has asked me to put together some of my impressions as I tried to jump back over the wide gulf that has opened between us and the solid land on which we stood a score of years ago. But I find it almost as hard to reconstruct the bland assumptions of 1904 as those of the time of St. Louis or Augustus.

" The twenty years have witnessed a more startling accumulation of human information, more astounding applications of ingenuity and, at the same time, a more tragic indictment of approved human institutions, than any of the stately eras into which we are wont to divide history. We have eaten of the tree of knowledge so freely that we are bewildered as no previous generation has ever been. For when good and evil tend to become matters of intelligence rather than of habit and routine, our old moorings are lost and we are tossed about on the waves

[16] *Op. cit.*, p. iii.

of illimitable doubt.   Former assurances turn into questions;
and solutions into problems. . . .

" Since the Neolithic Age all things appear to have been going
with extraordinary rapidity.   Twenty years ago I had little
" feel " for this and few others had.   Now it seems to me that
the history of the race since Menes I of Egypt (the first recorded human name in history) is a very brief period, and that
we are at the beginning of the beginning, as Mr. Wells conjec-
tures — rather than in a somewhat advanced and ultimate
phase of human achievement.   The human experiment seems
to me now about to start.   The curtain is up and the play is on.
The tempo of the overture has increased from largo to presto
and pretty soon, the nimblest fingers will not be able to keep up
with the score, unless we acquire unprecedented dexterity —
and we may." [17]

Robinson's growing interest in the genetic approach to
history, together with his conviction that we should study
the past in order better to understand the present, led him
ultimately into a primary interest in the interpretation of
historical material.   It was here that he developed those
methods, attitudes and concepts which made him the
leader of the " new history " in the United States.   With
Robinson the development of the so-called new history
was not the result of any *à priori* or systematic philosophy
of history, as was the case with Lamprecht and Henry
Adams, but was simply the inevitable outgrowth of the application of his type of mind to a consideration of the nature and meaning of historical data and historical study.
Once one makes use of his mind and thought-processes in
the field of history he of necessity becomes, consciously or
unconsciously, a convert to the " new history."   In fact,
the new history is nothing else than thoughtful history.

[17] *Loc. cit.*, p. 18.

As far as the writer knows, there has been no historian who has thoughtfully regarded the subject-matter of history and not acquired the genetic way of looking at things, the synthetic approach to the content of history, and a primary interest in the interpretation of historical data accumulated through patient research.

The reason why so many historians of real intellectual distinction have failed to espouse the dynamic trends in historical writing and teaching is that their thought-processes have been paralyzed or restricted by the dogmas of historical methodology and objectives which von Ranke and his associates found it necessary to instill in the minds of the historians of a century ago in order to obstruct the tendency towards such undocumented vagaries as the Hegelian and Comtian philosophies of history. These concepts were of the greatest value in promoting the development of the science of documentary investigation, but the general obsession with them in the nineteenth century prevented the historians from making any intelligent use of the materials which they had accurately and conscientiously gathered. So much time and attention were absorbed in investigation that none was left for intelligent reflection upon the significance of the material and facts discovered. The means entirely obscured the end. Robinson was never the slave of his facts or overwhelmed by them. To him they were only important in so far as they enabled him better to understand the genesis of man and culture. Robinson became the leader of the new history in the United States because he possessed to an unusual degree the training and the type of mind which are most conducive to curiosity and thoughtful reflection in dealing with historical subject-matter. These are bound to lead one beyond the confines and limitations imposed by the tenets of documentary criticism. In other words, he was historically-minded beyond all other American historians of his generation, with the possible exception of his student and colleague, Professor Shotwell, and he was the first in point of time to apply his talents to a reconsideration of the general problem of the nature and purpose of history.

While the " new history " and the discussions which it produced had an earlier origin in Europe than in America, it seems that Robinson was but little influenced by these European antecedents. He early read John Richard Green's *Short History of England* and was impressed by its emphasis upon social and cultural factors. McMaster's *History of the People of the United States* helped to make him discontented with the purely political narrative. He read Rambaud's *Histoire de la civilization française,* but his interests were in the Revolution rather than in a general survey of French history. He was also familiar with Charles Seignobos' general history of civilization, but there is no evidence that either Rambaud or Seignobos exerted any definitive influence upon him. Karl Lamprecht he neither read nor attempted to understand. He was repelled by Lamprecht's schematic presentation of history and his philosophical generalizations. Ernst Bernheim's *Lehrbuch der historischen Methode* unquestionably helped him to consider the more fundamental problems of the nature and objectives of history, but certainly did not convert him to the new history. He had little regard for Guglielemo Ferrero, mainly because Professor George W. Botsford, with whom he shared his office at Columbia, possessed for Ferrero ardent and articulate contempt. Robinson was considerably affected, however, by certain of the more dynamic authorities on the periods in which he was interested. The genetic interest which he derived from his study of the French Revolution was stimulated by the profound work of De Tocqueville on the socio-economic background of this movement. Likewise, he was very much taken by Janssen's comprehensive consideration of the social and intellectual background of the Protestant Revolt. Then, his interest in the history of ideas was helped along to a considerable degree by his enthusiastic cultivation of the works of Draper, W. E. H. Lecky, and Andrew D. White. But, by and large, Robinson's creation of the new history in the United States was an indigenous, personal and very gradual development.

The first stage in the development of Robinson's interpretative attitude was his consideration of the history of history itself. He began to raise the question of what history is all about and why. He pointed out how the historian had emphasized the necessity of studying the development of all forms of human thought and culture in the past, but had singularly and strangely neglected to apply this attitude towards the history of his own subject. Nothing is more potent in the promotion of serious reflection concerning the subject-matter and objectives of history than a consideration of what the various practitioners of the subject from Herodotus to Lamprecht have thought about the matter. How thoughtfully Robinson analyzed the theories of history past and present appears in his Columbia University lecture on the history of history, reprinted in amplified form as the second chapter of his *The New History*.

Next to his interest in the history of history, probably

the most potent influence in leading Robinson into his
conception of the " new history " was his growing interest
in the social sciences. A constant effort on his part to keep
abreast of the newer discoveries and inferences in regard
to man and human nature revealed to Robinson the existence and the work of the biologists, psychologists and
anthropologists. This had a fatal effect upon any earlier
presumption as to the adequacy of history as " past
politics."

The new history, according to Robinson, embraces a
number of definite conceptions and aspirations, namely:
(1) the genetic point of view; (2) comprehensiveness of
content; (3) an exploitation of the various social sciences,
which he regarded as " the new allies of history," supplementing the older allies of history: lexicography, paleography and *diplomatique;* (4) a primary interest in the
interpretation of historical data; and (5) a utilization of
historical knowledge in the interest of human betterment
and social reform. We have traced above the various influences and factors which led to Robinson's apprehension
of these basic tenets of the new history. We shall here
content ourselves with a few excerpts from *The New History,* designed to illustrate in his own words what the new
history meant to him:

" But history, in order to become scientific, had first to become historical. Singularly enough, what we now regard as the
strictly historical interest was almost missed by historians before the nineteenth century. They narrated such past events as
they believed would interest the reader; they commented on
these with a view to instructing him. They took some pains to
find out how things really were — *wie es eigentlich gewesen.*
To this extent they were scientific, although their motives were
mainly literary, moral or religious. They did not, however, in

general try to determine how things had come about — *wie es eigentlich geworden*. History has remained for two or three thousand years mainly a record of past events, and this definition satisfies the thoughtless still. But it is one thing to describe what once was; it is still another to attempt to determine how it came about. . . .

" Now — and this cannot be too strongly emphasized — the continuity of history is a scientific truth, the attempt to trace the slow process of change is a scientific problem, and one of the most fascinating in its nature. It is the discovery and application of this law which has served to differentiate history from literature and morals, and which has raised it, in one sense, to the dignity of a science. . . .

" When we turn to our more popular treatises on history, the obvious and pressing need of picking and choosing, of selecting, reselecting, and selecting again, would seem to have escaped most writers. They appear to be the victims of tradition in dealing with the past. They exhibit but little appreciation of the vast resources upon which they might draw, and unconsciously follow, for the most part, an established routine in their selection of facts. When we consider the vast range of human interests, our histories furnish us with a sadly inadequate and misleading review of the past, and it might almost seem as if historians had joined in a conspiracy to foster a narrow and relatively unedifying conception of the true scope and intent of historical study. . . .

" While, then, the historian has been busy doing his best to render history scientific, he has, as we have seen, left the students of nature to illustrate to the full the advantages of historical mindedness and to make two discoveries about mankind infinitely more revolutionary than all that Giesebrecht, Waitz, Martin or Hodgkin ever found out about the past. Today, he has obviously not only to adjust himself as fast as he can to these new elements in the general intellectual situation, but he must decide what shall be his attitude toward a considerable number of newer sciences of man which, by freely applying the evolutionary theory, have progressed marvelously and are now in a position to rectify many of the commonly accepted conclusions of the historian and to disabuse his mind of many ancient misapprehensions. By the newer sciences of man I mean, first and foremost, Anthropology, in a comprehensive sense, Prehistoric archaeology, Social and Animal psychology, and the Comparative study of religions. Political economy has already had its effects on history, and as for Sociology, it seems to me a highly important point of view rather than a body of discoveries about mankind. These newer social sciences, each studying man in its own particular way, have entirely changed the meaning of many terms which the historian has been accustomed to use in senses now discredited — such words as " race," " religion," " progress," " the ancients," " culture," and " human nature." They have vitiated many of the cherished conclusions of mere historians and have served to explain historical phenomena which the historian could by no possibility have rightly interpreted with the means at his disposal. . . .

" Hitherto writers have been prone to deal with events for their own sake; a deeper insight will surely lead us, as time goes on, to reject the anomalous and seemingly accidental occurrences and dwell rather upon those which illustrate some profound historical truth. And there is a very simple principle by which the relevant and useful may be determined and the irrelevant rejected. Is the fact or occurrence one which will aid the reader to grasp the meaning of any period of human development or the true nature of any momentous institution?

" It should then be cherished as a precious means to an end, and the more engaging it is, the better; its inherent interest will only facilitate our work, not embarrass it. On the other hand, is an event seemingly fortuitous, isolated, and anomalous, — like the story of Rienzi, the September massacres, or the murder of Marat? We should then hesitate to include it on its own merits, — at least in a brief historical manual — for, interesting as it may be as an heroic or terrible incident, it may mislead the reader and divert his attention from the prevailing interests, preoccupations and permanent achievements of the past. . . .

" If it be conceded that what we rather vaguely and pro-visionally call social betterment is coming to be regarded by large numbers of thoughtful persons as the chief interest in this game of life, does not the supreme value of history lie for us today in the suggestions that it may give us of what may be called the technique of progress, and ought not those phases of the past especially to engross our attention which bear on this essential point? . . . .

" At last, perhaps, the long-disputed sin against the Holy Ghost has been found; it may be the refusal to coöperate with the vital principle of betterment. History would seem, in short, to condemn the principle of conservatism as a hopeless and wicked anachronism." [18]

Almost the only respect in which Robinson's views were somewhat archaic and his attitude prejudiced was in regard to his opinions concerning sociology, a subject which he never mastered and the existence of which he would scarcely concede. Neither in his books nor in his conversations has Robinson revealed the reasons for this bias and antipathy. It is probable that he was at first repelled by the abstractions, vagaries and contradictions of the subject in its earlier days, and that he never took up a second time an investigation of this field of knowledge in the more mature period of sociological literature.

In his interpretation of historical materials Robinson quickly and logically came to believe in the primary impor-tance of the history of ideas in determining the successive stages in the growth of civilization. Some have con-tended that Robinson was led into his psychological inter-pretation of history and his interest in the history of ideas through enthusiasm for the conceptions of Granville Stan-ley Hall's genetic psychology. In a letter to the writer

[18] *Op. cit.*, pp. 2–3, 15–16, 62, 83–4, 252, 265.

Robinson has stated that this was not the case. He never read Stanley Hall until long after he had organized his course on the intellectual history of Europe. Robinson recognized that the general attitudes of mind on the part of the dominating classes in every age are likely to determine the prevailing characteristics of most other phases of culture. This led him to an outstanding interest in the intellectual history of Europe in his studies from about 1910 onward. Here his early training in psychology under James, together with its revival and elaboration through contact with Dewey and Thorndike, was of inestimable value. His great respect for natural science and for the sceptical and inquiring turn of mind, which characterizes the rationalist, led him to interpret the intellectual development of the race in the guise of a struggle between supernaturalism, dogma and bigotry, on the one hand, and critical thought and the inductive method on the other. His best work in this field was done in his lectures on the "History of the Intellectual Class in Europe," which became the most famous and popular course at Columbia University. Unfortunately, he has not yet given us the long-promised two-volume work embodying the substance of these brilliant and arresting lectures, but the general nature of the course and its dominating conceptions may be gleaned from the successive editions of the syllabus which he printed as a guide to this course of lectures. The general philosophy of the course is embodied in his *Mind in the Making* and *The Humanizing of Knowledge* and will be summarized briefly at the close of this chapter.

In an address given before the annual meeting of the Association of History Teachers of the Middle States and Maryland on November 28, 1925, Professor Robinson summarized his mature reflections in regard to the province, purpose and results of historical study. We may here quote the concluding section of this address as the essence of Robinson's views on the obligations and achievements of his profession:

" When Professor Cheyney came to give his presidential address before the American Historical Association a couple of years ago he took for his subject certain tendencies or laws which he thought emerged into one's mind from a study of the past. These were six in number: (1) Historical continuity (2) the impermanence of the nations (3) the general unity and interaction of all portions of humanity (4) the steady prevailing of democrary (5) the enlarging of freedom (6) the decrease of gratuitous cruelty and increase of kindness. I should say that the first three appear always to have been true of humanity; the last three seem to be characteristic of the past two or three centuries.

" All these tendencies appear to me to be unquestionably and essentially important for teachers to understand and to call to the attention of their students. As for the last one, it seems to me questionable whether there has been any considerable decrease in human cruelty, except in its more spectacular manifestations. But this is a matter well worth considering.

" I might accept my friend Cheyney's invitation to add a few other laws of history. There is the law of the sacredness of the familiar and of holy routine when they are called in question; and like unto it, the law of man's suspicion of innovators. There is the law of the timely rationalizing of institutions and habits when they come to be criticized. One can observe this in the case of religious intolerance, witchcraft, slavery and nowadays in the matter of war. One might suggest a law of wine, women and song, for all these have played an essential part in the development of mankind if we could but get at the intimate facts. There is a neglected law that whatever title, however exalted, we may give to a person he will remain a human being in nine tenths of his daily conduct, thought, prejudice, jealousy and initial ignorance. And lastly, it is another law that what passes for history in any generation is what Voltaire called *une fable convenue* — only one of the many, many stories which could be told of man's doings, — and usually an uncommonly dull one. . . .

"To me history is nothing more or less than all the things that we can find out about the doings, feelings, thoughts, aspirations, loves, hates, achievements, defeats, discoveries and mistakes of men and women. One can call it a *treasury* or a *jungle*. If a treasury, a selection must be made from its limitless wealth; if a jungle, there are innumerable new trails to be blazed besides the dusty old road which most of us feel bound to travel. Many of us are tired of it and little fruit seems to be left on the bereft trees which line it. . . .

"History is for me those recollections of man's origin and past behavior and thought which enable me to see the more clearly how he comes to act and think in the strangely successful and unsuccessful ways he now does. This is my way of reconciling the longing of a scientifically-minded person to take things as they are, and at the same time set forth an edifying tale. . . .

"I long ago tired of the odds and ends which textbook compilers have had the nerve to call the leading facts, essentials, or elements of history. For I found out that they were not anything of the sort. So I should suggest that you just find out as much as may be about the past; enrich your recollections and then, when you come to teach or write, call forth such of your memories as you think might be worth the attention of your audience. It is better to be misled now and then and to mislead — far better than to make history a profitless subject which leaves us just as considerable fools after we study it as we were in the beginning.

"History is the living past, to use Mr. Marvin's illuminating term. It must live in the teacher and writer, and be buzzing around in his head even when he is off on a vacation. . . . While the idea that we study history to understand the present has now become fairly generally recognized it is as yet rather an ambition or ideal than an achievement. And this for the simple reason that the old selection from the treasury of the past is still sanctified in examination papers and the old route, beaten hard by many weary feet, is still marked out in textbooks. And great will be the labor of establishing new paths that will lead to high points of vantage from which the human welter may be viewed with increasing understanding." [19]

Professor Robinson's professional life as a teacher of history revolved around some four courses: (1) the French Revolution; (2) the pre-Reformation; (3) the Middle Ages; and (4) the Intellectual History of Europe. These are listed above in the chronological order of their dominance in Robinson's historical interest.

Robinson's treatment of the Middle Ages was a novel departure from the conventional exposition of the history of this period. In the first place, his realization of the enormous time that man had been on the earth and of the relatively short period included in recorded history led Robinson to discard the customary periodization of history as "ancient, medieval and modern." He looked upon recorded history as practically one, and a relatively recent, period. He viewed the Middle Ages less as a break and collapse than as a period of continued, though slow, progress. To him the Middle Ages never started, because there was no such thing as the "Fall of Rome," and because pagan culture never ceased. Likewise they never ended. The Renaissance was as much a myth as the "Fall of Rome," for there never could be a rebirth of something which had never died. His interpretation of the medieval period itself was equally original and illuminating. The

[19] *Publications of the Association of the History Teachers of the Middle States and Maryland*, 1925.

Dark Ages were shown to be less murky than ordinarily supposed. He repudiated utterly the conventional view of the Middle Ages as a thousand years of unmitigated stagnation and unrelieved barbarism. He depicted them rather as a period of developing culture in a new area, this cultural progress becoming particularly notable from the twelfth century onward. Though the Middle Ages are ordinarily interpreted as preëminently the Christian "Age of Faith," Robinson was himself more interested in the hold-over of pagan culture and its revival by the Humanists than he was in the doctrinal developments and the ecclesiastical institutions and practices of the period. He was particularly delighted when discussing the cultured pagans of the medieval age, as well as the outstanding critics of the Church. Following the precedent of Maitland, he interpreted the Church itself as primarily a great international political system. This led to a break with Lecky's generally accepted views and to an original interpretation of heresy as political treason rather than as doctrinal perversity. It also determined the nature of his attitude towards the Protestant Reformation. Regarding this as a political rather than a religious development, he believed it better described as a " revolt " than as a " reformation." Yet one should not give the impression that Robinson was not interested in Church history. Indeed, he was always intensely interested in it, and retained his concern with it to the very close of his teaching days. His approach was, of course, that of Voltaire or Andrew Dickson White, and not that of Milman, Schaff or Janssen. What interested him in studying the history of the Christian Church was to discover the diverse sources of such extraordinary beliefs and customs as it adopted, created, fostered and perpetuated. He delighted in revealing the manner in which attitudes of mind and social practices, utterly foreign to the needs and inconsistent with the progress of our own age, had developed very naturally out of a quite different set of conditions from those which now prevail.

While Robinson rejected the views of Burckhardt and Symonds, who held that the Renaissance represented a distinct break with the Middle Ages and a new and unique birth of pagan culture, nevertheless he was much interested in Humanism as an age and a movement which espoused and promoted that pagan culture which he admired far more than he did the civilization of Christendom. In particular, he approved the enthusiasm of Petrarch for the literary masterpieces of the secularly inclined pagan antiquity; the urbanity, tolerance and mildly satirical tendencies of Erasmus; as well as the boundless tolerance and withering irony of Montaigne. He was generally sceptical of the ordinary notion that the Renaissance produced the Reformation. The most that he would concede was that " the mythical Renaissance may have produced the mythical Reformation." His fundamental thesis was that the Reformation killed the Renaissance. In interpreting the Protestant Revolt he held that it was chiefly the political secession of a number of princes in northwestern Europe from the great international ecclesiastical state with its headquarters at Rome — a view vaguely hinted at by Sleidanus in the Reformation period itself.

In studying the period of the Reformation he was much more interested in, and sympathetic with, the pre-Reformation figures like Erasmus than he was interested in, and sympathetic with, Luther, Calvin and Zwingli. He well recognized the fallacies of the Protestant apologists who have stressed the alleged revolutionary contributions of Protestantism to toleration and to freedom of thought. He made it clear at once that the pre-Reformation figures, such as Erasmus, were infinitely more enlightened and tolerant than Luther or Calvin. He looked upon the Protestant Revolt as the product of general forces rather than of the personality of Luther. His formula most frequently repeated in the course was: " The Reformation produced Luther, not Luther the Reformation." Even when the Reformation came, Luther remained its leader for but a short time, and soon turned toward the right wing in the movement. Robinson's interpretation of the Reformation is most thoroughly set forth in his world-famous article on that subject in the eleventh edition of the *Encyclopedia Britannica*. The only notable defect in his explanation of the Reformation lay in his general ignoring of the economic factors involved in the movement. The Reformation now appears to have been quite as vitally associated with the Commercial Revolution and with the rise of capitalism and the *bourgeoisie* as it was with the development of the national state system in northern Europe. This fact was not generally understood twenty years ago. Two of Robinson's foremost students have furnished the writer with illuminating descriptions of Robinson's treatment of the Reformation. Professor Preserved Smith describes his conception in the following manner:

" His view of the Reformation was determined by his larger conception of the Roman Catholic Church as fundamentally an international state. To him the Reformation was a nationalistic secession from this state, and should therefore properly be called the Protestant Revolt. The roots of his idea are found in the works of Maitland and Lea; and his conception of the movement as a whole was deeply colored by Janssen, from whom other Rationalists, like Nietzsche and Karl Pearson, have also taken their estimates of the Reformation. In Robinson's view there is much truth; its main defect is that he did not fully understand the effect of the Commercial Revolution upon the religious cataclysm. Nationalism is one important root of the movement, but it is only one. Robinson recognized to some extent the intellectual and ethical preparation for the religious upheaval; but at the time when I was his pupil no one had fully brought out the immense significance of the rise of capitalism and the growth of the power of the *bourgeois* class." [20]

Professor J. Salwyn Schapiro thus sets down his impressions of the course:

" In the course on the Protestant Revolution he made clear the many-sided character of the movement, with Luther being in the center and not on the left. His attitude towards the Catholics was sympathetic; he explained that they regarded the Reformation in very much the same way as political conservatives today regard radicals. His sympathies were of course with Erasmus, whose " culture " *motif* he explained in a remarkable series of lectures. One came out of the course puzzled but not confused. A most excellent thing! " [21]

In his treatment of the French Revolution, Robinson was almost exclusively concerned with the antecedents of this much studied episode. He believed that all of the fundamental achievements of the Revolution had been worked out prior to the dissolution of the National Constituent Assembly. He had little interest in, and devoted little or no attention to, those dramatic incidents of the Reign of Terror which had absorbed the time and space of most writers of the French Revolution.

[20] Letter to the writer, March 13, 1926.
[21] Letter to the writer, March 14, 1926.

Robinson thus pays his respects to the older sensation-alist students of the French Revolution, who were chiefly interested in a super-dramatic interpretation of a fictitious version of the Reign of Terror:

" We are ordinarily taught to view mankind as in a periodic state of turmoil. Historical writers do all they can, by studied neglect, to disguise the importance of the lucid intervals dur-ing which the greater part of human progress has taken place. They skip lightly from one commotion to another. They have not time to explain what the French Revolution was by ration-ally describing the *Ancien régime,* which can alone give it any meaning, but after the quotation from La Bruyère, regarding certain fierce animals, " black, livid, and burnt by the sun," and a repetition of that careless phrase, " After us the deluge," they hasten on to the Reign of Terror as the be-all and end-all of the bloody affair. And in this way they make a second St. Bartholomew's of one of the grandest and, in its essential re-forms, most peaceful of changes which ever overtook France or Europe." [22]

Robinson's own judicious summary of the historiography, causes and achievements of the French Revolution is con-tained in the chapter on " The Principles of 1789 " in *The New History,* while his best survey is embodied in the *Development of Modern Europe.* Professor Schapiro thus describes his impressions of Robinson's course on the French Revolution:

" In the course on the French Revolution Robinson was in his element. He never touched the Revolution itself but spent all his time on the causes. Then I saw the real Robinson, the Humanist became the Rationalist. Voltaire was his hero, if so sceptical a person can have a hero. Robinson's idea was that the French Revolution was over when the Constituent Assembly

[22] *The New History,* pp. 12–13.

dissolved. The folly of terrorism succeeded the folly of absolutism, with the real Revolution as a lucid interval." [23]

Whatever his earlier success as a teacher in the courses above described, there can be no doubt that the crowning element in Robinson's pedagogical career was his famous course on the "History of the Intellectual Class in Europe." Like his general philosophy of history, this course had a gradual development rather than being a conscious and abrupt product of any definite period in his teaching career. It began shortly after his call to Columbia with a small group of students reading selected sources on the intellectual history of a particular period. Then he later pieced together the intellectual history of the periods which he studied in his major courses, namely, the history of the intellectual life of the Middle Ages, the pre-Reformation period and eighteenth century France. Gradually the course departed more and more from a reading of, and commentary upon, the source-material, and took on the characteristics of an interpretation of the salient personalities and types of thought in each age. The course rapidly expanded in scope. The Middle Ages sent him back to pagan culture, pagan culture to the ancient Orient, oriental culture to the mental life of primitive man, and anthropology pushed him back still further into a study of comparative psychology and animal behavior. Similarly, his interest in science and criticism led him to go forward from the French Revolution to a study of the growth of modern science and its influence upon material culture and the world of ideas. The course thus became more universal in its scope and more interpretative in character. As it grew more popular and more propagandist, in the best

[23] *Loc. cit.*

sense of that term, it became more useful as a weapon for clarification of thought and for the promotion of social reform. The outstanding generalizations of the course have, fortunately, been made available for public consumption in *The Mind in the Making* and *The Humanizing of Knowledge*. Yet Robinson never lost touch with his interest in the study of historical sources for, along with this increasingly popular general course, he maintained a seminar in which his students read and discussed with him such things as Bakewell's *Source Book in Ancient Philosophy*, Cicero's *Nature of the Gods* and Augustine's *City of God*.

Most of Robinson's students and colleagues, however . much they may admire his literary efforts and his general lecturing, incline to the opinion that Robinson was at his best as a class-room teacher. While Robinson's historical interests changed much, his aims and methods as a teacher altered but little during his teaching career, except in so far as some transformation was forced by changes in the subject-matter of his courses. His foremost aim in his teaching was to make his courses vital and interesting or, rather, interesting because they were vital. His alert mind went immediately to the heart of things, and his originality of expression and penetrating interpretation of historical material at once aroused the interest and enthusiasm of his students. He was from the first absolutely devoid of what Mencken has so well denominated "the solemn-ass complex," which has ruined the usefulness of so many otherwise capable history teachers. He early made that fundamental distinction, so often and fatally missed, between seriousness and solemnity. He always made a discriminating use of wit and humor to intensify the interest of his students in the material at hand. Yet, his sallies of wit were always enlisted in the service of the course rather than making the course a vehicle for his jokes. He had a veritable genius for happy illustration, and for the illumination of a past event by comparison with some contemporary situation. He always avoided every semblance of bluffing or pedantry, freely admitted his ignorance when it existed, and made his students feel that he was one of them, even if their leader, in a common intellectual adventure.

The early appearance of those traits which made Robinson an almost unrivalled teacher of history, and their persistence throughout his entire professional career, is attested to by descriptions of his teaching from his Pennsylvania days to his last formal courses at the New School for Social Research. Professor Cheyney writes of his teaching at the University of Pennsylvania in the following manner:

" He was strongly interested from the beginning in getting across to the students what he wanted them to learn; that is to say, he is fundamentally a teacher. His lecturing and writing of special articles in magazines has never seemed to me his " long suit." His best work has been with his own classes, graduate and undergraduate, and through his text-books and monographic writings, and this has been true from the beginning of his academic career. Two early indications of this I can mention. One was his habit of writing an outline of his lecture on the blackboard before he began to talk to the students. I know it made a great impression on them to feel that he had in mind exactly the group of things he wanted to say, classified in the way he wanted to say them. The other proof is his share in the series of " Translations and Reprints " which he, Dana Munro and I began to publish through this department and which were kept up for a number of years. I do not remember whether he or in fact which one of us suggested the plan but we were a unit in our enthusiasm for it. The object was, of course, to give a sense of the reality of history to the students, to bring the subject of history down from the clouds into familiarity and normality.

" Mr. Robinson was always notable for the independence of his judgments. Whether it was because of his natural temperament or the characteristics of his training, or his habit of reading and talking with men outside of the historical fraternity, I was frequently struck by the freshness and indeed the paradoxes of his judgments. I remember that he deprecated giving so much attention to American History in the schools and the colleges on the ground that students would obtain far more mental training from studying about things they do not already know something of than about things they were already familiar with. His views on the essential elements in the French Revolution, the Reformation, etc., as contrasted with the habitual interpretation, were developed within the first few years of his teaching. Personally, I know I was very much influenced by his ideas, largely because of their originality and unfamiliarity. I think he has a mind of an unusual type. It is distinctly original and at the same time sufficiently receptive to suggestions to be able to express for other people what they recognize as their own belief, — what they possessed but had not yet formulated. In other words, he could draw material not only from his own sub-consciousness but from the sub-consciousness of other people.

" To sum up: James Harvey Robinson is a sound scholar, a first rate teacher, an original interpreter of otherwise meaningless facts, and a gifted leader in a movement of somewhat blind progress towards a better understanding and method of historical thought and teaching. I am not fond of the expression, the " New History," but I suppose Robinson exemplifies what the users of it mean by that term. All these characteristics are his by natural right; he showed them while he was still a teacher at Pennsylvania, and later surroundings have only modified them in details. Other ideas and ideals have been added to these early ones. He has grown, of course, in mental stature and has done much work of the most valuable character since he left Pennsylvania, but I am still convinced that his career amplifies the fact that a man is what he is by force of his natural endowment." [24]

Professor William R. Shepherd, one of Robinson's earliest students, and long his colleague, at Columbia, thus describes his impression of Robinson as a teacher:

" In the early days Robinson was regarded as a man of singular originality in ideas and methods. What interested him and those who heard him was the evolution of what had been thought about the phenomena of history, rather than the phenomena themselves. In his mind this took on a substantiality of fact, quite as real as recorded events and infinitely more important.

" Upon set notions, sacrosanct prejudices, solemn convictions, derived from conventional ways of viewing things bygone, Robinson cast an incredulous, critical eye. That something had happened and that a learned and hence indisputable, authority had told of it meant little to him. Even if its occurrence could be proved, the fact did not guarantee it value, unless it had a genuine meaning for life and thought at the present day. This value must be ascertained by the manner in which able intellects then or later judged it. Were a man's utterances in advance of his time, they became to Robinson more evidential of truth than the law and gospel hitherto prescribed and accepted.

" A merciless, though cheerful, iconoclast was Robinson, who took sheer, but never savage, delight in throwing down many a graven image of assertions about the past. If tradition had erected it for reverence by a docile posterity, then the sooner the descendants realized that, like their forebears, they too had a human world of their own where permanence in ideas and institutions is not to be mistaken for a changeless law of nature, the better would be man's estate — and woman's — on this earth.

[24] Letter to the writer, March 3, 1926.

" Such was Robinson's concept of history. He set it forth, moreover, with a keenness of discernment, a picturesqueness of apt illustration and a whimsicality of epigrammatic humor which had an irresistible appeal to all who came within the widening circle of his influence." [25]

Professor Alexander C. Flick, whose period of study at Columbia was contemporaneous with that of Professor Shepherd, records a similar opinion of Robinson's pedagogical acumen:

" If I were to sum up in a few sentences my impressions, I should say,

1. His courses grew out of his interest in intellectual progress.

2. His interest centered in the growth, development and evolution of human society and he believed that this could be demonstrated by history.

3. His aims as a teacher were to shatter preconceived judgments in his pupils and then let them reconstruct their opinions from the evidence.

4. His methods were first to awaken interest, then encourage study in the sources, and finally to let each student form his own conclusions." [26]

Professor Preserved Smith, who studied under Robinson a decade later than Professors Shepherd and Flick, presents an eloquent and discerning analysis of Robinson's prowess as a teacher:

" Robinson was the most exciting teacher I ever had. The extraordinary interest which he aroused in his pupils was due chiefly to three qualities, his humor, his realism, and his rationalism.

" Better than any man of his generation he saw the irony latent in the *comédie humanine* spread on the pages of history. The inconsistencies, the self-deception, even the gullibility of

[25] Letter to the writer, March 23, 1926.
[26] Letter to the writer, March 22, 1926.

some men and the hypocrisy of others seemed to him infinitely amusing. He presented historic situations with all the comedy there was in them. Never the buffoon or Cheap Jack joker, he nevertheless did not fear to find and to point out some element of humor inseparable from life. Wit he had too, though it was less characteristic than his humor.

" He saw history realistically — as it is and not as it ought to be; not as it has generally been presented with flowing garments and a halo. Nothing imposed on him. He saw through shams and pretences and, what is more difficult, through the drapery carefully adjusted to the naked form of facts by the piety and " good taste " of the too conscientious artist. He loved homely comparisons, especially when they were slightly ruffling to the prejudices. He delighted to compare the persecution of the heretics with modern intolerance of socialists, and to draw a parallel between the methods of the Roman Curia and those of Tammany Hall. Sometimes he was led into paradox — though his paradoxes were more instructive than other men's orthodoxies — as when he almost proved that the words of the Valensian Fragment on which were based all subsequent accounts of the Fall of Rome in 476, meant no more than that Odoacer knocked some bric-à-brac off the mantlepiece of Honorius; or as when he showed that the Declaration of the Rights of Man, so often censured for doctrinalism, was the most practical step possible in the circumstances of 1789.

" Best of all was Robinson's rationalism. In his textbooks he has made some concessions to popular prejudices, in his other works much less, in his lectures very little, and in his intimate conversation none at all. Fundamentally, he is the most rational and the most intelligently sceptical man I have ever known. To those who came to him from carefully sheltered homes and from country colleges, from the halls of which all winds of modern doctrine were carefully excluded as dangerous drafts, his biting blast of reason was the most healthful and bracing thing in their experience. He cleared his own mind, and the minds of others, of the cant not only of religion but of that superstitious morality based not upon reason but upon out-

worn custom, that morality which is really religious conduct
with the religious excuse for it taken away. In his lectures he
still consulted prudence by a studied moderation of language,
but in private conversation he was as trenchant as Voltaire.
' To no bad man in history,' he once said to me, ' do we owe so
damnable a doctrine as that of predestination which we owe to
Calvin.'

"When I was a student at Columbia — 1901–3 and 1906–7,
Robinson's classes were not very large and his seminaries were
small. To his classes he lectured twice a week. He placed the
main criterion of successful teaching in the ability of the professor to interest his students, and in this he was a past master.
He once told me that his aim was to get the student interested
in the first five minutes of the course and not to let his interest
flag to the end — and this aim he actually accomplished. The
subject made no difference — he could make Duns bright and
the *Leges Visigothorum* thrilling." [27]

Professor Carlton J. H. Hayes, who has succeeded to
Robinson's position as the most popular class-room
teacher of history in the Columbia graduate school, shares
the enthusiam of Professor Smith for Robinson's qualities
as a teacher:

" James Harvey Robinson was the greatest teacher I have
ever had. I say ' greatest ' not because he supplied me with
any vast quantity of facts in medieval history. As a matter of
fact all the notes I took from him during three years as a
student were incorporated in less than half of a very small
notebook. I say ' greatest ' because more than any other man
he made me think. He had a way of arousing the student's
curiosity and of filling the student with a great and firm determination to satisfy that curiosity; and the curiosity he aroused
— at least in me — was a curiosity about things which most of
us take for granted."

The writer, who attended Robinson's lectures regularly
or sporadically from 1915 to 1920 can testify to the fact

[27] Letter to the writer, March 13, 1926.

that the qualities described by Professor Shepherd as characteristic of Robinson's teaching as early as 1895, had in no sense disappeared after the lapse of a quarter of a century.

Robinson's method of presenting material to his classes inevitably varied somewhat with the transformation of his historical interests and the nature of his classes. At first his classes were extremely and delightfully informal. To his small classes he lectured in an intimate fashion, and interspersed his lectures with extensive reading from the sources and an interpretation of these documents. He was never a drill-master. So far was he from this type of teacher that the questions asked in the class were almost universally those asked by the students, which Robinson heartily welcomed. Even in his seminars Robinson was more interested in stimulating thought than in perfecting the esoteric technique of minute research. Professor Flick has furnished the writer with an excellent description of Professor Robinson's classroom procedure during Robinson's first two years at Columbia University:

" As a part of his work, he was constantly quoting the sources and urging students to read more widely in them. He enjoyed bringing an armful of books into the classroom which, after a brief description of their value, were passed around the class.

" From cards about the size of a postcard, which he took out of his right-hand coat pocket, he lectured to the class. His diction was slow, but his points were remarkably well organized, and his wit was subtle. He seldom asked questions of the class but encouraged questions from the class. I never saw a teacher who more frankly admitted his ignorance on unfamiliar points. He never posed and never bluffed. He seemed to enjoy smashing smug convictions and emphatic opinions. There was something stimulating in contact with him, and from the outset the handful of students with which he started increased in number with great rapidity.

" A seminar was opened to a few students in this general course. The four or five who were favored with membership were privileged to go to his home and spend the evening in his library. We read a tract in medieval Latin by Pierre Dubois on the recovery of the Holy Land and had rather a tough time with it but Robinson's comments were so interesting and illuminating that we thoroughly enjoyed our weekly sessions. Dante's *Vita Nuova* was also read but this time, fortunately for our peace of mind, in translation. Robinson was of the firm conviction that students of history should go to the sources. . . ." [28]

As his courses grew larger and more popular it was inevitable that his procedure should become rather more formal and less intimate, yet, even to the close of his teaching career, he never made use of rhetorical or dramatic methods. Though he was one of the most popular teachers of very large classes, his success was due to sheer intellectual ability and feats of psychic dexterity. There was in his procedure none of the thrilling cosmic flights or synthetic hypotheses of Shotwell, the perfection of organization and literary polish of Professor Shepherd, the dramatic intensity of Beard, or the histrionic perfection and engaging facetiousness of Hayes — the great Columbia teachers of history who have approached Robinson in popularity. Few teachers could have used his method of delivery and retained a dozen students in the class at the end of the year. Carl Becker is the only other history teacher known to the writer who has resembled Robinson in his class-room attitudes and mannerisms and still been a highly successful teacher. Robinson lectured even to his large class in intellectual history in a rather dry manner

[28] Letter to the writer March 22, 1926.

and in somewhat drawling tones characteristic of his temperament, rarely looking at his students, but more often with his eyes glued upon an upper corner of the ceiling. He never wrote out his lectures, but just talked and thought as he went along. He would frequently lecture for the whole hour with his arms folded without varying his position during the entire class period. His most brilliant flashes of wit were usually delivered without the slightest change of countenance, though occasionally, if the joke was on some eminent historical or contemporary character, such as St. Augustine or Chancellor Day, he would hesitate and laugh heartily with the class.

Nevertheless, with this method, so utterly devoid of dramatic appeal, Robinson interested and amused his students far more than any other teacher of history with whom the writer has ever had any association. This amazing result he achieved first and foremost by seizing upon the most important facts and generalizations related to the subject-matter of the lecture. He accustomed his students to anticipate an introduction to matters of real intellectual importance in each lecture, and they were rarely if ever disappointed. He never slumped off into irrelevant side issues, but kept the leading threads of the course continually before his students. His command of subtle but penetrating irony and satire was almost unique and served to keep his students intellectually alert at all moments. One of his brilliant students has remarked that Robinson was a supreme master of the art of teaching by the method of "wise-cracks," but, while this is in a sense true, Robinson's sallies were never obtrusive, but were subtle rapier-like thrusts, always brought in at exactly the right moment to provide real illumination of the material with which he was dealing. To the writer Robinson's success in the class-room in the last decade of his teaching experience will remain the outstanding example of what may be achieved in the way of pedagogical success through turning loose a profound but playful mind upon vital historical materials without any effort whatever at stage presence or " horse-play."

In spite of Robinson's success as a class-room lecturer and his great influence exerted through his students, it is probable that his most enduring and extensive impression upon the field of history has been executed through his books. Professor Schapiro has indicated in the following paragraph how Robinson's *History of Western Europe* brought into existence a new epoch in text-book writing in the field of history:

" The teachers of history in America owe a great debt of gratitude to Professor James Harvey Robinson, of Columbia University, chief protagonist and brilliant interpreter of the New History. In his *History of Western Europe,* Professor Robinson produced a history textbook that is at the same time a work of original scholarship. This volume was the first of its kind to give coherence and viewpoint to complex historical material and to emphasize social and cultural elements. After Professor Robinson, no one may now write an old-style textbook, a compendium of dry facts, mainly political and military, hastily put together by a hack writer or tired historian." [29]

A main reason for the great influence of Robinson as an historical writer is to be found in the straight-forward presentation of his subject-matter and the limpid clarity of his style. He not only had something to say, but gave far more than the usual amount of thought as to how to say it. Professor Hayes correctly emphasizes this fact:

[29] *Modern and Contemporary European History,* p. ix.

" One other point I should like to make about the impression James Harvey Robinson made on me, and that is that he represented a rare combination of scholarly honesty and literary and artistic appreciation. I am sure that he spent a great deal more time in writing out what he knew than in acquiring his knowledge. His knowledge was great and varied, but the clarity and simplicity of his presentation could be arrived at only through the greatest effort. This is a lesson which all aspiring students in the social sciences, particularly history, can with profit take to heart."

Robinson's critics have contended that he has never produced a weighty and voluminous monograph on any historical subject. They have maintained that his writings have been in the form either of textbooks or popular essays. The writer must admit the truth of this observation in relation to Robinson's standing as a " productive " historical scholar in the conventional sense of that term. No one could regret more than the present writer the loss which we have sustained in Robinson's delay in completing his *magnum opus* on the intellectual history of Europe. Yet, the very fact that his writings were chiefly textbooks or volumes for general consumption have, on the other hand, served to make his general influence upon history teachers, the thoughtful public and the coming generation far greater than that of any other contemporary historian. Further, the fact that he wrote many textbooks is quite obviously no indication of his lack of scholarly capacity. His literary product in the way of bibliographic and monographic articles was certainly equal to the comparable achievements of such men as Burr, F. J. Turner, Munro and Fling, admittedly among the most rigorous historical scholars this country has produced. While it is to be deplored that Robinson did not intersperse his series of textbooks with more substantial monographs, there is no doubt that, as between exclusive monographic publication or concentration upon textbooks and essays, a man of Robinson's qualities of mind and historical interests decided wisely in choosing the latter alternative. He published more in the way of the closest scholarly work than a number of men who have held the office of president of the American Historical Association, and to this achievement he added the most influential and progressive series of history textbooks yet written, the most stimulating of our books on the "new history," and the most popular historical work of the generation with the exception of the extraordinary *Outline of History* by H. G. Wells.

Robinson's first books, as we have pointed out above, were his *Original and Derived Features of the Constitution of the United States,* which was published in 1890; and *The German Bundesrat,* published in 1891. In 1899 came the *Petrarch: the First Modern Scholar,* in which he was associated with Professor Rolfe of Swarthmore.

It will unquestionably be the verdict of historians that Robinson's most influential work was the famous college text on the *History of Western Europe* which was published in 1903. This work, in the first edition, had a sale of 250,000 copies. Up to this time there had been no textbooks in this field except the erudite, but dry and relatively uninteresting conventional manuals of Professor Emerton, and the translation of Bémont and Monod's excellent but limited French treatise. Into the *History of Western Europe* Robinson put his best thought and manner at the time of his maximum intellectual vigor and enthusiasm, and he set an entirely new standard for textbook writing in the historical field. Its success has led many

to imitate the book, and, though as yet no one has succeeded in duplicating it, the efforts along this line have
notably improved the tone of history textbooks in the last
generation. The outstanding characteristic of the *History
of Western Europe* lay in Robinson's effort to single out
the vital essentials of medieval and modern European history and to trace these leading threads through with clarity and consistency. He repudiated the usual assumption
that historical material was preëminently constitutional,
dynastic and diplomatic history, and for the first time
made a positive effort to include much material on economic, social and cultural life as an integral part of the
volume. Added to these achievements were the human
touch and sprightly style which served to give vividness
to the volume. The chief weaknesses in the work lay in
the failure to appreciate the significance of the Commercial Revolution, the rise of capitalism, and the Industrial
Revolution, and in the inadequacy of the treatment of the
constitutional development of England. These defects
are remedied in the second edition. Robinson's emphasis
upon the historical and pedagogical value of source-material led to the preparation and publication of the two volumes of *Readings in European History* in 1904–5 as a supplement to the *Western Europe*. He brought out a revised
edition of the *History of Western Europe* in two volumes
in 1925.

Next came the two volumes on the *Development of
Modern Europe*, written with the collaboration of Charles
Austin Beard and published in 1907. This was an epoch-
making book, in that it was the first real college textbook
on modern European history published in the English language. It was also the first manual on European history

to take into account the stupenduous influence of the Industrial Revolution. Next to the chapters on the Industrial Revolution and the novelties in contemporary civilization, the most striking section in this work was the ninth chapter, dealing with the Rationalists of the 18th century. No subsequent textbook has rivalled this analysis of the place of rationalism in the history of modern civilization. The *Development of Modern Europe* was, however, prepared rather hastily to meet a particular market at a given time, and was by no means the finished type of work which the *History of Western Europe* exemplified. It has since been superseded by a number of more thorough manuals, but it will be credited in the history of American textbooks as the pioneer treatise in this field. It is to be reissued in a new and greatly improved form. The two volumes of readings published to accompany this work on modern European history were, if anything, more illuminating than those prepared to supplement the *History of Western Europe*.

Aside from the revisions of his college texts, Robinson's subsequent achievements in the field of textbook writing have been limited primarily to high-school texts, where he enlisted the assistance of the distinguished Chicago orientalist, James Henry Breasted. Here the teaching profession owes directly to Robinson the responsibility for inducing Professor Breasted to write his *Ancient Times*, a book which has done for ancient history what Robinson's *History of Western Europe* did for medieval and modern times.

In 1911 Robinson brought together his more original essays on the purpose and content of history in his well-known work, *The New History*. In the opinion of the writer this collection of essays will constitute the chief criterion by which Robinson's ultimate place in the history of historiography will be determined. It represents his confession of faith in the newer history, and forecasts the gradual shift of his interest from the field of history, conventionally speaking, to that of social betterment and intellectual reform. This work did as much to stimulate and improve the thinking of historians concerning their subject as the *History of Western Europe* achieved with regard to the advancement of history teaching.

Robinson's contributions to the exploitation of the lessons of history in the interest of reform and human betterment are embodied in his *The Mind in the Making* and his *The Humanizing of Knowledge,* published in 1921 and 1923 respectively. An analysis of these works will be reserved for the latter part of this chapter, which will be devoted to Robinson as a modernist and reformer. In his article in the *Survey* for October 1, 1924, from which we have earlier quoted, Robinson expounds his view of the primary purpose and utility of history as an aid in the improvement of the cultural outlook and social institutions of man:

" History I am inclined to describe as an effort to recall those reminiscences of the past which cast most light on the present. It is an extension of our personal memories. Memory alone renders us sane and able to make judicious terms with things. History properly conceived should vastly augment our insight by widening our memories. . . .

" From this standpoint most history books are poor, dull things, written by unimaginative people with the temperament of faithful clerks. Conscientiousness and Insight seem suspicious of one another, and yet they might be friends. Careless talk about the past is just as bad as reckless statements about

the present. An indefinite amount of slavish work is necessary
to mine out the raw materials essential to forming any just estimates of the past — and there seem to be a good many willing
to undertake this laborious kind of work. It is far more difficult to find those who can reduce crude information to wisdom
and supply us with enlightening reminiscences. . . .

" All this kind of business (conventional historical research)
is fine and fundamental and it makes no difference how dull it
may be, since those who know how to use it clearly perceive its
value. All such books form the *scientific* basis of history. I
plead however for a sharp distinction between meeting the needs
of the professional historian and those of the public. And the
two are often confused, as may' be seen in innumerable historical
works which fail to suit either class very well. . . .

" History — the illuminating reminiscences of times gone by,
as I conceive it — should work for sophistication. And sophistication means understanding and insight and wisdom. It is no
trivial and supercilious affectation, but something most fundamental. We cannot attack our political, religious, economic,
educational and social standards directly, although we may well
suspect that they must *per force* be anachronisms. They may
all, however, issue into a clearer light when we think how everything that now goes on has come about. So history might be
the great illuminator. As yet it is highly imperfect; but some
day it may well become the most potent instrument for human
regeneration." [30]

While Robinson has retained his contact with historical
writing and teaching through successive revisions of his
textbooks and through occasional addresses at meetings of
historians, his interest in the last decade has been more and
more absorbed by contemporary problems and the broad
issues of intellectual improvement. This transformation
was forecast even in *The New History*, particularly in the
fourth, fifth and eighth chapters of that book. Robinson

[30] *Loc. cit.*, p. 19.

was led to this field of interest and activity in a natural and gradual manner. He who views history in an intelligent fashion inevitably comes to the ultimate conclusion that historical study and reflection are largely useless unless they can be turned to some practical account in the way of advancing contemporary progress. Robinson's life-long interest in natural and applied science led him to contrast the remarkable achievements executed in the field of material culture with the archaic nature of our social thought and institutions, which have been but slightly altered since the days prior to the scientific and industrial revolutions. Finally, his knowledge of the miseries of the human past inevitably awakened a humanitarian spirit which was directed towards a lively interest in the unnecessary waste and suffering in the contemporary period. The close relation between Robinson's historical work and his ideas as a social critic, together with his abhorrence of the "snouty" uplifter, appear clearly in the following section from a recent letter to the writer:

"Of course the long row of books for high schools and colleges which I have written, helped write or edited and which have required many adjustments and recastings and "bringings-up-to-date" have taken a great part of my attention and should be reckoned as a main achievement. In all conferences on historical instruction in which I took part, the first in 1891 at Madison, I have urged that history for students and readers should always be directed to an understanding of the present conditions and problems. I have scarcely been a reformer in any other sense. History exactly corresponds to the genetic approach in the natural sciences.

"I am no social reformer. I believe that intelligence underlies the kind of goodness we most need nowadays in making fresh adjustments. I have a tendency to share and impart what I learn but no great anxiety to "better" my fellow-beings.

That desire has come to seem a very arrogant and crude enterprise based usually upon some suspicious psychic mechanism..
Reformers of the more fanatical type approach paranoiacs.
There is a sort of persecution-complex, and some element of re-
sentment and revenge enters in. But you see my point. I do
not want to be confused with the naïve uplifter."

As a critic of the contemporary order and a man interested in educational betterment Robinson is in no sense a
fanatic or bound down by any system or program of social reform. He has conspicuously avoided becoming a
victim of what Francis Bacon called "the idol of the the-
atre." In fact, Hendrick Van Loon, in reviewing his *The
Mind in the Making,* vigorously criticized Robinson for
failing to present any clear-cut panacea for remedying contemporary social ills. He likened him unto Achilles sulk-
ing in his tent. Nor is Robinson a thoroughgoing "red"
in the conventional sense of that term, in spite of the sub-
sidized attack upon him by one Harré in Mr. Ralph Eas-
ley's *National Civic Federation Review* in the spring of
1919. He appears content to put his faith in a mitigated
and more efficient capitalism and in a chastened political
democracy.

Indeed, it seems that the genesis of Robinson as a social
critic was brought about by much the same situation that
made him an exponent of the more progressive trends in
history. As soon as he began thinking about history he became a "new historian," while as soon as he started to
think about contemporary problems he equally naturally
and inevitably became a critic of existing institutions, put-
ting his chief trust in a better type of education. In fact,
his historical studies helped him along in this attitude, for
these researches had revealed to him most effectively the

archaic and outgrown elements in contemporary culture. As he calmly surveyed the contemporary system, with its unbelievable wastes, its notorious inefficiency, its injustices, its intolerance, and its regimentation and standardization, he was repelled by it as he was by the superstitions and restrictions of the medieval period, and by the intellectual savagery of the Reformation. As Voltaire and others had stimulated him in his reaction against Christian bigotry, so Veblen was his chief stimulus in his critical attitude towards contemporary capitalistic society. Under the guidance of Veblen and later of Tawney, he came to see that capitalism and plutocracy cramp and hamper man today as supernaturalism and religious superstitions had restricted his potential development during the Middle Ages.

Robinson's only suggestion as to a remedy for this situation has been to allow the free play of the human intellect over the problems which confront us, trusting to its efficacy, if unhampered, in suggesting adequate modes of controlling the complex and baffling problems of the present day. As he once remarked in class, " our minds may be poor things, but they are the best little things we have." This view is clearly stated in the following quotation from *The New History:*

" In the career of conscious social adjustment upon which mankind is now embarked, it would seem as if the history of thought should play a very important part, for social changes must be accompanied by emotional readjustments and determined by intellectual guidance. The history of thought is one of the most potent means of dissolving the bonds of prejudice and the restraint of routine. It not only enables us to reach a clear perception of our duties and responsibilities by explaining the manner in which existing problems have arisen, but it promotes that intellectual liberty upon which progress fundamentally depends." [31]

Hence, the first step must be found in a battle against the forces of reaction and conservatism which prevent the full and complete operation of available human intelligence. It is on this ground that Robinson opposes the conservative with the " Lusking " propensity to crush out the spirit of free inquiry. Few writers have formulated the case against the conservative as the enemy of intellectual freedom and progress more effectively than has Robinson in the closing chapter of the *New History* and the last two chapters of *Mind in the Making*. Particularly vigorous is his opposition to the whole notion of censorship. This he expressed trenchantly in a contribution to a symposium on censorship conducted by the *Literary Digest* for June 23, 1923:

" I am opposed to all censorship, partly because we already have Draconian laws, and police willing to interfere on slight pretense in cases in which the public sense of propriety seems likely to be shocked; partly because, as Milton long ago pointed out, censors are pretty sure to be fools, for otherwise they would not consent to act. Then I am a strong believer in the fundamental value of sophistication. I would have boys and girls learn early about certain so-called ' evils ' — and rightly so-called — so that they may begin to reckon with them in time. I have no confidence in the suppression of every-day facts. We are much too skittish of honesty. When we declare that this or that will prove demoralizing, we rarely ask ourselves, demoralizing to whom and how? We have a sufficiently delicate machinery already to prevent the circulation of one of Thorstein Veblen's philosophic treatises and Mr. Cabell's highly esoteric romance. For further particulars see the late John

[31] *Op. cit.*, pp. 30–31.

Milton's " Areopagitica " *passim.* To judge by the conduct of some of our college heads the influence of this work is confined to a recognition of its noble phraseology, with little realization of the perennial value of the sentiments it contains." [32]

Robinson's own faith in the gospel of " Open-Mindedness " is admirably set forth in one of his most recent articles, contributed to the *American Hebrew* for September, 1925:

" Liberalism — and I have no great love for the word — may be conceived as the mood of the explorer, who notes the facts as he goes along. He does not know beforehand what he is going to find over the next mountain or across the next river or lake. He learns as he goes, and adjusts his beliefs to his increasing information. We have only just begun to explore man's nature and the world in which he is placed. We have new methods of research which were not available half a century ago. New experiments are being tried on a large scale, and conditions are vastly different from those with which our ancestors had to deal. Dogmas — ancient teachings which are protected in various ways from the fermentive influence of increasing knowledge — are still congenial to a creature such as man. But, while they are sometimes harmless, their chance of being suited to the present needs and best insight of men is so slight that we should have no least hesitation in calling them in question. The open-minded will do this in so far as their powers permit. Open-mindedness, like dogma, demands faith and loyalty. It is a lofty ideal and one implying a new type of the mortification of the flesh — a new conception of righteousness and salvation. Whether one strives to fulfill the behests of ancient dogma or to follow those of open-mindedness, he will often stumble and have his moments of contrition and his renewals of faith. But the new gospel places far more onerous restraints on our natural impulses than did the old. It has its promises and its rewards — sometimes its beatific vision, but these glories are as yet for a scattered few. Yet the communion of saints grows daily." [33]

[32] *Loc. cit.,* p. 29.   [33] *Loc. cit.,* p. 595.

Robinson's general program of the discrediting of ancient dogmas and the application of critical and scientific thought to the solution of modern problems is best brought together as the dominating conceptions of his *The Mind in the Making* and *The Humanizing of Knowledge*. *The Mind in the Making*, delivered originally as the Kennedy Lectures before the New York School of Social Work, is to be regarded as the harbinger of his general history of human ideas. As an intellectual history of Europe the volume is pathetically inadequate, but as an effort to present the leading generalizations which might be drawn from a long and assiduous cultivation of the field of intellectual history the book is nothing short of a magnificent achievement. Indeed, it is the calm and deliberate judgment of the writer that no other book by an historian can be said to equal this one as a presentation of the more significant generalizations of history for the use of thoughtful citizens. As a withering attack upon the conventional utilization of history to justify the sacred anachronisms in our own civilization the book is both unrivalled and invaluable.

The material in the book is arranged according to the consideration of the following topics: (1) the futility of past efforts at reform because of an ignorance of the mechanisms of the human mind; (2) the chief types of thinking, with special reference to the contrast between secondary rationalization and creative thought; (3) the development of the human mind in its thought content from the animal stage to that manifested in contemporary civilization; (4) the indictment of the puritanical-capitalistic-nationalistic-pietistic " acquisitive society " of the present day; and (5) an analysis of the bearing of a review of the genesis of the

modes of human thought upon the problem of social reform in its widest implications. Throughout the book
there is always evident an effort to show the relation of
the facts of psychology and history to the present and future of human society. Yet there is no attempt to advocate
any special type of reform measure.

The significant message of Professor Robinson's volume
may be epitomized in the following manner: The basic
need of today is to bring our thinking in the field of the
social sciences up to the same level of scientific objectivity
that now prevails in the realm of the natural sciences.
Mankind has experimented unsuccessfully with three
methods of reform, namely, tinkering up social machinery,
moral uplift, and education through inculcation of " the
collective wisdom of the past." We can understand why
these have failed only by an investigation of the prevailing
modes of thought, their genesis and method of operation.
We tend to respect and remain satisfied with the so-called
" wisdom of the ages," though every forward step taken
by the race has been in defiance of this moss-embellished
sagacity. This we do because most of our thinking is derived from a subconscious level, where instinct, habit and
tradition dominate. Most of our " basic principles " of
conduct are but secondary rationalization of primitive
reactions.

Our only escape is through the encouragement of creative thought, based upon the experimental and pragmatic
method. Yet creative thought is obstructed on every hand
by many forces, the variety and potency of which can only
be understood after a review of the history of the chief
stages in the formation of our present mental content and
psychic operations. These stages are those of the genesis

of our animal mind, the development of our savage mind, and the formation of our traditional civilized mind. Man's long period of existence as an animal developed in him the variety of instinctive reactions which he possesses, the method of learning by trial and error, and a certain docility and intellectual inertia. The period of human savagery was far longer than that of civilization, and has left its indelible impress upon our modes of thinking. It generated our animistic and mystic tendencies, our strange deference to authority, and our unbelievable conservatism. Most of the basic elements in our religious and ethical beliefs date from this stage of human psychogenesis. Taboos, ideas of "principle," symbolism, notions of the "sacred," and dream logic are some of the more conspicuously powerful vestiges of savage thought which still remain to plague our civilized age.

The background for the emergence of a civilized mind was provided by the Egyptians, who invented writing and many practical arts, by the Babylonians, who excelled in commercial life and in astrology, and by the Hebrews, who developed to an unusually high degree the religious views they had drawn from a primitive era. Working on these and additional data the Greeks first evolved creative thought. "They discovered skepticism in the higher and proper significance of the word, and this was their supreme contribution to human thought." But the Greek intellectual life tended towards metaphysical abstractions and away from experimental and applied science. When the possibilities of metaphysics were exhausted, Greek thought inevitably entered into a period of stagnation and decay. The medieval age brought with it intellectual reversion and deterioration. Christianity, aided by Neo-platonism and the Oriental mystery cults, substituted faith and emotion for reason and critical thought. A crude and primitive scheme of creation, life and ultimate destiny was elaborated into a divinely authoritative epic, belief in which was enforced by the powerful Roman Catholic Church. Man was significant only as the possessor of an immortal soul to be saved from eternal torment. The monks and Augustine introduced and established in European intellectual and ethical tradition that impurity-complex which, with additional impulses from Protestant Puritanism and the rationalized apologia of Immanuel Kant, has served to prevent any scientific consideration of the problem of sex, right down to our own day. An extensive system of secondary rationalization, supplying an elaborate and sophisticated explanation and justification of these primitive reactions on metaphysical grounds, was provided by the Scholastic philosophy, which culminated in Aquinas. The medieval age added little or nothing of a progressive nature to the thought of the Greeks, but rather revived a vast mass of primitive superstitions which have survived to obstruct the critical and scientific thought of the modern age.

Our modern civilization has been an outgrowth of a totally new type of thinking, which was partially foreseen by Roger Bacon and definitely heralded by Francis Bacon — critical thought and experimental science. This was on all points opposed to the dialectical method of the Greeks and Scholastics, and has proceeded on the notion that " nature is more subtle than any argument." Though opposed by the Church and long by professional scholars, it has triumphed and made possible an entirely new material world through its applications to industry. Yet the great potential benefits of modern applied science have been but very partially and imperfectly realized, owing to the lack of adequate development of moral and social control over the new technique, which is in danger of developing into a Frankenstein monster. The two chief obstacles to a proper socialization of modern applied science are the profit-making objective of all modern economic life, and modern nationalistic patriotism, which diverts so much human energy and wealth into processes of mutual destruction. But those in control of modern civilization believe that they stand to gain by the modern theory of business enterprise and by unreasoning patriotism. Hence, they oppose all efforts at reform under a mass of defensive rationalizations known collectively as " the philosophy of safety and sanity." The challenge of the World War to the old social order increased the activity of its guardians and we have had as a result the Palmer Inquisition, the " Lusking " of New York State, and the " law and order myth " associated with ex-Governor Coolidge, of Massachusetts. Yet, if history proves anything, it is that excessive repression of progressive tendencies is as ill-advised on the part of the vested interests as it is detrimental to society at large. Stupidly thorough repression merely postpones change, makes it violent and expensive, and costs the vested interests more dearly in the end. Conservatism is partially a savage and primitive trait and partially a sort of collective neurosis — the mechanism through which the guardians of the existing order seek to avoid facing the social realities of the present day.

Without bravely facing these realities which demonstrate the " sickness of the modern acquisitive society," however, we cannot hope to improve our social order. With the gradual elimination of the belief in the providential nature of social causation and supernatural interference with human institutions, we have come more and more to see that our civilization will be neither better nor worse than we will that it shall be; that man holds his destiny in his own hands. Until the leaders in modern society fully recognize this fact and intelligently accept the responsibility which this carries with it the "race between education and catastrophe" will continue, with the odds wholly favoring catastrophe.

Professor Robinson's book is an eloquent appeal to social initiative, but one knows that it was read only by a small minority of the population and appreciated only by a small percentage of those who read it. In the meantime the guardians of the modern order and the masses who support them will continue to trust in "the tried wisdom of the ages," the "findings of mankind," "the sturdy virtues of manhood and womanhood," "the sagacity of the Fathers," the "hard-headedness and practical shrewdness of the modern business man," and "the adroitness and astuteness of the modern politician and diplomat." The outlook is not entirely encouraging or wholly conducive to optimism, and Professor Robinson's book is a convincing demonstration that one can derive little assurance or comfort amidst the novel and diverse problems of the modern age from the perennial conservative rejoinder that somehow things have always come out all right in the past, in spite of the calamity howlers of earlier ages.

The Humanizing of Knowledge is the logical sequel to his remarkably successful and widely-read *Mind in the Making*. In the earlier work he traced the evolution of our contemporary modes of thinking, indicating the historical basis for the mental patterns of contemporaries, so

far separated as Calvin Coolidge and William J. Bryan,
on the one hand, and John Dewey and Thorstein Veblen,
on the other. Some critics felt, however, that he had left
his task incomplete, as he had not offered any very definite suggestions as to how we might escape from the stu-
pidities which encompass us in Lusking, Sumnerizing and
Ku Kluxing. *The Humanizing of Knowledge* is the answer to this challenge. The main theses of this book
follow:

There has been a general indifference to the scientific
point of view through the ages, so that even today the more
intelligent citizens are still dominated in their thinking
by the attitudes and methods of the mystic, poet, rhetor-
ician or shaman. The revolutionary scientific advances
of the last three hundred years have, in their deeper implications, scarcely affected the thinking of mankind at
large. This has been due in the main to the fact that
science has tended to develop in an esoteric and detached
fashion, in part necessitated by the need for self-protec-
tion. It has also tended towards excessive specialization
and departmentalization, which has often resulted in
amazing ignorance on the part of scientists of material
outside of their own subjects, and in such abstruseness in
scientific writing that even the average college graduate
who is not a specialist could find little which is intelligible
in such works. The great need of the future is not to make
scientific specialization, research, and discovery less extensive or effective, but to accompany this process by
an intelligent and persistent effort to make available for
the intellectual class the general implications of scientific
discovery in every field, and to produce something like a
general tendency towards critical and " reflective think-

ing." Eventually this may possibly be achieved by a rational integration and reconstruction of our educational institutions and curriculum, but for the time being it may be most effectively advanced by the compilation of books of sufficient clarity and brevity to commend themselves to the intelligent general reader. The alacrity with which this class took up Mr. Wells' *Outline of History* indicates that readers would not be lacking for competent books of this sort and offers some hope that if enough such books were available many of those now on the side of Mr. Bryan would come to line up behind men like Professor Robinson. Until something like the same degree of objectivity can be produced in the social sciences that exists in regard to natural science, we are likely to continue with our common-sense and rule-of-thumb methods in economics, politics, and modes of social conduct, a procedure which is becoming yearly more dangerous and menacing with the increasing complexity of modern life. If this extension of scientific control over society is an impossible aspiration, then the " jig is up " with the human race. The following citations sum up fairly adequately his thesis and positive program:

" Modern scientific research, in spite of its professed aloofness and disregard of human feelings and motives, has succeeded in unfolding to our gaze so new a world in its origin, development, workings and possibilities of control in the interests of human welfare, that practically all of the older poetic and religious ideas have to be fundamentally revised or reinterpreted.

" Scientific knowledge, ingeniously applied and utilized by inventors and engineers has, with the assistance of business men and financiers, metamorphosed our environment and our relations with our fellow men.

" Lastly, our notions of our own nature are being so altered that should we discreetly apply our increasing knowledge of the workings of the mind and the feelings, a far more successful technique might finally emerge for the regulation of the emotions than any that has hitherto been suggested. This is at least an exhilarating hope.

"Now if all this be true we are forced to ask whether it is safe, since our life has come to be so profoundly affected by and dependent on scientific knowledge, to permit the great mass of mankind and their leaders and teachers to continue to operate on the basis of presuppositions and prejudices which owe their respectability and currency to their great age and uncritical character, and which fail to correspond with real things and actual operations as they are côming to be understood.

"A great part of our beliefs about man's nature and the rightness or wrongness of his acts, date from a time when far less was known of the universe and far different were the conditions and problems of life from those of today.

"Do we not urgently need a new type of wonderer and pointer-out, whose curiosity shall be excited by this strange and perturbing emergency in which we find ourselves, and who shall set himself to discover and indicate to his busy and timid fellow creatures a possible way out? Otherwise how is a race so indifferent and even hostile to scientific and historical knowledge of the preciser sort — so susceptible to beliefs that make other and more potent appeals than truth — to be reconciled to stronger drafts of medicinal information which their disease demands but their palates reject? . . .

"We should have a dynamic education to fit a dynamic world. The world should not be presented to students as happily standardized but as urgently demanding readjustment. How are they to be more intelligent than their predecessors if they are trained to an utterly unscientific confidence in ancient notions, let us say of religion, race, heredity and sex, now being so fundamentally revised. . . .

"The problem has apparently two phases. One, how is human knowledge to be so ordered and presented in school and college as to produce permanent effects and an attitude of mind appropriate to our time and its perplexities; the other, how is knowledge to be popularized and spread abroad among adults who have become dissatisfied with what they know and are eager to learn more. . . .

" We need, therefore, a new class of writers and teachers, of which there are already some examples, who are fully aware of what has been said here and who see that the dissipation of knowledge should be offset by an integration, novel and ingenious, and necessarily tentative and provisional. They should undertake the conscious adventure of humanizing knowledge. There are minds of the requisite temper, training and literary tact. They must be hunted out, encouraged and brought together in an effective if informal conspiracy to promote the diffusion of the best knowledge we have of man and his world. They should have been researchers at some period of their lives, and should continue to be researchers in another sense. Their efforts would no longer be confined to increasing knowledge in detail but in seeking to discover new patterns of what is already known or in the way to get known.

" They should be re-assorters, selectors, combiners and illuminators. They should have a passion for diffusing, by divesting knowledge as far as possible of its abstract and professional character. At present there is a woeful ignorance even among persons who pass for intelligent, earnest and well read, in regard to highly important matters that are perfectly susceptible of clear general statement.

" The re-assorters and humanizers should combine a knowledge of the exigencies of scientific research with a philosophic outlook, human sympathy, and a species of missionary ardor. Each of them should have professional familiarity with some special field of knowledge, but this should have come to seem to him but a subordinate feature of the magnificent scientific landscape." [34]

Opinions will naturally differ as to the feasibility and practicality of Professor Robinson's scheme, but it is the

[34] *The Humanizing of Knowledge,* pp. 40–42, 69, 83, 90–92.

writer's firm conviction that there is no other promising or possible way out of our present intolerable and perplexing impasse, though of course the writing of clear books setting forth the new knowledge is but a phase of the program, which would need to be supplemented by such effective assaults upon the conventionally accepted standards as are being launched by Shaw and Mr. Mencken and his followers, and such fact-finding and disseminating organizations as are suggested by Mr. Lippmann in his *Public Opinion*.

Robinson proposes to devote a considerable proportion of his spare time during the rest of his life to the furthering of this program of adult education as expounded in *The Humanizing of Knowledge*. Beyond this, Robinson assures the writer that he intends to finish his own *magnum opus* on the intellectual history of Europe, which will ultimately be published as *The Story of Man's Notions of Himself and His World*.

INDEX